The New York Times
EASY CROSSWORD PUZZLES

Edited by Will Shortz

St. Martin's Paperbacks

THE NEW YORK TIMES EASY CROSSWORD PUZZLES

ISBN: 0-312-98975-X

Printed in the United States of America

St. Martin's Paperbacks edition / June 2003

St. Martin's Paperbacks are published by St. Martin's Press, 175 Fifth Avenue, New York, NY 10010.

10 9 8 7 6 5 4 3 2 1

The New York Times
EASY CROSSWORD PUZZLES

ACROSS

1 Friendly
5 Pro ___ (perfunctory)
10 Vegas calculation
14 Lip balm ingredient
15 Ryan or Tatum
16 Urban unrest
17 National monument dedicated 10/28/1886
20 Show respect for
21 Dress
22 Fairy tale villain
25 Spies' org.
26 PC key
29 47-Across poet
35 Farce
37 "___ Like It Hot"
38 Clear the blackboard
39 Ambulance wail
41 Coffee alternative
42 Catnapper
43 First month of the año
44 Bed-and-breakfasts
46 Kids' indoor ball material
47 Poem inscribed on 17-Across, with "The"
50 Draft org.
51 Place for thieves
52 Send out
54 Lawrence of Arabia portrayer
58 Cry of delight
62 President who dedicated 17-Across
67 Take it easy
68 Adhesive resin
69 Huron, for one
70 Watcher
71 "The Divine Comedy" poet
72 Examine closely

DOWN

1 Do the dishes
2 Palo ___, Calif.
3 Horse with a gray-sprinkled coat
4 "Ditto"
5 Enemy
6 Songstress Yoko
7 N.B.A. official
8 ___ de mer (seasickness)
9 Silverstone of "Clueless"
10 Lunch box treat
11 Grime
12 Biblical verb
13 Eye inflammation
18 Prod
19 Burned brightly
23 Apt. divisions
24 Strong feeling
25 Make pure
26 German city north of Cologne
27 "Rise and ___!"
28 Seven-time A.L. batting champ Rod
30 Prayer responses
31 Elvis ___ Presley
32 Utterly destroys
33 Computer operators

34 Feudal workers
36 First planet: Abbr.
40 Piece of pasta
45 Total
48 Gave a longing look
49 Small, medium or large
53 Turnpike tabs
54 Give a longing look
55 Waiter's load
56 Seep out
57 Finished

59 W.W. II females' service grp.
60 Durante's "___ Dinka Doo"
61 Idyllic place
63 Tax return preparer, for short
64 Actor Chaney
65 Abbr. after a telephone number
66 Eustacia of "The Return of the Native"

ACROSS

1 Pequod skipper
5 Mizzen and jigger, e.g.
10 Engine disks
14 Lascivious look
15 Abbr. on a record label
16 Skin cream ingredient
17 Song a. k. a. "Somewhere, My Love"
19 Noon, in Nantes
20 Potbelly, e.g.
21 Society page word
22 Black, in poetry
23 1982 Meryl Streep film
27 Gangsta ___
29 Gymnast's goal
30 Word before rod or staff, in Psalms
31 Brother of Jacob
33 Gallery display
35 Prom couples
40 Popular mail order company
44 Look of contempt
45 Bit of paronomasia
46 Floor square
47 Patty Hearst's kidnap grp.
50 Foot in the forest
52 Nile viper
53 Saul Bellow's Pulitzer-winning novel
59 Out of port
60 Hubbub
61 Cowardly Lion portrayer and family
64 Thanksgiving dishes
65 "Anything that can go wrong will"
68 Freudian topics
69 "Green ___"
70 Singer Tennille
71 Lucy's partner
72 "Now you ___, now . . ."
73 Pique

DOWN

1 "___ Well That Ends Well"
2 Miami five
3 Lockheed Martin field
4 Acclaim for Pavarotti
5 Pin location
6 Volcanic fallout
7 Vista
8 Most docile
9 Cry at an awards ceremony
10 Minor role
11 Excuse
12 Oregon Indian
13 English Channel feeder
18 Be Kind to Editors and Writers Month: Abbr.
24 "___ me out"
25 Crucifix letters
26 Jekyll's counterpart
27 Races, as a motor
28 Z ___ zebra
32 Salt Lake City athlete

Puzzle 2 by Randall J. Hartman

34 Spigot
36 Dramatize, with "out"
37 Iron man event
38 Wriggly fish
39 Escalator part
41 Approximately
42 Has dinner
43 Hidden catch
48 Alpaca cousins
49 Bring forward as evidence
51 Scheming

53 Did fieldwork?
54 Grammarian's concern
55 Office notes
56 Deep voices
57 Baseball manager Joe
58 Prison protests
62 Punjabi princess
63 Hot Lips Houlihan player
66 Canton-born architect
67 Former White House inits.

ACROSS

1 Blue-ribbon position
6 Tiny aquatic plant
10 Radar screen dot
14 Thespian
15 "Crazy" bird
16 Moreno of "West Side Story"
17 School essay
18 Pepper's partner
19 "Oh, woe!"
20 Start of a comment by critic George Jean Nathan
23 Like hen's teeth
26 "I surrender!"
27 Part 2 of the comment
32 Washington Mayor Marion
33 Sharpens
34 Puppy's bite
37 Opera singer Pinza
38 Virile
39 Zola courtesan
40 Kind of whisky
41 Ill-fated ship Andrea___
42 Olympian's prize
43 Part 3 of the comment
45 Atlantic fish
48 Fish-eating hawk
49 End of the comment
54 Helps
55 Natural balm
56 Prefix with -pedic
60 Prefix with logical
61 Not the front or back
62 Arctic, for one
63 Sign gas
64 "___ Dreams" (1994 documentary film)
65 Nairobi's land

DOWN

1 More than hefty
2 "___ bin ein Berliner"
3 Expy., e.g.
4 Hat for a siesta
5 Excessively sweet
6 As well
7 Goof off
8 Game on a green
9 Not pro
10 Intellectually gifted
11 State flower of New Hampshire
12 "Darn ___!"
13 Old hat
21 Joey ___ & the Star-liters (60's group)
22 Chicago team
23 Cavalry sword
24 Nutso
25 Eagle's nest
28 Swiss ___ (vegetable)
29 Gin's partner
30 China's Zhou ___
31 Actress Susan
34 Ralph who wrote "Unsafe at Any Speed"
35 Silly
36 Very friendly
38 Dairy farm sound
39 Chief Joseph's tribe
41 Dumbbell

Puzzle 3 by Pauline V. Wilson

42 Identified wrongly
43 Special boy
44 Overly
45 Beau
46 Rebuke
47 Bucking bronco event
50 "Candy / Is dandy . . ." humorist

51 Mishmash
52 Kind of list
53 Mondale or Quayle, e.g.
57 Countdown start
58 Cow chow
59 Go ___ diet

ACROSS

1 Irene of "Fame"
5 B.A. and B.S., e.g.
9 Try to avoid a tag
14 Throat clearer
15 Eye amorously
16 Kitchen counter?
17 1996 Clinton challenger
18 Stand in line
19 More slippery
20 How to succeed as a stripper?
23 Opposite WNW
24 Letterman's network
25 Heir's concern
28 Vandalize
30 Start with down and out
32 Fourposter, e.g.
33 Stops
35 Areas between hills
37 How to suceed as a retailer?
40 Voting districts
41 Go light (on)
42 Getting on in years
43 Govt. book balancers
44 Lucky plant
48 Puts in office
51 "Tsk!"
52 First lady
53 How to succeed as a demolition crew?
57 Fine dinnerware
59 Ready and willing's partner
60 Finito
61 "Prizzi's ___"
62 Hit alternative
63 Just in case
64 They're cutting, sometimes
65 Sports figure?
66 Greek god of love

DOWN

1 Bummed
2 What Richard III offered "my kingdom" for
3 Load off the mind
4 "You can say that again!"
5 Somewhat pessimistic
6 "Yikes!"
7 Smooth-talking
8 ___ good example
9 Mudholes
10 On the up and up
11 Worthy of copying
12 "Look at me, I'm Sandra ___"
13 Miscalculate
21 Means of approach
22 One of Lee's men
26 Ball props
27 Asner and Begley
29 Kind of test or rain
30 Addict's program
31 Takes advantage of
34 Flower supporter
35 Jumps with a pole
36 Brand for Bowser

Puzzle 4 by Nancy Salomon

37 Room connector
38 Bossing
39 Most safe
40 Grief
43 Sugar suffix
45 Presidential nixer
46 Nonetheless
47 Racks the pins again
49 Trapper transport
50 Russian autocrats:
    Var.
51 Oklahoma city
54 Thanksgiving potatoes

55 Passing notice
56 In neutral
57 ___ Guevara
58 Coal carrier

ACROSS

1 Garbage boat
5 Ingrid's "Casablanca" role
9 I.O.U.'s
14 Singer Guthrie
15 "Get a ___ of that!"
16 Nouveau ___
17 Nightgown-clad nursery-rhyme character
20 Reverse image, for short
21 ___ the lily
22 Be present at
23 Grow dim
24 Jackie's second husband
25 Heavens
26 Saying of Caesar
31 Banishment
32 Put on
33 No, to Nikita
37 Towering
38 Item
40 Snapshot, Mad. Ave.-style
41 Captain Hook's assistant
42 Tic-tac-toe win
43 Nearsighted Mr.
44 1960 Terry-Thomas film farce
48 Tie the knot
51 Fleur-de-___
52 Bloody
53 Twenty questions category

55 Concerning
56 Alternative to a subway
59 Shakespearean comedy (original spelling)
62 Smooth and glossy
63 Persian sprite
64 Brainstorm
65 "___ la vista, baby!"
66 Former spouses
67 Bruce or Laura of Hollywood

DOWN

1 Cut, as a log
2 Prairie Indian
3 Designer Cassini
4 "Unbelievable!"
5 Fighting ___ (Big Ten team)
6 Lounged around
7 Port ___, Egypt
8 Summer cooler
9 Rex Reed, e.g.
10 Help for the puzzled
11 Clinton staffer Harold
12 Use your brain
13 Squalid
18 "___ at the office"
19 Bandleader Fred
23 Actor Dafoe
24 Door-to-door cosmetics company
26 Docs for dachshunds
27 Quiz
28 Cairo's river
29 Dialect

Puzzle 5 by Stephanie Spadaccini

30 Odious reputation
34 Berra or Bear
35 Prince William's school
36 Grabbed
38 "___ a Mockingbird"
39 Works in the garden
43 French mothers
45 Where Nome is home
46 Pay no heed to
47 Action star Chuck

48 Former 49ers coach Bill
49 W.W. II's ___ Gay
50 Jackknife and others
54 Encounter
55 Wild goat
56 Presage
57 Exploiter
58 Getz or Kenton
60 Imitate
61 Pot top

ACROSS

1 State firmly
5 Born's partner
9 Famous rib donor
13 Heart
14 Stead
15 Teacake
16 Like Hawthorne's "Tales"
18 Peer
19 "My Fair Lady" scene
20 Second-stringer
22 Five-to-one, e.g.
26 St. Teresa of ___
28 Some stock buys
30 Galley type appropriate for this puzzle?
32 Speaker's place
33 "Darn!"
35 Pretend
36 Addl. telephone off a main line
37 Hamlet
39 Rita Hayworth spouse ___ Khan
40 Page of music
42 Speak to the hard-of-hearing?
43 Dog biter
44 Has contempt for
46 Alternative to Nikes
48 Valued violin
49 Publish lies about
50 Queen ___ lace
52 Short trip
56 Compel
58 Extra-base hit
62 Contract signer
63 Official language of Pakistan
64 Vogue rival
65 Head honcho
66 Tournament passes
67 Fine pajama material

DOWN

1 Official proceedings
2 Wedding exchange
3 The Red
4 45's and 78's
5 Sandwich order
6 ___ Bravo
7 Slippery one
8 Garb
9 Get
10 Gobbledygook
11 Santa ___ (Pacific wind)
12 Sportscaster Allen
15 Sycophantic
17 And more
21 It'll take you for a ride
23 Spelling of "Beverly Hills 90210"
24 "Paradise of exiles": Shelley
25 Workers in stables
27 Soap plants
28 Mexican state
29 " "
31 One-named Irish singer
32 Assts.
34 Oregon's capital
37 Ernest or Julio Gallo

Puzzle 6 by Eileen Lexau

38 Elation
41 Hypnotic states
43 Searches for provisions
45 "Sprechen ___ Deutsch?"
47 Lower California, familiarly
51 Ticket remainder
53 Good fruit with a bad name?

54 Dickens girl
55 Quite a trip
56 Stretch the truth
57 Warbler Yoko
59 Kind of humor
60 Lyric poem
61 School transportation

ACROSS

1 One of the Three Bears
5 Dog restraint
10 "___ It Romantic?"
14 Misfortunes
15 Dramatist Edward
16 Swirl with a spoon
17 School cutup
19 Moon goddess
20 Basic belief
21 "You said it!"
22 Garden of Eden man
23 Slept noisily
25 Muscular
27 Pony's gait
29 Like some committees
32 Young 'uns
35 Between-meals eater
39 Hubbub
40 Drink cooler
41 Art student's subject
42 On, as a lamp
43 Pie ___ mode
44 Longtime PBS series
45 Artist Paul
46 Kind of sentence
48 ". . . one ___ two!"
(Welk intro)
50 Gobbles (up)
54 Wreck, as a train
58 1970 Kinks hit
60 Poker players' markers
62 Catch cowboy-style
63 "We try harder"
company
64 Head of P.E. class
66 ___-majeste

67 "Stand and Deliver"
star Edward James ___
68 Mister, in Munich
69 Pretentiously cultured
70 Harvests
71 "That's clear"

DOWN

1 Early Brits
2 Revolutionary hero
Ethan
3 City in north Texas
4 Declares
5 Fond du ___, Wis.
6 Scat queen Fitzgerald
7 Manhattan Project
project
8 Underground passage
9 Redhead's dye
10 Cuba, e.g.
11 Quiet schoolroom
12 Ship of 1492
13 Coal car
18 Suffix with trick or
prank
24 Fashion's Karan
26 Cautious
28 Perfectly
30 "Garfield" dog
31 Pigeon's home
32 Fibber
33 Rights defender, for
short
34 Honor for the A-team?
36 Alphabet trio
37 Dance at a Jewish
wedding

Puzzle 7 by Fran and Lou Sabin

38 Improve
41 Model ___ Nicole Smith
45 Pakistani port
47 Playwright Sean
49 Oscar ___ Renta
51 Hardship
52 Christopher Morley's "Kitty ___"
53 Highest, in honors
55 Grave matter?
56 River to the Rhone
57 Actor Peter
58 Bit of a song refrain
59 Partner of "done with"
61 "Knock it off!"
65 Road curve

ACROSS

1 Help in a heist
5 Neighbor of St. Pete
10 ___ podrida
14 Etna output
15 "Our Town" role
16 Close
17 Cereal "for kids"
18 Pitcher Ryan
19 Restrain
20 John Stuart Mill treatise
22 Senator Hatch
23 Airport sched. abbr.
24 "Erotica" singer
26 Part of a place setting
30 Angola's capital
32 Stinging wasp
34 Amtrak stop: Abbr.
35 Colorless
39 Party to a defense treaty
40 Old-time anesthetic
42 Cunning trick
43 Fluctuate repeatedly
44 West of Hollywood
45 Sadistic sort
47 Diamond arbiter
50 Small fry
51 Spat
54 Early Beatle Sutcliffe
56 Single entities
57 In a precarious situation
63 "Make ___" (captain's directive)
64 Astronomer Tycho
65 Just
66 Scrabble piece
67 Russo and Magritte
68 Christmas tree topper
69 Bullring cheers
70 Idolize
71 Bill Clinton's birthplace

DOWN

1 Like Charlie Parker's sax
2 Farm building
3 Wicked
4 It's hailed by city dwellers
5 Principle
6 Lacking principles
7 Jazz bassist Hinton
8 Schoolyard friend
9 Novelist Rand
10 1963 Drifters song
11 Live's partner
12 What Mr. Chips taught
13 Gladiator's place
21 Nota ___
22 Peculiar
25 Cost ___ and a leg
26 Open carriage
27 Sport shirt
28 Paris airport
29 Rodgers and Hart musical
31 Theater employee
33 Site of Super Bowl XXX
36 Milieu for Lemieux
37 "I cannot tell ___"
38 Hive dwellers
41 Fitted

Puzzle 8 by Gregory E. Paul

46 Sundries case
48 "___ Doubtfire"
49 Book before Job
51 Capital just south of the equator
52 "Wait ___ Dark"
53 Supermarket section
55 "___ Eyes" (1969 song)
58 Prefix meaning "one-billionth"
59 Snack
60 Passionately studying
61 Thunder sound
62 Bronte heroine
64 Maidenform product

ACROSS

1 Dish of leftovers
5 Ink problem
9 Ill-tempered woman
14 Turkish official
15 Money to buy a car, maybe
16 Kind of fairy
17 1981 Treat Williams film
20 Followers of Xerxes
21 Socks cover them
22 Nevertheless
23 Weep
24 Groups entering Noah's ark
25 Yield, as a dividend
26 Actress Arthur and others
27 Taxi
30 Knight's horse
33 Jai ___
34 Middling
35 1945 Mel Torme song
38 Thin
39 Start of a counting-out rhyme
40 Like an old bucket of song
41 Memorable period
42 E-mail, e.g.
43 "It's freezing!"
44 Fountain order
45 Butt
46 ___ Vegas
49 Mail-related
52 Spy for the U.S.
54 1996 Hillary Clinton best seller
56 Purloined
57 More than ajar
58 ___ of Man
59 Crossed one's fingers
60 Ice block
61 Toot

DOWN

1 One of the Seven Dwarfs
2 Go along (with)
3 Polo or tee
4 Storied boy with silver skates
5 Not sharp, as eyesight
6 Off one's rocker
7 Clods
8 Explosive
9 Ones copying from Dictaphones
10 Pawns
11 Disturb
12 Suffix with kitchen
13 Philosophers' questions
18 Loud insect
19 Michener best seller
24 Moist-eyed
25 Job benefit
26 Mixture
27 Boil or broil
28 "___ forgive our debtors"
29 Former German capital
30 Enticing store sign

Puzzle 9 by Marilynn Huret

31 Ivan or Nicholas
32 Sicilian mount
33 Rocket stage
34 Lead player
36 Compass part
37 Everyday
42 Wet through and through
43 Sheep noise
44 Unfresh

45 Missouri or Delaware
46 Renter's paper
47 Polygon's corner
48 At quite an incline
49 "Nonsense!"
50 Palindromic emperor
51 Halt
52 Superman attire
53 Silver-tongued
55 Weep

ACROSS

1 Half a school yr.
4 Part of CD
8 Brings home
13 "American Gigolo" actor
14 Capri, e.g.
15 German sub
16 Halo
17 "Coming of Age in Samoa" author
18 Tycoon J. Paul ___
19 60's singer who "walks like a man"-servant?
22 Chinese gambling game
23 Sprinted
24 "Yuck!"
27 Airport abbr.
28 Ancient Brit
31 Actress Reynolds
33 Talks up, so to speak
35 Depend (on)
36 Life-style expert who's a perfect housekeeper?
40 Bargain seeker's event
41 Radio woe
42 Sign of acne
45 Basics
46 ___ Lanka
49 Critic ___ Louise Huxtable
50 Paris's ___ de la Cite
52 Miss Prynne of "The Scarlet Letter"

54 PBS host who's good in the kitchen?
57 Nichelle Nichols's role on "Star Trek"
60 ___ Fein
61 Lariat
62 Folk or rap, e.g.
63 Awestruck
64 Ripened
65 Environs
66 Hankerings
67 Fenced-in area

DOWN

1 "Sunday in the Park With George" painter
2 Gofer's chore
3 Intended
4 Reduce in size
5 "You're clear"
6 Eastern European
7 Lebanese tree
8 Conductor Ormandy
9 Assist in crime
10 Degenerate badly
11 Revolutionist Turner
12 Pigpen
13 Faux pas
20 Fini
21 Young chap
24 Above, in Berlin
25 Decorate expensively
26 "Watch it!"
29 Cartoonist Addams
30 Head, in Italy
32 Bric-a-___
33 Get ready, for short

Puzzle 10 by Stephanie Spadaccini

34 Pierce
36 One of "the help"
37 ___ mater
38 Some prints
39 Older but ___
40 Health resort
43 Walt Whitman bloomers
44 Actor Wallach
46 Moe, for one
47 Begin again, as a debate

48 Annoyed
51 Russell Baker specialty
53 Leftover piece
54 Operatic solo
55 Buster Brown's dog
56 Any day now
57 She played June in "Henry & June"
58 "Ben-___"
59 Exploit

ACROSS

1 Came apart at the seams
5 Ann ___, Mich.
10 Without
14 Mimics
15 Actress Rigg
16 Show appreciation at a concert
17 Complimentary close
19 ___ mater
20 Smeltery input
21 Old-fashioned poems
22 More sedate
24 Muffin ingredient
26 Shrewd
27 German spa
28 Deli side order
31 Spanish houses
34 Singer Crystal
35 Flamenco exclamation
36 Desertlike
37 Brooklyn's ___ Island
38 Czar before Feodor I
39 Ballpoint, e.g.
40 University of Florida footballer
41 ___ Litovsk (1918 treaty site)
42 Quit for the day
44 Pod occupant
45 Ice skating figure
46 With 43-Down, a complimentary close
50 Old Iran
52 ___ Lee cakes
53 Madhouse, so to speak
54 Guinness and others
55 Complimentary close
58 Madden
59 Formal goodbye
60 Kind of hygiene
61 Lock openers
62 "You've got the wrong guy!"
63 Nota ___

DOWN

1 Forbidden
2 Soap ___
3 Change, as a clock
4 Superlative suffix
5 Sneaker brand
6 Out of bed
7 "A Christmas Carol" cries
8 Singleton
9 Mischievous
10 Musical ladders
11 Complimentary close
12 Dub
13 Box, but not seriously
18 Ordinary bait
23 James who wrote "A Death in the Family"
25 Necklace ornament
26 More coquettish
28 Church law
29 Despondent comment
30 Traveled
31 Andy of the funnies
32 Region
33 Complimentary close
34 "I have the answer!"

Puzzle 11 by David Levinson Wilk

37 Native of old China
38 Seniors' nest eggs, for short
40 1958 movie musical
41 Sired, in biblical times
43 See 46-Across
44 Chase
46 Sheik's bevy

47 Sky-blue
48 Fastballer Ryan
49 Holmes's creator
50 Place the car
51 "Night" author Wiesel
52 Diamonds or spades
56 Prefix with meter
57 ___ blind

ACROSS

1 Proficient
6 Greek promenades
11 Vestment for the clergy
14 Rival of Paris
15 Tin Woodman's quest
16 Animal house
17 "Cheyenne" star
19 Prom wear
20 Cause of strain pain
21 Musical Horne
22 Wind dir.
23 Hoosier pro
26 Fr. holy woman
29 Tourmaline, e.g.
30 Jacuzzi
31 Tones
33 "Red Roses for a Blue Lady" singer
36 Swashbuckler Flynn
40 Not a blood relative
42 Sal of song
43 "Lorna ___"
44 Turkish title of old
45 Freudian interests
47 Semiquaver, e.g.
48 "___ alive!"
50 Cone bearer
52 Voting aye
53 Meadowlark Lemon, once
59 Calif. airport
60 Fishing item
61 Military command
65 Friend of Francois
66 1982 Harrison Ford film
68 Last letter in London

DOWN

69 Charlton Heston epic
70 Certain rocket engine
71 Before, to poets
72 Takes out
73 Hives

1 St. Louis landmark
2 Welfare, with "the"
3 Arabian bigwig
4 Helsinki coin
5 Hauling around
6 ___ Na Na
7 "I cannot ___ lie!"
8 Like some buckets
9 Madison Square Garden and others
10 Out of cash
11 Tenochtitlan resident
12 No-goodnik
13 Kind of shorts
18 Got wet up to the ankles
24 Screen presentation
25 Hitter of 755 home runs
26 Side-wheeler, for one
27 Sushi staple
28 Congers
32 Master, in Calcutta
34 Pester
35 Up in the sky
37 Part of the mouth
38 Aware of
39 Lascivious look
41 It may rock you to sleep

Puzzle 12 by Randall J. Hartman

46 Ravi Shankar's instrument
49 Cry in "A Streetcar Named Desire"
51 Half of a round trip
53 Shiny coating
54 More hobbled
55 Fe$_2$O$_3$, e.g.

56 Don't just stand there
57 "Golden" song
58 1966 hit "Walk Away ___"
62 Pantry pests
63 Spanish muralist
64 Son of Aphrodite
67 Sullivan and Asner

ACROSS

1 Shortly
5 NaCl
9 Kind of cheese
14 Letterman rival
15 Wash's partner
16 Noodles
17 Traveling ice-cream seller
20 Acapulco gold
21 Active person
22 Assistants
23 Overcast
25 Denver of "The Dukes of Hazzard"
26 Fire residue
27 Gorbachev policy
31 List components
34 Press, as clothes
35 Prevaricate
36 1976 film about a Little League team
40 Oliver North's rank: Abbr.
41 Syncopated songs
42 Vast chasm
43 Getting a move on
46 Lobster eater's accessory
47 Possess
48 Outstanding athlete
52 On land
55 Not in use
56 "Honest" President
57 1958 best seller set in Southeast Asia
60 Oslo's land, on stamps
61 Scored 100 on
62 Henri's head
63 Brilliantly colored fish
64 Unites
65 Rabbit dish

DOWN

1 Choir members
2 India's first P.M.
3 Tie ___ (get smashed)
4 Yuletide beverage
5 Rushing sound
6 Yellow fever mosquito
7 Lion player of 1939
8 Capote, familiarly
9 Turns bad
10 Head of a pen
11 "Woe ___ I"
12 Walk of Fame symbol
13 ___-serif (type style)
18 Ukraine port
19 Central American pyramid builders
24 Mary's pet
25 Snow-cleaning vehicles
27 One of the Allman Brothers
28 Oil of ___
29 Sexist letter start
30 Dick Tracy's love
31 Seven-year phenomenon
32 10 C-notes
33 Wriggly fish
34 Foolish
37 Utter nonsense
38 One who dips out water

Puzzle 13 by Fred Piscop

39 Subsides, as the tide
44 However
45 Some T-shirts
46 Has an open wound
48 Carrying guns
49 Be silent, in music
50 Diminish in intensity

51 Ask for more Time?
52 "___ added expense"
53 Boutique
54 Wife of Zeus
55 Confront
58 Go off course
59 Part of T.G.I.F.

ACROSS

1 Charlie Chan portrayer Warner
6 Letters after a proof
9 1908 Peace Nobelist Fredrik
14 Auger or drill
15 ___ Today
16 A McCoy, to a Hatfield
17 747 and DC-10
19 "___ which will live in infamy": F.D.R.
20 Greek earth goddess
21 British submachine gun
22 Temporary stay
26 Literally, face to face
29 Accents in "resume"
30 Precooking solution
31 18-wheelers
32 Founder of a French dynasty
33 Meadow
34 Ninnies
35 Seeker of the Golden Fleece
36 Take ___ at (criticize)
37 Singer Kamoze
38 Spanish gent
39 "Zorba the Greek" setting
40 Genius
42 Attired for a frat party
43 Convertibles
44 Additional helpings
45 Moonshine containers
46 Phnom ___
47 Old adders

49 Nickname for DiMaggio
54 Italian bowling game
55 Record speed: Abbr.
56 Role for Valentino
57 Some sharks
58 Caribbean, e.g.
59 Circumvent

DOWN

1 Goal: Abbr.
2 Singer Rawls or Reed
3 Pitcher's pride
4 Lincoln's state: Abbr.
5 Small parachutes
6 Wicked "Snow White" figure
7 "Como ___ usted?"
8 Prosecutors, for short
9 Skedaddles
10 Like the Incas
11 "Les Miserables" protagonist
12 C.P.R. administrant
13 Deli bread
18 See 30-Down
21 Theda Bara, e.g.
22 With more attitude
23 Pacific islands, collectively
24 Single calisthenic
25 Big name in elevators
26 Gaseous mist
27 Conceptualized
28 Where oysters sleep?
30 With 18-Down, home canning items

Puzzle 14 by Dean Niles

32 ___ Major (southern constellation)
35 Army vehicles
36 35-Across's vessel
38 Cheap cigars
39 Apache chief
41 Plaster finish
42 Camp sight
44 Alabama city
46 Pontiff

47 Defense syst.
48 Feathered stole
49 Some namesakes, for short
50 Gretzky's grp.
51 Game, in France
52 Ending with human or planet
53 Supplement, with "out"

ACROSS

1 Bushy coif
5 Belle or Bart
10 "Dancing Queen" pop group
14 It goes with runners
15 Army Corps of Engineers construction
16 Burrow
17 In direct competition
19 Mid 12th-century date
20 Long fish
21 Rich Little, e.g.
22 Drew out
24 Three-sided sword
25 Savage
26 One of the Greats
29 Half step, in music
32 Partner of ways
33 Shack
34 Corn crib
35 Early Andean
36 More rational
37 Diplomat's skill
38 Fr. holy woman
39 Burger King, to McDonald's
40 Where the loot gets left
41 Autumn drink
43 Crave, with "for"
44 "You Must Remember This" author
45 Kennel cry
46 Browning automatics
48 Effrontery
49 Menlo Park initials
52 Shut noisily
53 Kind of combat
56 Gambling, e.g.
57 ___ orange
58 Mitch Miller's instrument
59 Squint
60 Firefighting need
61 Old TV detective Peter

DOWN

1 Connors defeater, 1975
2 Hightail it
3 Not imagined
4 Roulette bet
5 Inclined
6 Snicker
7 Say it's so
8 New Deal proj.
9 Jesus Christ, with "the"
10 Virtually
11 One after the other
12 Ill temper
13 Saharan
18 Uses a camcorder
23 Resort near Copper Mountain
24 Soprano Berger
25 Angle on a gem
26 Plain People
27 Slowly, in music
28 In-person, as an interview
29 Sub detector
30 Recess
31 Computer command
33 Wealthy ones

Puzzle 15 by Gregory E. Paul

36 Two-headed lady exhibit, e.g.
37 Part of L.S.T.
39 Liturgy
40 Film producer Ponti
42 More tranquil
43 Horse restraint
45 Sheriff's star, e.g.

46 Invitation letters
47 Tennis's Nastase
48 Pesky insect
49 No-no: Var.
50 Erelong
51 First place
54 Simile center
55 Not a sharer

ACROSS

1 Spring
5 Upper-story room
10 Ali who said "Open sesame!"
14 Latin journey
15 Material for uniforms
16 Arab prince
17 Plot size
18 "Greetings!"
19 Suffix with million
20 Chickens that lay brown eggs
23 Toward shelter
24 Old French coin
25 Mad ___ (Wonderland character)
28 Pedaler's place
33 Kitchen garment
34 Interstate hauler
35 Actress Myrna
36 Attraction for winter vacationers in the South
40 ___ Aviv
41 Followers: Suffix
42 ___ the Barbarian
43 Soup crackers
46 ___ Anderson of TV's "Baywatch"
47 Half of dos
48 Play part
49 Easy-gaited saddle horse
57 Pitcher Nolan
58 Bridal walkway
59 Not for
60 "Rule Britannia" composer
61 Like certain dentures
62 Tide type
63 Ground grain
64 Snoozes
65 Remove, in editing

DOWN

1 Pinocchio, at times
2 Make art on glass
3 Pertaining to aircraft
4 Lion or coyote
5 Sorer
6 "One of ___ days, Alice . . ."
7 Money drawer
8 1985 movie "To Live and Die ___"
9 Kind of cap
10 Face hardship bravely
11 She's a sweetie in Tahiti
12 Wren or hen
13 Greek Mars
21 1985 Nicholas Gage best seller
22 Buck's mate
25 Sword handles
26 Cop ___ (negotiate for a lighter sentence)
27 Folklore dwarf
28 Defeats
29 Radio host Don
30 Skirt type
31 Having a key, in music
32 "Laughing" animal

Puzzle 16 by Sally Jo Walther

34 Encl. for a reply
37 Jurassic Park revival
38 La ___ opera house
39 One's birthplace
44 Burrow
45 Ending with nectar or saturn
46 ___ that be
48 Rent again

49 Mine vehicle
50 Jane who loved Mr. Rochester
51 Zola novel
52 Ex-Cleveland QB Brian
53 Intuitive feelings
54 Where the patella is
55 And others: Abbr.
56 Properly aged

ACROSS

1 ___ blocker
5 Cabbie
9 Desert flora
14 Latin 101 word
15 Cousin of a Tony
16 Autumn color
17 Singer McEntire
18 Give the slip to
19 Squirrel away
20 Alien art form, some say
23 Magnum and others, for short
24 Give it ___ (try)
25 "Now, about . . ."
26 Getaways
28 Hilton Head Island, for one
30 Prohibitionists would like to prohibit it
33 Caught but good
36 Danish money
37 Agreement
40 Interrupt, as a dancer
42 Parroted
43 Fitzgerald and others
45 Bee and snake products
47 Boo-boos
49 Turkey moistener
53 Cartoon skunk ___ Le Pew
54 TV ad
56 "Norma ___"
57 SASE, e.g.
59 Fruit pastry
62 Ravel work, with "La"
64 Legal scholar Guinier
65 Villa d'___
66 "Give peace ___ time, O Lord": Morning Prayer
67 Prime time hour
68 Mets stadium
69 Gently gallops
70 Pub round
71 Like a Granny Smith apple

DOWN

1 Where train commuters drink
2 Come to the fore
3 No-nos
4 Pronto!
5 Kind of medicine
6 Call off a takeoff
7 50's western "The ___ Kid"
8 Ship's central beam
9 Russian horseman
10 Take steps
11 Auto disassembly site
12 Actress Hatcher
13 Gets one's goat
21 Singer Irene
22 Building wing
27 Quagmire
29 Recorded
30 Point after deuce
31 Single
32 Conducted
34 Disposable diaper brand

Puzzle 17 by Elizabeth C. Gorski

35 Bordeaux summer
37 Foot: Lat.
38 The works
39 Carriage horse sound
41 People who don't count
44 Evening meals
46 ___ Hari
48 Each
50 Country singer Yearwood

51 Resurrection Mass day
52 Warm up again
54 Escargot
55 Tubular pasta
57 Stephen King topic
58 Prefix with second
60 Arm bone
61 Hornets' home
63 Take to court

ACROSS

1 Wood-turning tool
6 Welcome smell
11 Undergrad degrees
14 Disney mermaid
15 Site of golfing's Ryder Open
16 Genetic trait carrier
17 Make an error
19 Consume
20 Part to play
21 Teacher in a turban
23 Conciliate
27 Gotten back, as land in battle
29 Villain
30 Capital of Tasmania
31 Welles of "Citizen Kane"
32 Golden Horde member
33 Premium cable channel
36 Diana of the Supremes
37 Munchhausen's title
38 Lima, e.g.
39 Suffix with superintend
40 Rubbernecker
41 Fanny ___ of the Ziegfeld Follies
42 Area of Manhattan
44 Lighthouse light
45 Artist's studio
47 Make manhattans and such
48 Ear parts
49 Is up
50 Zoo bird
51 Be outrageous
58 ___ room
59 Deceive
60 Charge
61 "For shame!"
62 Mystery writer's award
63 Nairobi's land

DOWN

1 Terhune's "___: a Dog"
2 Opposite of "Dep." on a flight board
3 Tijuana uncle
4 With it, 40's-style
5 It loops the Loop
6 Dancer Astaire
7 Caftan
8 ". . . man ___ mouse?"
9 ___ de mer
10 Selected athlete
11 Get a party going
12 "What's in ___?"
13 Luxurious sheet material
18 Hydrant hookup
22 Card game for two
23 Dean Martin song subject
24 Juan of Argentina
25 Not take responsibility
26 1961 space chimp
27 Copter part
28 Israeli statesman Abba
30 Quarters in a sultan's palace
32 Grow narrower

Puzzle 18 by C. F. Murray

34 Breakfast sizzler
35 Upturned, as a box
37 Cotton bundle
38 Baby sitter's nightmare
40 Chewy part of meat
41 Bananas
43 Hearty drink
44 Alternative to a shower
45 With ears pricked
46 Weighty books

47 Ulan ___, Mongolia
49 ___ carotene
52 Help
53 Beer barrel
54 Feed lines to
55 Massachusetts cape
56 Braggart knight of the Round Table
57 H, to Greeks

ACROSS

1 Courtyards
6 ___ d'etat
10 Part of a gateway
14 Middays
15 Facilitate
16 Denver's home: Abbr.
17 Disoriented
20 Dancers Fred and Adele
21 ___-Japanese War
22 Actor Sparks
23 ___ end (very last part)
25 Prime-time hour
26 Soviet labor camp
30 Party to a defense pact
31 Spirited horse
32 Prophet who anointed Saul
34 Mimic
37 Disoriented
40 Jet to Heathrow
41 Vigorous
42 Actress Spelling
43 Operatic prince
44 Dead, as an engine
45 Had been
48 Guinness Book suffix
49 One of the Gershwins
51 Once more
53 Captain Picard series
58 Disoriented
61 State south of Ky.
62 Kind of smasher
63 Sharp as ___
64 Chair
65 They hold hymnals
66 Where Seoul is

DOWN

1 Paul who sang "Having My Baby"
2 Shipping units
3 Cheer (for)
4 Andean of old
5 Inquiring
6 Relinquished
7 Schmoes
8 G.I. entertainers
9 Each
10 Rights protection grp.
11 Chicken house
12 In the ball park
13 Board, as a trolley
18 "Able was I ___ . . ."
19 Historic county of Scotland
23 Botches
24 Native Alaskan
26 Wanders (about)
27 "Exodus" author
28 Endure
29 Roseanne's former network
30 Love, in Lourdes
32 Urban woes
33 Monastery V.I.P.
34 Over
35 Where the Amazon originates
36 Make a change for the verse?
38 China and environs, with "the"
39 One ___ time
44 Noted site of Egyptian ruins
45 Floats gently

Puzzle 19 by Sidney L. Robbins

46 Be of one mind
47 Finnish bath
49 News paragraphs
50 "Far out"
52 "Money ___ everything!"
53 Pack

54 Dog in Oz
55 Bring up
56 Suffix with exist
57 America's first commercial radio station
59 Seance sound
60 Dined

ACROSS

1 Rushes (along)
5 Amassed
10 They cover Highland heads
14 Neglect
15 Mes numero uno
16 "In a cowslip's bell ___": "The Tempest"
17 One nourished by daydreams?
19 Rotten to the ___
20 One of "Them!" things
21 Author O'Brien
22 Ready for framing
24 Genealogical chart
25 New Rochelle college
26 One who counts calories?
32 Perspiration perforations
33 Alternative to a watering can
34 Khan married to Rita Hayworth
35 Detective Charlie
36 Dress style
38 Classic art subject
39 Elephant's weight, maybe
40 Israeli Abba
41 "For ___ sake!"
42 One with a high-iron diet?
46 Hollywood giants?
47 Jemima, for one
48 Farm trough
51 ___ .45
52 Dallas school, for short
55 Strip of wood
56 One fond of dining on tongue?
59 Florence's river
60 Destroy
61 Motion supporters
62 High schooler's test, briefly
63 Went out with
64 Key letter

DOWN

1 "J'accuse" author
2 Springsteen's "___ Fire"
3 English P.M. called "The Great Commoner"
4 Alphabet trio
5 Carolina river
6 More ridiculous
7 "I ___ Song Go Out of My Heart"
8 Before, to a poet
9 Member of Alice's tea party
10 Popular breath mint
11 Loads
12 Slough
13 Burpee's bit
18 Some Bosnians
23 ___ Morrow Lindbergh
24 Feds
25 Clothes presser
26 Not at all
27 Heavens: Prefix

Puzzle 20 by Jonathan Schmalzbach

28 Tableware
29 ___ cuisine
30 Presbyter
31 Deli loaves
32 Election numbers: Abbr.
36 Sucked up
37 Statutes
38 Its eye is needed in a "Macbeth" recipe
40 Slight advantage
41 Sophia's Carlo
43 Boiling mad

44 "Tao Te Ching" author
45 Quieted
48 Part of an envelope
49 Auricles
50 Lab burner
51 Layer
52 Hebrides island
53 Make the acquaintance of
54 Twinkling bear
57 Man-mouse link
58 Taxi

ACROSS

1 Poverty
5 Mutual of ___
10 Track tipster
14 Neighborhood
15 Artist Bonheur and others
16 Like Solomon
17 Watch face
18 Whitney's partner in airplanes
19 Pizazz
20 1970's New York Knick's nickname
23 Western alliance: Abbr.
24 Sidestep
28 Grotto
32 20- and 51-Across, e.g.
35 States firmly
36 To ___ (precisely)
37 "___ the season to be jolly"
38 Hank Ketcham comic strip
42 Purpose
43 Harrow's rival
44 Dog: Fr.
45 When American elections are held
48 Rio ___ (border river)
49 Take care of, as duties
50 Nearly worthless coin
51 1960–66 N.B.A. scoring leader, informally
59 Jellystone Park bear
62 "I don't give ___!"

63 Scent
64 G.I. addresses
65 Jazz singer Vaughan
66 Burn soother
67 Didn't part with
68 Pickpocketed
69 Physics unit

DOWN

1 Walk in the baby pool
2 La Scala solo
3 Not distant
4 Six-foot or more
5 Annie, e.g., in the comics
6 Folkways
7 "Rush!"
8 Abhor
9 30's movie dog
10 Midnight
11 Source of Rockefeller money
12 Red, white and blue initials
13 Hamilton's bill
21 Trunks
22 Seminary subj.
25 Reach
26 Cleared, as a winter windshield
27 Ancient Palestinian
28 West Pointers
29 Boulevard
30 Buyer
31 Suffix with east or west
32 One of the Three Musketeers

Puzzle 21 by Gregory E. Paul

33 MTV's target viewer
34 Haw's partner
36 Bar member: Abbr.
39 Poseidon's realm
40 Pale colors
41 Shelter grp.
46 Double curve, as in yarn
47 "How ___ love thee? Let me . . ."
48 "Faust" dramatist
50 Sand bar

52 Sweetheart
53 "Anything but ___!"
54 Bullfight bull
55 "The Wind in the Willows" character
56 Without thought
57 Diving bird
58 Chestnut or walnut
59 Talk, talk, talk
60 Unlock, in poetry
61 Republicans, collectively

ACROSS

1 Pitchers
6 Take to the dump
11 Say "pretty please"
14 Republican politico Alexander
15 Skip the big wedding
16 Genetic letters
17 1978 Faye Dunaway film
20 I.B.M. or 3M, e.g.: Abbr.
21 In this place
22 Taboos
23 ___ of war
24 Luxuriate, as in the sun
25 Tone down
26 Incredible bargain
28 Boeing product
29 The "I" in T.G.I.F.
30 George Bush's home now
34 Peer Gynt's mother
35 1932 Will Rogers film
37 Tofu source
38 Late singer named for a Dickens character
39 Midmorning
40 Douglas ___
41 Adagio and allegro
45 Pennsylvania, for one
47 Food inspection inits.
50 Suffix with convention
51 Kind of closet
52 Italian princely family name
53 Mata ___

54 1948 Ava Gardner film
57 N.Y.C. subway operator
58 Olympic judge
59 Come up
60 Prodigy competitor, for short
61 Used colorful language
62 40- and 51-Across, e.g.

DOWN

1 Puts into office
2 Exit
3 Come out
4 Bronchitis symptom
5 Full house sign
6 Tennis's Monica
7 Co-worker of Lois and Jimmy
8 Libertine
9 30-day mo.
10 Subject for George Washington Carver
11 Wave, as a weapon
12 Along the way
13 Helium and neon, e.g.
18 Mortgage agcy.
19 Teeming group
24 Hard punch
25 French assembly
27 On-board greeting
28 Bishop of old TV
31 Loosen, as laces
32 Recipe directive

Puzzle 22 by Elizabeth C. Gorski

33 "Long" or "short" amount
34 "Don't look ___ like that!"
35 Fait accompli
36 Singer Coolidge
37 53 minutes past the hour
39 Puget Sound city
40 Frenzies
42 Villain
43 Look over

44 Record-setting van Gogh canvas
46 ___ King Cole
47 Fallen house of literature
48 Squirrel away
49 Rock's ___ Leppard
52 Outside: Prefix
53 Munchen Mr.
55 Detroit labor grp.
56 Grape masher's work site

ACROSS

1 Garb for Superman
5 Ice cream dessert
10 Work detail, for short
14 Singer Guthrie
15 Ness of "The Untouchables"
16 ___ Strauss (jeans maker)
17 What a ghost may give you
19 Coup d'___
20 Boundary
21 Meat cuts
22 Stockholmer
23 Wise one
24 Pay no attention
26 Georgia city where Little Richard was born
29 Western hero
31 Keeps away from
33 "Whose Life ___ Anyway?" (1981 movie)
34 Suffix with cash
37 Factory on a stream
38 Department at an auto shop
40 Fairy tale starter
41 Tally (up)
42 Bundled cotton
43 "Well said!"
45 Honkers
48 A Musketeer
49 Pass ___ (make the grade)
50 Poll amts.
52 Bar for a bird
53 California lake resort
55 Notwithstanding, briefly
58 Actress Chase
59 With feet pointing in
61 Above, in Berlin
62 Not moving
63 Singer Fitzgerald
64 Articulates
65 Go along (with)
66 Enemy's opposite

DOWN

1 Hamster's home
2 "East of Eden" brother
3 Slog (through)
4 Dawn goddess
5 Obscure
6 Hardy and North
7 Bearing
8 Most domineering
9 Numerical ending
10 Quite a few, after "a"
11 "Network" co-star
12 Dodge, as a question
13 Commend
18 African antelope
22 Perturbed state
23 Loam
25 Grain for grinding
26 Baby doll's cry
27 Enthusiastic
28 One way to quit
30 Personnel person
32 Outpouring
35 Reverberate
36 "Cheers" actor Roger
39 Emulating Paul Revere

Puzzle 23 by Stephanie Spadaccini

40 Inning parts
42 This and that
44 Granola-like
46 Katharine Hepburn has four
47 Globe
49 Opera star Nellie
51 "Veddy" British actor Robert

52 Papal name
54 Finish for teen or golden
55 Auto commuter's bane
56 "War is ___"
57 Singer Anita
59 Actress Zadora
60 Wonderland drink

ACROSS

1 Poland's Walesa
5 Fine violin
10 With 39-Across, featured boxing match
14 "As Long ___ Needs Me" ("Oliver!" song)
15 Two-door
16 Capital on a fjord
17 Gallows reprieve
18 Quite healthy
20 Eternally, to poets
21 Downwind
22 "We ___ the World"
23 Not firsthand
25 Biting
29 Patisserie employee
30 Application information
31 Downhill runner
33 Amusement park features
35 Uncles and others
36 Around
38 "___ Ruled the World" (1965 hit)
39 See 10-Across
41 Rope-a-dope exponent
42 Angers
45 Angers
46 Rural way
48 Comes to the rescue
50 Teaches the A B C's
51 Self-defense art
54 Like some humor
55 Kind of chop
56 Kovic of "Born on the Fourth of July"
57 "Designing Women" co-star
61 Pinochle combo
62 Food bar
63 An archangel
64 Baseball's Rose
65 Talon
66 Litigants
67 Hullabaloo

DOWN

1 Light in a light show
2 Lauder of cosmetics
3 "The Most Beautiful Girl" singer
4 "Yo!"
5 Tackle box gizmos
6 "And so ___"
7 Hold sway over
8 Imitate
9 Spectacular failure
10 Part of MOMA
11 "Unaccustomed ___ am . . ."
12 Spot in the mer
13 Visual O.K.
19 To avoid the alternative
21 Parliamentary stand
24 Current status
25 Tax filer's dread
26 1978 Gerry Rafferty hit
27 Ammonia-derived compound
28 Parts of dollars

Puzzle 24 by Thomas W. Schier

30 Played a flute in a march
31 Temporary protectors
32 New Hampshire's state flower
34 Actress Bonet and others
37 Colorado city
40 "I saw," Caesar-style
43 Oedipus' foster father
44 Marine fishes
47 Servilely defer (to)
49 H-L connectors
51 Wild card
52 Conductor Georg
53 Secondary to
55 ___-dieu (pew part)
57 Medic
58 Angled annex
59 Pasture
60 It neighbors Braz.
61 AWOL hunters

ACROSS

1 Desert plants
6 Swap
11 Stomach muscles, for short
14 Extraterrestrial
15 King or queen
16 Do some softshoe
17 Big name in video rentals
19 Kimono accessory
20 Musical partner of Crosby and Stills
21 Madison Avenue worker
23 Big monkeys
27 French artist Henri
29 Adjusts to fit
30 Extreme cruelty
31 Religious factions
32 Top floor
33 Rainbow shape
36 Lodge members
37 Air raid alert
38 Words of comprehension
39 Tiny bit, as of cream
40 Asia's ___ Peninsula
41 Bus station posting: Abbr.
42 Mickey of "National Velvet"
44 Word said to a photographer
45 Split with a hatchet
47 Scorched
48 Contract with a car dealer
49 Limerick, e.g.
50 Bic filler
51 Yegg
58 "We're number ___!"
59 Eskimo boat
60 Lariat's end
61 Neighbor of Isr.
62 Little finger
63 Soaked

DOWN

1 Quick way around town
2 The whole shooting match
3 A.F.L.'s partner
4 Gumshoe
5 Tied up
6 Supporting beam
7 "High priority!"
8 Supermodel Carol
9 Ruby or Sandra
10 Unpredictable
11 Cyclotron
12 Rum cakes
13 Vertebra locale
18 Prohibits
22 Malign, in slang
23 Established
24 Writer ___ Rogers St. Johns
25 Exhausting task
26 Chooses
27 Chum, to a Brit
28 Tennis score
30 Homeless animal
32 Felt crummy

Puzzle 25 by Fred Piscop

34 Pee Wee of Ebbets Field
35 Yielded
37 Having one's marbles
38 Cake finisher
40 Advances
41 Tribal healers
43 Western treaty grp.
44 Sonny's ex
45 Advertising awards

46 Comedian Bruce
47 Overly selfconfident
49 Mountain
52 "___ Blue?" (1929 #1 hit)
53 Five smackeroos
54 Dove sound
55 Keystone character
56 Sixth sense, for short
57 Juan Carlos, e.g.

ACROSS

1 Anesthetize, in a way
4 Some chain clothing stores
8 Video game hub
14 Play the part
15 Zone
16 Stops the tape temporarily
17 "Little" extraterrestrials
19 Passe
20 Had a bug
21 Inspirationalist Norman Vincent ___
23 Before, in verse
24 Home on the Black Sea
26 Smart-alecky
28 Pop duo with the album "Swamp Ophelia"
34 Reply to a masher
38 Satellite ___
39 Bunk
40 Actress Anderson
41 Newton or Stern
43 Actress Thurman and others
44 Small choir
46 Outfielder's cry
47 Oct. precursor
48 Drinks with gin, Cointreau and lemon juice
51 Greeting at sea
52 Undignified landing
56 Hardly Mr. Right
59 Facilitates
62 Unpaid factory worker

64 "All ___!"
66 Some Gainsborough forgeries
68 Ice cream parlor order
69 Two-wheeler
70 Sometime theater funder: Abbr.
71 Be at
72 French holy women: Abbr.
73 Blow it

DOWN

1 Crazy (over)
2 Pungent
3 Inscribed column
4 Leader called Mahatma
5 Tattoo place
6 Coop sound
7 Psychologically all there
8 Noted Harlem hot spot, with "The"
9 Durham's twin city
10 Bossy's chew
11 Connors opponent
12 ___ John
13 Isabella d'___ (Titian subject)
18 Continental trading org.
22 Khyber Pass traveler
25 1941 Glenn Miller chart topper "You ___"
27 Reverent
29 Lets down

Puzzle 26 by Elizabeth C. Gorski

30 "Let me repeat . . ."
31 Where the Vatican is
32 Giant hop
33 Method: Abbr.
34 Leisurely
35 Ness, for one
36 One doing a con job?
37 Michelangelo masterpiece
42 So-so grades
45 Iran's capital
49 Stinking rich
50 Shopping binges

53 Defensive tennis shot
54 Have ___ to pick
55 One who's not playing seriously
56 Home for la familia
57 Go up against
58 Word of warning
60 Drops off
61 Cut
63 Pre-1917 ruler
65 Fruit juice
67 Hawaiian music maker

ACROSS

1 Ravioli base
6 Numbered hwys.
10 Nicholas was one
14 Sour
15 The Emerald Isle
16 "What's ___ you?"
17 18-wheelers
18 Communication means for computer-phobes
20 Grotesque imitation
22 Eat like a rabbit
23 Trees with cones
24 Tries again
25 Cornell's home
27 Passover event
28 Spanish gold
29 Moral principle
31 Convened again
35 Eggheady sort
37 "Cheers!" in Cherbourg
39 Dumb ___ (scatterbrain)
40 Length of yarn
42 Spud
44 Q-U link
45 Agrees (with)
47 Bang and buzz, e.g.
49 Graphed
52 "Lorna ___" (1869 romance)
53 Reddish brown
54 Comes to light
57 Communication means at the office
59 Eat away
60 Once, once
61 Blue-pencil
62 "The Thinker" creator
63 Henna and others
64 Old newspaper section
65 Sugary

DOWN

1 Auld lang syne, with "the"
2 Perfect server
3 Communication means at sea
4 "Jeopardy!" staple
5 "___ makes the heart . . ."
6 Takes five
7 Minuscule
8 Period of history
9 Trawled
10 Having trees
11 Knifes
12 Like Pisa's tower
13 Parts
19 Pepsi bottle size
21 Train reservations
24 Split the cards again
25 Charged particles
26 "Star ___"
27 "___ Marner"
30 More than disliked
32 Communication means for emergencies
33 Language spoken in Dingwall
34 Does lacework
36 Upsets

Puzzle 27 by Mary E. Brindamour

38 Jose Carreras, for one
41 British fertilizer
43 Ones at the top of their business?
46 Stapleton Airport site
48 Lined up
49 Pent up
50 "Faster!"
51 Belittle
52 Because of
54 Tizzy
55 Actress McClurg
56 Faxed
58 Bachelor's last words

ACROSS

1 Pickle container
4 Motionless
9 Fashion
14 Matriarch of all matriarchs
15 Actor Romero
16 Boiling
17 Weighed in
20 Light lunches
21 To any extent
22 List-ending abbr.
23 Moo juice container
25 Grp. overseeing toxic cleanups
28 Perfect rating
29 Most prudent
31 Become raveled
32 Painful spots
33 Carroll adventuress
34 Caused disharmony
38 Napping spots
39 Magazine exhortation
40 Break in relations
41 Out of business
43 Compaq products
46 ___ Miss
47 Engulfs in amusement
48 Cream ingredient
49 Tear to shreds
51 Part of MOMA
53 Blabbed
57 ___ pedis (athlete's foot)
58 Take to the stump
59 Certain shirt
60 Anxiety
61 Wanderer

62 Japanese honorific

DOWN

1 High-fliers
2 Fly
3 Change tactics
4 Like an eclair
5 Composer Rorem and others
6 Superlative ending
7 Short cheer
8 Firestone features
9 Clergyman
10 Kind of surgery
11 Indoor court
12 Indian with a bear dance
13 Some M.I.T. grads
18 Chum
19 Leave be
23 Wielded
24 Partner of search
26 Warsaw ___
27 Word of assent
29 Canton cookware
30 Land west of Eng.
31 Current
32 Sing "shooby-doo"
33 Out for the night
34 Aggravate
35 Part of a church service
36 Piano-playing Dame
37 Ariz.-to-Kan. dir.
38 Sign of stage success
41 Professor Plum's game
42 Pomeranian, for one

43 Stitched folds
44 Window of an eye
45 Breath mint brand
47 Sloppy-landing sound
48 Suffix with stock
50 France's ___ de Glenans

51 Queens team
52 Follow the code
53 ___ Puf fabric softener
54 Wrestler's goal
55 Have a go at
56 Gen. Arnold of W.W. II fame

ACROSS

1 Not fiction
5 Prefix with legal or chute
9 Fire starter
14 Hand lotion ingredient
15 At any time
16 Macho dude
17 Author Fleming and others
18 Extinct bird not known for its intelligence
19 Sky-blue
20 Louisa May Alcott classic
23 Envision
24 Deli loaves
25 Participants in a debate
27 World's fastest sport, with 2-Down
29 Footfall
32 Sounds of satisfaction
33 Thomas ___ Edison
35 "Woe is me!"
37 Walkway
41 Nightgown wearer of children's rhyme
44 Four-door
45 It has a keystone
46 Lass
47 "Now ___ seen everything!"
49 Store, as a ship's cargo
51 Aye's opposite
52 Woven cloth or fabric
56 Not able to hear
58 "___ Believer" (Monkees hit)
59 Don Ho standard
64 Sprite
66 Destroy
67 ___ one's time
68 It's a piece of cake
69 Atlanta arena, with "the"
70 "What's ___ for me?"
71 Affirmatives
72 Endure
73 Kett of the comics

DOWN

1 Flunk
2 See 27-Across
3 Artificial
4 Irritable and impatient
5 Place for a statue or a hero
6 Affirm
7 Give a makeover
8 Fragrance
9 Major Chinese seaport
10 Candy that comes in a dispenser
11 Tickle the funny bone
12 Harder to find
13 Strike zone's lower boundary
21 "___ Miserables"
22 Memorable time
26 Taking advantage of
27 Shark tale
28 Sheltered from the wind

Puzzle 29 by Shannon Burns

1	2	3	4		5	6	7	8		9	10	11	12	13
14					15					16				
17					18					19				
20				21				22			23			
	24						25			26				
27	28			29		30	31		32					
33			34		35			36		37		38	39	40
41				42				43						
44					45					46				
			47		48		49			50		51		
52	53	54			55			56		57				
58				59			60	61				62	63
64			65		66					67				
68					69					70				
71					72					73				

30 First name in scat
31 Couples
34 Watch for
36 Religious splinter group
38 Miser
39 Trevi Fountain coin
40 Slippery
42 People asked to parties
43 Murder mystery
48 Yale grad
50 World Wide ___
52 A bit blotto
53 Writer Zola
54 The line y = 0, in math
55 Register, as a student
57 60's protest leader Hoffman
60 City in Arizona
61 Storage containers
62 Do magazine work
63 ___ high standard
65 Skating surface

ACROSS

1 Some sports cars, for short
5 Foundation
10 Yield
14 Grimm villain
15 Novelist Jong
16 Jump at the Ice Capades
17 British heavy metal group
19 Canned meat brand
20 Disney's Dwarfs, e.g.
21 Printings
23 Support for Tiger Woods?
24 Pop singer Peeples
26 Prepares leather
27 Do a few odd jobs
32 ___ Ababa
35 Cape Cod resort town
36 Acuff of the Country Music Hall of Fame
37 Androcles' friend
38 Headgear for Hardy
39 Celebration
40 Worshiper's seat
41 Bruce Wayne's home, for one
42 Valentine's Day gift
43 Inexpert motorist
46 Klondike strike
47 Org. that advises the N.S.C.
48 Computer key abbr.
51 One who works for a spell?
55 Sauteed shrimp dish
57 Not this
58 Huck Finn portrayer, 1993
60 Bring to ruin
61 As a companion
62 To be, in Tours
63 Afrikaner
64 London length
65 Fortuneteller

DOWN

1 Ceiling supporter
2 Conform (with)
3 Search blindly
4 E-mailed
5 "Hit the bricks!"
6 Jackie's second
7 Pro or con
8 Chilled the Chablis
9 Hygienic
10 Dealer's employer
11 Film box datum
12 Cain of "Lois & Clark"
13 Stately shaders
18 Luncheonette lists
22 Tropical root
25 Look after, with "to"
27 Wrestler's goal
28 Diamond flaw?
29 Decorative heading
30 Bit of marginalia
31 Changes color, in a way
32 European chain
33 The Almighty, in Alsace
34 Reduce in rank

1	2	3	4		5	6	7	8	9		10	11	12	13
14					15						16			
17				18							19			
20							21			22				
23				24		25			26					
			27				28	29				30	31
32	33	34			35					36			
37				38					39			
40				41				42				
43			44				45					
	46					47			48	49	50
51	52			53	54		55		56			
57				58		59					
60				61					62			
63				64					65			

38 Class distraction
39 On behalf of
41 Having a Y chromosome
42 Boxer's stat
44 Alter deceptively
45 Countenance
48 Overplay onstage
49 Fern fruit
50 Autumn beverage
51 Hit, as the toe
52 "You gotta be kidding!"
53 Model Macpherson
54 Very funny fellow
56 Makes one's jaw drop
59 Dad's namesake: Abbr.

ACROSS

1 Sandwich shop
5 Fitzgerald and others
10 "We're looking for ___ good men"
14 North Carolina college
15 Gettysburg victor
16 Pepsi, for one
17 41339
20 Sweet liqueur
21 Gallic girlfriends
22 Ascot
23 ___-Coburg-Gotha (British royal house)
25 62060
33 Affixed with heat, as a patch
34 ___ number on (mess up)
35 Campground letters
36 20's gangster Bugs ___
37 Each of the numbers in this puzzle's theme
38 Being a copycat
40 They: Fr.
41 ___ Tse-tung
42 Tone deafness
43 49236
47 "Horrors!"
48 Hawaiian wreath
49 Companionless
52 They're handy by phones
57 97352
60 I in "The King and I"
61 Heathen
62 Glow
63 Cheer (for)
64 Lodge member
65 Reading light

DOWN

1 "It was ___ vu all over again"
2 Enthusiasm
3 Graph points
4 Signs, as a contract
5 Sentiment
6 Of the pre-Easter season
7 TV's Ricki
8 Summer refresher
9 Thurmond, e.g.: Abbr.
10 Shrewdness
11 Points of convergence
12 Actress Sommer
13 Streets and avenues
18 Places atop
19 Metered vehicle
23 Ladled-out food
24 Pie ___ mode
25 Copycat
26 On ___ (proceeding successfully)
27 Back: Prefix
28 Pig ___ poke
29 Dialect
30 Approving
31 Ancient Aegean land
32 Late astronomer Carl
37 Like the Marx Brothers
38 More pale
39 Taro dish

Puzzle 31 by Richard Hughes

41 "Hi ___!" (fan's message)
42 Common solvent
44 Like many diet products
45 Quaker pronoun
46 Actress Massey et al.
49 Slightly open
50 Late-night host
51 ___ consequence (insignificant)
52 Canceled
53 Bells' sound
54 Water, to Joaquin
55 College student's home
56 Rice Krispies sound
58 Engine speed, for short
59 ___ Paulo, Brazil

ACROSS

1 Scores for the Maple Leafs
6 Heavyweight champ dethroned by Braddock
10 In this way
14 Hold, as the attention
15 Any of three English rivers
16 Wax's opposite
17 In solitary
18 Dressed
19 As before, in footnotes
20 Batman and Robin, e.g.
22 Evening, informally
23 G.I. dinner
24 Kitty ___
26 Where to find Chile powder?
29 Vinegar: Prefix
31 Statement of belief
32 Obliquely
36 Diamond Head locale
37 Kind of mill
38 Within: Prefix
39 It's about thyme!
41 Impels
42 Expunge
43 Miniature map
44 50's-60's pitcher Don
47 Einstein's birthplace
48 Declare
49 Tinkers-Evers-Chance forte
56 New Zealander
57 Cartoonist Peter
58 Tylenol competitor
59 Mideast carrier
60 ___ Hari
61 Wouk work
62 Beach, basically
63 Kind of car
64 Handle a baton

DOWN

1 Mortarboard wearer
2 Overly smooth
3 View from Stratford
4 Horne who sang "Deed I Do"
5 Restrained, as a flow
6 Game with wooden balls
7 "___ Lang Syne"
8 Jacob's twin
9 Aromatic
10 One-time Manhattan sight
11 Equestrian's garb
12 Bring together
13 Jewish feast
21 Apr. payee
25 Communications corp.
26 Give ___ (care)
27 Royal Crown Cola brand
28 Condition in kids' card games
29 ___ B. Toklas
30 Amontillado holder
31 Subjects for Barron's: Abbr.
32 Sp. ladies

Puzzle 32 by Fred Piscop

33 "Picnic" writer
34 Manuscript mark
35 Dawn goddess
37 Sporty Pontiacs
40 Palindromic preposition
41 Not intentional
43 "Well, ___ be!"
44 Aral and Caspian Seas, really

45 Spanish tourist center
46 "Laugh-In" co-host
47 W.W. II predator
50 Kind of thermometer
51 Biblical preposition
52 Farm need
53 ___ Strauss jeans
54 Swear
55 "Gimme a C . . . !" is one

ACROSS

1 Org. that guarantees bank holdings
5 Poets
10 Egyptian snakes
14 Moon goddess
15 German sub
16 Patricia who co-starred in "The Fountainhead"
17 Late newsman Sevareid
18 Waken
19 The Supremes, e.g.
20 1989 Spike Lee film
23 French school
24 Weights
25 Letter before beth
28 Kapow!
30 Top 3 hit of 1963 and 1977
34 Mont Blanc is one
37 "Play it ___ lays"
38 Studio sign
39 Light bulb, in cartoons
40 Happened upon
41 Moonshine
43 Camp beds
44 Suns
45 ___-Kettering Institute
48 Chilled meat garnish
51 Unwelcome sight in the mail
57 In the past
58 Finger-pointer
59 Cake finisher
60 Backside
61 States

62 Jasmine or morning glory
63 Commits a sin
64 Present, for example, in English class
65 Mini-whirlpool

DOWN

1 Vamoosed
2 Five-peseta coin
3 Any part of J.F.K.: Abbr.
4 Ornamental container in a flower shop
5 Grand Canyon transport
6 Irate
7 Cheek cosmetic
8 Elan
9 Proofer's mark
10 "La Marseillaise," e.g.
11 Printing flourish
12 Benjamin Moore product
13 Trudges (through)
21 Classical nymph who spoke only by repetition
22 Holier-___-thou
25 Economist Smith
26 Emit coherent light
27 Perform copy desk work
28 Formal order
29 Wedding dance
31 Eradicate, with "out"
32 Burden

33 One of the Bobbsey twins
34 Appends
35 Onion relative
36 Bears' hands
39 Like Mount St. Helens, now
41 "___ Lisa"
42 Wading bird
43 Supplies the food for
45 Plant reproductive part
46 Unsocial sort

47 Award for "Braveheart"
48 Saatchi & Saatchi employees
49 Litigators
50 Intrinsically
52 Tiny pest
53 Roof overhang
54 Battery fluid
55 Repair
56 Wolves, for wolfhounds

ACROSS

1 Cobblers
5 City near Phoenix
10 "Half-Breed" singer
14 Med. sch. course
15 All possible
16 Part of A.P.R.
17 Nimble
18 Dancer Jeanmaire
19 Persia, today
20 The Boy King
21 Sculpture in the Louvre
23 Madalyn O'Hair, e.g.
25 "Norma ___"
26 Deborah's role in "The King and I"
27 Reason for a small craft advisory
32 Paris newspaper, with "Le"
34 Blow one's top
35 Circle segment
36 Baker's dozen
37 Sign of spring
38 Headliner
39 What Dorian Gray didn't do
40 "___ Irish Rose"
41 Computer device
42 Dogpatch dweller
44 Author John Dickson ___
45 Bill's partner
46 Costa Rican export
49 Former Ford offering
54 Org. that sticks to its guns
55 Bread spread
56 Memorable ship
57 Count calories
58 Gen. Bradley
59 Modify
60 ___ Domini
61 Precious metal
62 Lascivious looks
63 He was a "Giant" star

DOWN

1 Naples noodles
2 Enter, as data
3 1955 hit for the Crew-Cuts
4 Pig's digs
5 Mother ___
6 The Super Bowl, e.g.
7 Diner's card
8 Nov. electee
9 Tears?
10 "___ and Misdemeanors"
11 Mata ___
12 Useful Latin abbr.
13 Gambler's mecca
21 Ivy plant
22 It may be Far or Near
24 Brings to a close
27 Town ___ (early newsman)
28 Regrets
29 Apollo mission
30 Intervals of history
31 Farm measure
32 Repast
33 Today, in Turin

Puzzle 34 by Gregory E. Paul

34 Southernmost Great
Lake
37 Irregular
38 Carolina rail
40 "___ Ben Adhem"
(Leigh Hunt poem)
41 Tailless cat
43 International
agreement
44 Wickerworkers

46 Sketch comic John
47 Sports center
48 Squelched
49 Synthesizer man
50 "Tickle Me" doll
51 Genuine
52 Where Bill met Hillary
53 Lo-fat
57 Father figure

ACROSS
1 Poet Sandburg
5 Sand bar
10 Jemima, e.g.
14 Guy with an Irish Rose
15 "College Bowl" host Robert
16 Chew (on)
17 Off-color
19 New York theater award
20 Escalator alternative
21 Boat propellers
23 "___ Maria"
24 Tear-jerker in the kitchen
26 "Bald" baby bird
28 Big toe woe
30 Patsy's pal on TV's "Absolutely Fabulous"
31 Dapper fellow
32 Foe
34 Numbskull
37 Catch sight of
39 Saccharine
41 Garbage boat
42 Chartres chapeau
44 "Deutschland uber ___"
46 High season, on the Riviera
47 Before the due date
49 African antelopes
51 Actress Loren
53 Four-time Gold Glove winner Garvey
54 Chicken ___ king

55 ___ platter (Polynesian menu choice)
57 Bug's antenna
61 What not to yell in a crowded theater
63 Off-key
65 Tied, as a score
66 Revolutionary patriot Allen
67 Lo-cal
68 Funnyman Foxx
69 Horned zoo beast
70 Son of Seth

DOWN
1 Elliot of the Mamas and the Papas
2 Be next to
3 Latvia's capital
4 French Foreign ___
5 Rap or jam periods
6 Stetson, e.g.
7 Betelgeuse's constellation
8 Thomas Edison's middle name
9 Looked lecherously
10 In the past
11 Off-center
12 Innocent
13 Sound from an aviary
18 Sgt. Bilko
22 Stated
25 Street sign with an arrow
27 Wildebeests
28 Pedestal

Puzzle 35 by Stephanie Spadaccini

29 Off-guard
30 Embroidered hole
31 Cotillion V.I.P.
33 Director Brooks
35 Bunkhouse beds
36 Female sheep
38 "You bet!"
40 It's used for a call in Madrid
43 Excursion
45 Lifeguard, sometimes
48 Giver of compliments

50 Thread's partner
51 Morley of "60 Minutes"
52 Martini garnish
53 Japanese dish
56 ___ helmet (safari wear)
58 Reclined
59 Inner: Prefix
60 1 and 66, e.g.: Abbr.
62 Finis
64 Campbell's container

ACROSS

1 "Let's go!"
5 Miss Cinders of old comics
9 Stravinsky's "Le ___ du printemps"
14 It's pulled on a pulley
15 Music for two
16 Farm units
17 Once more
18 Schooner part
19 Signified
20 Hit NBC comedy
23 Passing grade
24 Director Howard
25 X's in bowling
27 It's behind home plate
32 Sugar source
33 "___ American Cousin" (1859 comedy)
34 Results of big hits?
36 "Gandhi" setting
39 Shiite, e.g.
41 1997 has two
43 Brothers and sisters
44 Flattens
46 Plains home
48 Tam-o'-shanter
49 Yin's counterpart
51 Not the subs
53 Liberace wore them
56 A.F.L.'s partner
57 Tempe sch.
58 Novelty timepiece
64 Cinnamon unit
66 ___-Seltzer
67 First name in supermodeldom
68 Actress Berry
69 Alice doesn't work here anymore
70 Campus authority
71 Buzzing
72 Organic fuel
73 Klutz's utterance

DOWN

1 Pack in
2 "___ Lisa"
3 Like a William Safire piece
4 Alternative to J.F.K. and La Guardia
5 Oiler's home
6 Molokai meal
7 For fear that
8 Esqs.
9 Belushi character on "S.N.L."
10 Expert
11 Bartender's supply
12 "Walk Away ___" (1966 hit)
13 ___ Park, Colo.
21 Pear type
22 Like some stocks, for short
26 Lodges
27 Part of an old English Christmas feast
28 Atmosphere
29 Hodgepodge
30 Cross out

Puzzle 36 by Elizabeth C. Gorski

31 Glazier's items
35 Back-to-school time: Abbr.
37 Building support
38 Egyptian threats
40 Romeo
42 Maine's is rocky
45 Tee-hee
47 Psychiatrist Berne
50 Bearded creature
52 "Holy ___!"

53 Russian-born violinist Schneider, informally
54 These, in Madrid
55 Rascal
59 "Twittering Machine" artist
60 Neighbor of Kan.
61 Nondairy spread
62 Bit of thunder
63 Dolls since 1961
65 Cato's 151

ACROSS

1 "Too bad!"
5 Sen. Lott
10 Hardly colorful
14 Parks who wouldn't take discrimination sitting down
15 12-inch stick
16 Superb
17 Water conduit
18 China's Zhou ___
19 Do, re or mi, e.g.
20 "Little Orphan Annie" character
23 "There ___ young . . ." (common limerick start)
24 WNW's reverse
25 Plant dripping
28 ___ Kippur
31 Newsman Pyle
35 Puts up
37 Spigot
39 Switch positions
40 Santa Claus
44 Noted business conglomerate
45 Great Lakes cargo
46 C_2H_6
47 Sweetie
50 1040 grp.
52 Last name in cosmetics
53 Photo ___ (media events)
55 Supreme Court Justice Black
57 Nobel author, informally
63 Pack (down)

64 To no ___ (worthless)
65 Snake eyes
67 Lemon go-with
68 Menu at Chez Jacques
69 One of the corners at Four Corners Monument
70 Blockhead
71 Gouged sneakily
72 Akron product

DOWN

1 It may be slung in a sling
2 Dumptruckful
3 Where China is
4 B.L.T., e.g.
5 Deuce toppers
6 Takeoff site
7 Actress Raines
8 Not distant
9 Cree or Crow
10 Martha Graham, e.g.
11 Castle, in chess
12 Orkin targets
13 Quilting party
21 "The Divine Comedy" poet
22 Take advantage of
25 Install to new specifications
26 Poet's Muse
27 Brawl
29 Partner for this and that, with "the"
30 Spoil
32 Wanderer

Puzzle 37 by Gregory E. Paul

33 Absurd
34 Ruhr Valley city
36 Box-office letters
38 Bit of Trivial Pursuit equipment
41 Dernier ___
42 Coach Amos Alonzo ___
43 Discard
48 Went one better than
49 Place for a little R and R
51 Devout Iranian

54 Rough cabin
56 Proceeding independently
57 Item for Jack and Jill
58 Bullets and such
59 Writer Hunter
60 Stallion's mate
61 The "A" in ABM
62 Vintage
63 Special attention, for short
66 "___ Drives Me Crazy" (1989 #1 hit)

ACROSS

1 Certain drapes
6 Atlantic food fish
10 Gator's kin
14 Cop ___ (confess for a lighter sentence)
15 White-tailed flier
16 Deli offering
17 Colt 45, e.g.
19 List member
20 "That's a lie!"
21 Household
23 70's-80's robotic rock group
25 The United States, metaphorically
27 Uris hero
28 Dance, in Dijon
29 Member of the 500 HR club
30 Rock impresario Brian
31 Surgical fabric
33 Ant, in dialect
35 "Texaco Star Theater" host
39 Cut down
40 Brilliance
43 High dudgeon
46 Mai ___
47 Go on to say
49 "Bravo!"
50 It once settled near Pompeii
53 Part of a whole
54 Kangaroo movements
55 Hayfield activity
57 Prefix with China
58 Kind of cereal
62 Shade of red
63 Conception
64 Bizarre
65 Bronte heroine
66 Pre-1821 Missouri, e.g.: Abbr.
67 He had Scarlett fever

DOWN

1 Uncle of note
2 New Deal prog.
3 Stream deposit
4 "I can't ___" (Stones refrain)
5 Morton product
6 "Rocky II," e.g.
7 Diabolical
8 Due halved
9 Words of assistance
10 "I ___" (ancient Chinese text)
11 Record again
12 Where to find Eugene
13 Awaken
18 Early Shirley role
22 Signed up for
23 U.N's Hammarskjold
24 Former polit. cause
26 ___ of the Unknowns
28 Like some greeting cards
32 Nine-digit number, maybe
33 Ultimate point
34 R.N.'s offering
36 Send
37 Trompe l'___

Puzzle 38 by Alan Arbesfeld

38 Stretch
41 He KO'd Quarry, 10/26/70
42 Asian holiday
43 Tipple
44 "Didja ever wonder . . . ?" humorist
45 Successful escapee
47 Incarnation
48 Spanish Surrealist

51 Certain investment, informally
52 More competent
53 Jesse who lost to Ronald Reagan in 1970
56 Composer Stravinsky
59 Ending with quiet
60 N.Y.C. subway
61 Modern information source, with "the"

ACROSS

1 Pre-entree dish
6 Sit in the sun
10 Cozy home
14 Reflection
15 Opposing
16 Go ___ (exceed)
17 The "N" of U.S.N.A.
18 "Forever"
19 "Get going!"
20 Go
23 Withdraw from the Union
26 Those going 80, say
27 Med. cost-saving plan
28 And so on
30 Historical period
31 Teen woe
33 It makes an auto go
35 ___ latte
40 Go
44 Intuit
45 Hankering
46 Castle's protection
47 Chef's measure: Abbr.
50 Something to go to a bakery for
52 Wash. neighbor
53 Delivered a sermon
58 Comments to the audience
60 Go
62 Milky-white gem
63 Sacred Egyptian bird
64 War story, Greek-style
68 Chant at a fraternity party
69 Swiss painter Paul
70 The brainy bunch
71 George Washington bills
72 Arid
73 Cousin of a Golden Globe

DOWN

1 Transgression
2 Doc's org.
3 Restroom, informally
4 Wide-open
5 Deceive
6 False god
7 Black cattle breed
8 Treeless plain
9 Mouth, to Ralph Kramden
10 One always on the go
11 Call forth
12 Cut off
13 Lock of hair
21 "Take your hands off me!"
22 Instruct
23 Pre-Ayatollah rulers
24 Host
25 Sir Arthur ___ Doyle
29 Saturn, for one
32 Mag workers
34 Pigpen
36 Order between ready and fire
37 Result of a bank failure?
38 Distress signal
39 ___ Park, Colo.

Puzzle 39 by Stephanie Spadaccini

41 "Go get it, Fido!"
42 Jitterbug's "cool"
43 First digital computer
48 Arab leaders
49 Little rock
51 Inuit
53 Kind of ID
54 Wisconsin college
55 Story, in France

56 Ayn Rand's "___
    Shrugged"
57 Less moist
59 South Sea getaways
61 Words of
    comprehension
65 Business abbr.
66 Simile's middle
67 ___ es Salaam

ACROSS

1 Smart
5 Diminished by
10 E, in Morse code
13 Nimbus
14 Makes amends (for)
16 Morn's opposite
17 Part of B.P.O.E.
18 Like some regions
19 Levy
20 No middle ground, successwise
23 Corn serving
24 Mornings, for short
25 Like some history
28 "Beau ___"
31 Not guzzle
32 ___ firma
33 Sounds from the stands
34 Approximately
36 Trial judge Lance
37 Dad's mate
38 Bit of hope
39 Turndowns
40 Words before taking the plunge
43 Certain breakout
44 Channels
45 Married
46 Newspapers
47 At bats, e.g.
48 Eternal queen, of book and film
49 Former Mideast merger: Abbr.
50 Eventually
56 Hawaiian necklace
58 ___ to go (eager)
59 The Clintons' alma mater
60 Possess
61 Pindar's country
62 Class with a Paul Samuelson text
63 Entreat
64 Pothook shapes
65 1958 Presley #1 hit

DOWN

1 One whose work causes a stir?
2 Robust
3 Actress Chase
4 Pampers
5 Estate home
6 Anatomical passage
7 Foul
8 Free
9 Appears
10 Hoped-for effect of having a big military
11 Eggs
12 Cowhand's nickname
15 ___ Lanka
21 ___ kwon do
22 Christmas carol
26 Cases for insurance detectives
27 Maidens
28 Operates, as a hand organ
29 Patronize restaurants
30 Highlighting
31 In an undetermined place, in dialect

Puzzle 40 by John R. Conrad

32 Attempt
34 Back-to-work time: Abbr.
35 Paddle
37 ___ Olson (ad character)
41 Director Preminger
42 Eastern thrushes
43 In formation
46 Buddy

48 Trap
49 Prods
51 Assoc.
52 A long time ago
53 Sandwich with fixin's
54 Carolina college
55 1996 Tony musical
56 High return
57 Farm mother

ACROSS

1 Title car in a 1964 song
4 Month after marzo, in Mexico
9 Indian prince
14 Urban music
15 Tired
16 Uneven, as the border of a leaf
17 Oscar director for "Gentleman's Agreement"
19 ___ Moore stew
20 N.Y. neighbor
21 Oscar actress for "The Accidental Tourist"
23 Dramatist Eugene
25 Taboo
26 Oscar actress for "Shampoo"
30 Doctrine: Suffix
33 Easy golf putt
36 In ___ land (spacy)
37 Make eyes at
38 Pleasingly mirthful
39 Rocker Brian
40 ___ water (facing trouble)
41 In unison, musically
42 Johann Sebastian ___
43 Stop holding
44 ___ de mer
45 Oscar actor for "Forrest Gump"
47 Bank job?
49 Shoot-'em-ups

53 Oscar actor for "The Color of Money"
58 Region
59 Beckon to enter
60 Oscar actor for "Harry and Tonto"
62 Depart
63 Fiend
64 "___ Got Sixpence"
65 Concentrated beam
66 Plant disease
67 Always, to a poet

DOWN

1 Artist El ___
2 Eagle's claw
3 Think out loud
4 Parrot's cry
5 Snoopy, for one
6 Bring down the house
7 Hymn "Dies ___"
8 City northeast of Boston
9 Measles symptom
10 Suffix with sect
11 Oscar actor for "Coming Home"
12 Italian wine center
13 Cries of surprise
18 Dye ingredient
22 "___ Karenina"
24 Pre-Easter season
27 Flash of light
28 Cowhand's home
29 Hilo hello
31 Work long and hard

Puzzle 41 by Thomas W. Schier

32 "Take ___ your leader"
33 Monorail unit
34 Verdi opera
35 Oscar actor for "Watch on the Rhine"
37 Poor movie rating
40 Actress Chase
42 Snack for a dog
45 Leather worker
46 Sarge, for one
48 Martini garnish

50 "Sesame Street" regular
51 Christopher of "Superman"
52 Pop singer Leo
53 Cast a ___ over
54 On the briny
55 Walk in the surf
56 60's TV horse
57 "Look ___!"
61 Literary olio

ACROSS

1 It's hailed by city dwellers
5 "The final frontier"
10 Philosopher David
14 Plow pullers
15 Director Welles
16 Ukraine's Sea of ___
17 One socially challenged
18 Scottish estate owner
19 "Oh, my!"
20 Bad news
23 Philosopher John
24 It comes from the heart
28 Tampa neighbor, informally
31 Maladroit
33 "Common Sense" pamphleteer
34 Equestrian's handful
36 Smidgen
37 Lots of activity
41 Baseball stat
42 Like Superman's vision
43 Less tanned
44 Kickoff response
47 TV journalist Poussaint et al.
48 Highway curves
49 Window cover
51 Like some chicken
57 Talk
60 Alternatives to suspenders
61 Keen
62 One for the road
63 $100 bill

64 Reply to the Little Red Hen
65 "That was a close one!"
66 Planted
67 Word with high or hole

DOWN

1 Chinese dynasty
2 Skater's move
3 Dry: Prefix
4 Slothful
5 Comfort giver
6 Short-sheeting a bed, e.g.
7 Stage remark
8 Part of a parachute
9 Prefix with -morph
10 Upper part of a barn
11 Terrorist's weapon
12 Swab
13 "The Three Faces of ___"
21 "Psycho" setting
22 Sturdy furniture material
25 Tot's noisemaker
26 Rose's home, in song
27 Common vipers
28 Globe
29 Ford model
30 Galileo's kinsmen
31 Amos's partner
32 Part of "www"
34 Luke preceder
35 Santa ___, Calif.

Puzzle 42 by Brendan Emmett Quigley

38 First-rate: Abbr.
39 Flip over
40 Shoal
45 Confer (upon)
46 Volcano detritus
47 Got the suds out
49 "Look out ___!"
50 Starbucks serving
52 Kindergarten instruction

53 Gambling game
54 The Bard's river
55 Toy with a tail
56 Singer Brickell
57 Beret
58 "Come again?"
59 Noshed

ACROSS

1 Employee's reward
6 Person from Muscat
11 Civil War alliance: Abbr.
14 ___-garde
15 Repairman
16 Cause friction
17 Nervousness
19 Slippery fish
20 Lover of Sir Lancelot
21 Dawn goddess
22 Take it easy
23 Chooses
25 Computer-telephone link
27 Some New Year's resolutions
29 Gallows loops
32 Muppeteer Henson
35 Former pro footballer, briefly
37 Like mountains in winter
38 Very dry
40 Batman's sidekick
42 Yemeni port
43 Hotel employee
45 Words mouthed at a TV camera
47 "We ___ Not Alone" (1939 film)
48 Short sock
50 "Frasier" character
52 Red wine
54 Outline
58 Part of Q.E.D.
60 Prof's deg.

62 Jelly used for fuel
63 Coffee maker
64 Numbskulls
66 Ripen
67 Out-of-date
68 Stan's partner, for short
69 Actress Susan
70 Place for grandma's trunk
71 Yorkshire city

DOWN

1 "___ in Toyland"
2 Small egg
3 Birth-related
4 Loose, as shoelaces
5 Sign painter's aid
6 Not at work
7 Miss's equivalent, in a saying
8 Adage
9 Actor Liam
10 April check payee: Abbr.
11 Certain soft drink
12 Mideast canal
13 Skillful
18 Open up a rip again
22 Hotelier Helmsley
24 ___ Brewery Co., of Detroit
26 Opposite of no-nos
28 Polio vaccine developer
30 Pitcher
31 Auld lang ___

Puzzle 43 by Janet R. Bender

32 Jakarta's island
33 Ayatollah's land
34 Small allowance for a schoolchild
36 Copycat
39 Took out
41 Like a win-win situation
44 "Nightline" host Koppel
46 Cough drop ingredient
49 Formal headgear
51 "The Spectator" essayist

53 Treasure container
55 Papal vestment
56 Ruined
57 What everything's coming up, in song
58 College area
59 Encourage
61 Lucy's husband
64 Bean counter, for short
65 Dry, as wine

ACROSS

1 Start to form, as a storm
5 "___-Dick"
9 Christie's Miss Marple
13 Exude
14 Village Voice award
15 Miser Marner
17 Where this answer goes
19 Singing syllable
20 Mysterious loch
21 Utah mountains
22 Villa d'___
23 Up to the task
24 Goodyear fleet
27 Train storage area
31 W.W.II hero Murphy
32 Seas, to Cousteau
33 Go a-courtin'
35 What this answer does
38 Suffix with ranch
39 ". . . unto us ___ is given"
40 Contemptible one
41 Narrow-necked bottle
44 Cried like a baby
45 Word with slicker or hall
46 Guns, as an engine
47 "Lucky" dice rolls
50 ___ over (carry through)
51 Point of decline
55 What this answer seems to have
57 Book with legends

58 The triple in a triple play
59 Author Bagnold
60 Exude
61 Phoenix neighbor
62 Thanksgiving dishes

DOWN

1 Ring engagement
2 First sound in an M-G-M film
3 Poet Pound
4 Little piggy's cry
5 Some MOMA paintings
6 More than plump
7 Strained pea catchers
8 Biblical affirmative
9 Small bus
10 Heaps
11 Cape Canaveral org.
12 Gentlemen: Abbr.
15 Expertise
16 Without obligation
18 Picasso-Braque movement
22 Bahrain bigwig
23 Hammerin' Hank
24 Bundled, as straw
25 Riches
26 Manner of speaking
27 Scouting mission
28 Horrendous
29 Stir from slumber
30 Parceled (out)
32 Like fine netting
34 Chinese philosopher

36 Football team quorum
37 Starts a crop
42 Polar feature
43 Pixie and Dixie's nemesis, in the cartoons
44 Mythological woman with unruly hair
46 Laughfests
47 Mineral springs

48 Suffix with cigar
49 Reprehensible
50 Veracious
51 Sicilian peak
52 Cup lip
53 Political campaigns
54 Mr. Turkey
56 Susan of "Looker"

ACROSS

1 Hairdo
5 Inquired
10 Surrender
14 Stratagem
15 "Mars Attacks!" genre
16 They can take a yoke
17 Cake finisher
18 Guardian of Crete, in classical myth
19 Actor Arnaz
20 Agatha Christie title
23 "All ___ day's work"
24 Legal thing
25 Keats's work on melancholy
28 Biased
32 Grp. that oversees I.C.B.M.'s
35 Ironworker's workplace
37 Decree
38 Kent's state
39 Investigative tool
42 "EZ Streets" actor Ken
43 Mars: Prefix
44 Playful aquatic animal
45 Old TV comedian Louis
46 Hi-fis
48 Aegean, e.g.
49 Worker with a stethoscope
50 Ex-G.I.
52 Dismiss lightly
61 Work over Time
62 Profit
63 687 days on Mars
64 Bridge site
65 Jeune ___ (girl, in France)
66 Word repeated in "It's ___! All ___!"
67 Russian autocrat
68 Skedaddles
69 Word ending a threat

DOWN

1 Lit ___ (college course, informally)
2 "That hurts!"
3 Words of enlightenment
4 Physicist Enrico
5 Stellar
6 Old wound mark
7 Drug shipment, maybe
8 ___ effort
9 Separate
10 Musical finales
11 Prez
12 Where a student sits
13 Geraint's lady
21 Miniature map
22 Scarlet
25 Go ___ a tangent
26 Frilly place mat
27 Bert's "Sesame Street" buddy
29 Ere
30 Gunpowder ingredient
31 California-Nevada resort lake
32 Some immunizations
33 Evangelist McPherson

Puzzle 45 by Teresa M. Hackett

34 Army attack helicopter
36 Powell or Westmoreland, e.g.: Abbr.
38 Halloween mo.
40 Grain byproduct
41 Units of medicine
46 Drunkard
47 Seeds-to-be
49 Restrain through intimidation
51 Mint family member

52 Lady's escort
53 Altar vows
54 MasterCard alternative
55 Wicked
56 Cotton quantity
57 Make angry
58 Trompe l'___
59 Pre-air conditioning coolers
60 Gratis

ACROSS

1 Singer-actress Lane
5 "___ Mia" (1965 hit)
9 Choreographer Agnes de ___
14 Watery
15 Stratford-Avon link
16 Firefighter Red
17 TV/film actor Jack
19 Comparatively modern
20 Scott's "___ Roy"
21 Got a move on
22 Honeybunch
23 Humdingers
25 Octave followers, in sonnets
28 It's hoisted in a pub
29 T'ai ___ ch'uan
30 Phillips University site
31 Writer Jack
34 Form 1040 completer
35 Scourge
38 Idolize
39 Escritoire
40 "Boola Boola" singer
41 Pugilist Jack
43 Savoir-faire
45 Skater Midori
46 Superaggressive one
50 Barrow residents
52 Licked boots?
54 Grasslands
55 Crash diet
56 Absorbed, as an expense
57 AOL memos
59 Movie actor Jack
61 Haggard
62 "Garfield" dog
63 Grid coach ___ Alonzo Stagg
64 Loquacious, in slang
65 Kind of blocker
66 Sit in the sun

DOWN

1 Oscar and Obie
2 Wisconsin college
3 Psycho talk?
4 Manage to get, with "out"
5 Doll
6 Church recesses
7 Crucifix
8 Gloucester's cape
9 Currycombs comb them
10 Imagine
11 Lyricist Jack
12 "The check is in the mail," maybe
13 Blow it
18 Kind of wine
22 Clears for takeoff?
24 Word of Valleyspeak
25 High-pitched
26 Much of a waiter's income
27 Mount Rushmore's site: Abbr.
29 Former New York governor
32 Transmits
33 "Golden Boy" dramatist

Puzzle 46 by Fred Piscop

35 ___ noire
36 Griever's exclamation
37 Golfer Jack
39 Twosome
42 Sister of Calliope
44 Some commercial promotions
47 Poisonous atmosphere
48 Caused to go
49 Danish city

51 Like beer
52 Unspoken
53 Actor Milo
55 Bona ___
57 "Rotten" missile
58 Ewe's sound
59 San Francisco's ___ Hill
60 Part of a science class

ACROSS

1 Enter
5 Throaty utterance
9 Up, as the ante
14 Ancient alphabetic character
15 Singer Guthrie
16 Get straight A's, e.g.
17 Lot of land
18 "Greetings ___ . . ." (postcard opening)
19 Opinions
20 Lose some weight
23 Looks perfect on
24 Not pos.
25 Flier Earhart
29 Part of T.G.I.F.
30 Place to crash
33 Recluse
34 60's hairdo
36 ___ fide
37 Criticize formally
40 God of war
41 Where the Mets meet
42 Pulitzer winner Pyle
43 Actor Beatty
44 Senor Guevara
45 Certain marbles
46 "We ___ the Champions" (Queen tune)
47 He loved Lucy
49 Nears, as a target
56 Hardly the brainy type
57 "Othello" villain
58 Golfer's cry
59 The Little Mermaid
60 Quite a rarity
61 Writer Lebowitz
62 Raison ___
63 Marquis de ___
64 Jodie Foster's alma mater

DOWN

1 Pate de foie ___
2 "That hurt!"
3 Concerning
4 Exigency
5 Basket material
6 Stop, in France
7 Puts on the brakes
8 Splendor
9 Variety shows
10 Getting rid of
11 Decorated, as a cake
12 Uses needle and thread
13 Overhead trains, for short
21 Blazing
22 "___ of Old Smoky"
25 Nebbishy comic Sherman
26 Sculptor Henry
27 Signed off
28 Diamond, of gangsterdom
29 "___ la Douce"
30 Gist
31 Vanity Fair photographer Leibovitz
32 Palm tree fruits
34 Word with head or heart
35 Enemy

Puzzle 47 by Stephanie Spadaccini

36 Silent film star Theda
38 Hearth residue
39 On the up and up
44 New Orleans cuisine
45 On dry land
46 Yellowish-brown
47 Rigg or Ross
48 Pushed, with "on"
49 Take on, as an employee
50 Leave out
51 Grande and Bravo
52 Questionable
53 "A Doll's House" heroine
54 Like much testimony
55 Hawaii's state bird
56 Good, in street talk

ACROSS

1 The beans in refried beans
9 Snail ___ (endangered fish)
15 City south of Tijuana
16 Register
17 Battle site where the Athenians routed the Persians
18 Ford flops
19 Scene of Operation Overlord
21 Old paper currency
24 Gaffer's assistant
29 Friends' pronoun
30 Pound part
33 Druidic worship sites
34 Science shop
35 In ___ (properly placed)
36 When Browning wanted to be in England
37 Montana massacre locale
41 Tired of it all
42 Some nest eggs: Abbr.
43 "Take me as ___"
45 Hill dwellers
46 Michael and Peter
48 Sunday seats
49 Site of many flicks
51 Poet Teasdale et al.
52 1781 surrender site
56 Violinist Menuhin
60 1862 Maryland battle site
64 Obliterates
65 Infant
66 Heat up again
67 Candidate Harold et al.

DOWN

1 Opposite of masc.
2 Genetic inits.
3 Neighbor of Leb.
4 Dream girl in a Foster song
5 Where to put the cherry of a sundae
6 "The Wizard of Oz" actor
7 Brother of Jacob
8 Yemen's capital
9 Role in TV's "Hunter"
10 Capp and Gump
11 B.&O. et al.
12 Boot part
13 Add-on
14 "Treasure Island" monogram
20 Peacock network
21 Letters on a Cardinal's cap
22 Where Attila was defeated, 451
23 Religious experience
25 "___ the mornin'!"
26 Obstacle
27 1945 island dogfight site
28 Couturier initials
30 Heating fuel
31 Southwestern Indian
32 Ancient kingdom on the Nile

Puzzle 48 by Jonathan Schmalzbach

35 Criterion: Abbr.
36 Cries of delight
38 Exam
39 Like "to be": Abbr.
40 Heating fuel
41 Flock sound
44 What eds. edit
46 Oriental philosophy
47 Hafez al-Assad's land: Abbr.
48 Juries
50 Actress Winona
51 Kind of cheese

53 Okla. neighbor
54 Carpenter's fastener
55 Other: Sp.
56 "Get ___ Ya-Ya's Out!" (Stones album)
57 Poet's "before"
58 Turn left
59 "Land of the free": Abbr.
61 Knot
62 Raggedy doll
63 Brit. sports cars

ACROSS

1 Classic film star Greta
6 Howled like a hound
11 This instant
14 Extraterrestrial
15 Popeye's sweetie
16 Gardner of Tinseltown
17 Restaurant gadabout
19 Blend
20 Pesky insects
21 Christians' ___ Creed
23 Surfeit
26 Made fractions
27 Fold, as paper
28 One-dimensional
29 Forebodings
30 Zippy flavors
31 Uneaten morsel
34 Chaney Jr. and Sr.
35 Hats' stats
36 Fencing blade
37 Dehydrated
38 Star-to-be
39 Montreal baseballers
40 Held responsible (for)
42 "Accept the situation!"
43 Bing Crosby or Rudy Vallee, e.g.
45 Penny-pinching
46 Coarse-toothed tool
47 Stun gun
48 Egyptian snake
49 Dazzling performer
54 Victory sign
55 Cassettes
56 Speak
57 Be mistaken
58 Bewildered
59 Former Russian sovereigns

DOWN

1 Gangster's gun
2 Chicken ___ king
3 Barbecued treat
4 Antwerp residents
5 Unity
6 Pirates' plunder
7 Zurich's peaks
8 Sharp bark
9 Periods just past sunset
10 Infers
11 Egotistical conversationalist
12 Sheeplike
13 Like shiny floors
18 Despise
22 Spy org.
23 Chide, as a child
24 Knight's protection
25 Adolescent rock fan
26 Mel's on "Alice," for one
28 Lolled
30 Track official
32 Try to stop a squeak again
33 Snappish
35 To an extent
36 Quotes in book reviews
38 Rummy variation

Puzzle 49 by Patrick Jordan

39 Depose gradually and politely
41 ___ Angeles
42 Pugilist's weapon
43 Desire deeply
44 Part of a stairway
45 Term of address in "Roots"
47 Overly precious, to a Briton

50 Photo ___ (pol's news events)
51 Local educ. support group
52 Always, in verse
53 Southern Pacific and others: Abbr.

ACROSS

1 Quark's place
5 Some are filled out
10 Org. for 7-Down
14 Command on a submarine
15 Beethoven dedicatee
16 Get ___ the ground floor
17 "Stop" sign
20 Costa del ___
21 Cleanse
22 One of the Brothers Karamazov
23 "Unforgettable" singer
24 Gas or elec., e.g.
25 To pieces
28 Lustrous fabric
30 Sailor
33 Assail
34 Ted's role on "Cheers"
35 "Dies ___"
36 "Stop" sign
40 Connecticut Ivy Leaguers
41 ___ de la Cite
42 Marconi's invention
43 Cub's home
44 To whom Tinker threw
46 Alamogordo event
47 Bouillabaisse, e.g.
48 Table d'___
50 Chairs on poles
53 Angler's luck
54 Guy's date
57 "Stop" sign
60 German article
61 Colorful rock
62 "Pistol Packin' ___"
63 Cherished
64 Wankel engine part
65 Procedure part

DOWN

1 Tacks on
2 Novice: Var.
3 Track shape
4 Kitten's cry
5 Untamed
6 Mount of ___ (site near Jerusalem)
7 Astronaut Sally
8 N.Y.C. sports venue
9 When to sow
10 This meant nothing to Nero
11 Operating without ___ (taking risks)
12 Skyrocket
13 "The King ___"
18 Three sheets to the wind
19 Ugandan dictator
23 Game featuring shooters
24 Where Provo is
25 Invited
26 English dramatist George
27 Supped at home
29 Starwort
30 School division
31 Watering hole
32 Infatuate
35 Furious

Puzzle 50 by Gerald R. Ferguson

37 Exceptional, as a restaurant or hotel
38 Went by plane
39 Gadget for cheese
44 Sicilian volcano
45 Religion of Japan
47 Not a spendthrift
49 Aquatic mammal
50 Scurried

51 Buffalo's lake
52 Actress Merrill
53 Tuckered out
54 Midge
55 Crowning point
56 "Able to ___ tall buildings . . ."
58 Freudian factor
59 Early hrs.

ACROSS

1 Comedian Mort
5 Small dent on a fender
9 Picket line crossers
14 Margarine
15 Cookie with a creme center
16 Diamond weight
17 Vegas card game
19 Dress style
20 Bullfight bull
21 Marx who wrote "Das Kapital"
23 Sault ___ Marie
24 Flue residue
26 Suffix meaning "approximately"
28 Lucille Ball, e.g.
30 Where the Eiffel Tower is
32 Feed bag contents
34 Distinctive doctrines
35 Fast-growing community
37 Housebroken animal
39 Savior
42 Till bill
43 Yearned (for)
46 Weapon in a silo, for short
49 Found's partner
51 Muse of love poetry
52 Organized absenteeism of police officers
54 Turf
56 "The ___ in the Hat" (rhyming Seuss book)
57 Writer Fleming
58 Greek letter

60 Ark builder
62 Greek letter
64 Stew vegetable
68 Build
69 Forearm bone
70 Indonesian island
71 Appears
72 Christmas carol
73 Settled, as on a perch

DOWN

1 Cry loudly
2 Start (and end) of the Three Musketeers' motto
3 London airport
4 Kooky
5 Martial arts schools
6 Rhymester Gershwin
7 Giraffe's prominent feature
8 Racing vehicle
9 Burn with hot water
10 Baseball's Ripken
11 Gets up
12 Small chicken
13 Spirited horses
18 Actress ___ Scott Thomas
22 Set a top in motion again
24 Police radio alert, briefly
25 ___ Paulo, Brazil
27 Inventor Elias
29 ___ and yon (in many places)
31 "Hi, honey!" follower

33 Egyptian symbols of life

36 Verdi opera based on a Shakespeare play

38 Incited

40 Kooky

41 Of the windpipe

44 Greek letter

45 "i" piece

46 Long-billed wading birds

47 Actress Bloom

48 Jumper's cord

50 Exceed in firepower

53 Decrees

55 Basketball's Shaquille

59 Woody Guthrie's son

61 Rhyme scheme for Mr. Eban?

63 1900, on a cornerstone

65 Opposite WSW

66 Rhyming boxing champ

67 Annual basketball event: Abbr.

ACROSS

1 Sluggers' stats
5 Theme of this puzzle
10 Capital of Italia
14 Burn soother
15 Filibuster, in a way
16 Hawaiian music makers
17 Editor's definition of this puzzle's theme
20 Prevent legally
21 Popular beverage brand
22 Shea nine
25 More crafty
26 Allowable
30 Beckon
33 University of Maine site
34 ___-do-well
35 Dickens protagonist
38 Mapmaker's definition of this puzzle's theme
42 Compass heading
43 Pseudonymous short-story writer
44 Backing for an exhibit
45 Peaceful
47 Sentient
48 Insurance giant
51 Negative in Nuremberg
53 Competed in the Hambletonian
56 Ribeye, e.g.
60 Physician's definition of this puzzle's theme
64 Bank claim
65 Battery part
66 Second in command
67 Driver's license prerequisite
68 The ___ Prayer
69 Interested look

DOWN

1 Genre for Notorious B.I.G.
2 Depressed
3 Charged particles
4 Split-off group
5 Stylish auto
6 Man-mouse link
7 Back muscle, familiarly
8 Redding of 60's soul
9 "Open 24 hours" sign, maybe
10 Muss up
11 Animal with zebra-striped legs
12 Actress Oberon
13 Questioner
18 Indian drum
19 Political cartoonist Thomas
23 Kid's make-believe telephone
24 Elude the doorman
26 Canter
27 Ayatollah's land
28 Dunce cap, essentially
29 ___ pinch
31 Where St. Mark's Cathedral is
32 Investment vehicle, for short

Puzzle 52 by Jeff Herrington

35 Famous tower locale
36 Roman road
37 See 49-Down
39 Enzyme suffix
40 Shanty
41 Bird's cry
45 Purpose
46 "Phooey!"
48 Not perfectly upright
49 With 37-Down, famous W.W. II correspondent

50 Big handbags
52 Wight and Man
54 List shortener
55 Singer Martin, to friends
57 Therefore
58 In awe
59 Basketball's Malone
61 Neither's companion
62 Do basic arithmetic
63 Society column word

ACROSS

1 The ex-Mrs. Bono
5 Money owed
9 Pharmacy items
14 Composer Schifrin
15 Anatomical passage
16 Like "The Twilight Zone" episodes
17 Actress Lena
18 This ___ of tears (life)
19 Do watercolors
20 Secondhand store
23 Showed respect for the national anthem
24 Sister of Osiris
25 Mr. O.
28 Cinematographer Nykvist
30 Arthurian sorcerer
32 Harvest goddess
35 Pass, as laws
38 Verdi heroine
39 John Glenn's Mercury spacecraft
43 Type assortment
44 Card catalogue entry after "Author"
45 Before, in verse
46 Overage
49 Boat propellers
51 Loaf with seeds
52 ___ to the throne (prince, e.g.)
55 Laid, as a bathroom floor
58 Member of the police
61 Without ___ in the world

DOWN

1 Drain problem
2 Angels' headgear
3 Ness of "The Untouchables"
4 Musical movements
5 Stockholder's income
6 Catchall abbr.
7 Attorney Melvin
8 Lock of hair
9 Remove from office
10 Harvest
11 Spoon-bender Geller
12 Rummy game
13 Matched items
21 Made on a loom
22 That guy
25 Kicking's partner
26 Contract add-on
27 Nonsensical
29 Political cartoonist Thomas
31 "Norma ___"
32 Bidder's amount
33 Stockholder's vote
34 Subsequently
36 Letter before psi

64 Prefix with China
65 Nat King or Natalie
66 ___ says (tots' game)
67 ___-do-well
68 Popular fashion magazine
69 Israeli port
70 Microbe
71 Do one of the three R's

Puzzle 53 by Stephanie Spadaccini

37 Maverick Yugoslav leader
40 High season, on the Riviera
41 Railroad station area
42 Printing flourish
47 Singer Easton
48 Ocean
50 Deli machine
53 Cake decoration
54 "Walk Away___" (1966 hit)
56 French school
57 Singer Reese
58 Univ. teacher
59 German border river
60 Marsh stalk
61 Cigarette waste
62 K.G.B.'s cold war foe
63 "___ the only one?"

ACROSS

1 Procter & Gamble bar
6 Native Alaskan
11 Spoil
14 Midwest airport hub
15 Sergeant at TV's Fort Baxter
16 Diamonds
17 Place to place a wallet or handkerchief
19 ___ Na Na
20 Thanksgiving meat request
21 "Entry of Christ Into Brussels" painter James
23 Scott Adams's put-upon comics hero
27 Nautical spar
29 Body parts shaped like punching bags
30 W.W. II Philippine battle site
31 Horse in a harness race
32 1924 Ferber novel
33 Little newt
36 It's NNW of Oklahoma City
37 Rounded lumps
38 Nicholas I or II, e.g.
39 Mule of song
40 Nash's two-l beast
41 Hardly elegant
42 Easy two-pointers
44 Concert halls
45 Starts of tourneys
47 Last course
48 Peres's predecessor
49 "___ That a Shame"
50 Eggs
51 "Come on!"
58 ___ canto (singing style)
59 Characteristic
60 Confuse
61 Right-angle joint
62 Steinbeck migrants
63 Dapper

DOWN

1 ___ a plea
2 "Now I see!"
3 Beatnik's exclamation
4 Skill
5 Sweetheart's assent
6 Cancel, as a launch
7 Drub
8 Lodge member
9 Luau instrument
10 Alternative to a purse
11 Err on stage
12 Cause for blessing?
13 Get ready for battle again
18 Average figures
22 Org. for Bulls and Bullets
23 Fools
24 Ex-Mrs. Trump
25 Four-time Emmy-winning comedienne
26 Ran, as colors
27 ___ the Hutt, of "Star Wars"
28 Medical suffix

Puzzle 54 by Brendan Emmett Quigley

30 Certain mikes
32 Knee hits
34 Mountebank
35 Lovers' engagement
37 Rather morose
38 Suns
40 Deceiving
41 Nuclear treaty subject
43 "The Greatest"
44 ___ cava (path to the heart)
45 Explore

46 "Bolero" composer
47 They're losing propositions
49 French friend
52 Bother
53 ___ tai (drink)
54 Nutritional abbr.
55 N.Y.C. summer clock setting
56 Model Carol
57 Lock opener

ACROSS

1 Mad dog worry
5 Spy ___ Hari
9 Aware, with "in"
14 Water color
15 Valentine's Day matchmaker
16 Hawaiian veranda
17 "Brilliant idea!"
20 Ice Follies venue
21 Maid's cloth
22 Veteran
26 Pennilessness
30 ___ Strait (Russia-Alaska separator)
31 Confront
32 Wide shoe specification
33 Police operation
34 Knob
35 Nos. on a road map
36 Classic Bill Clinton phrase
39 Giant Mel et al.
40 Jazzy Fitzgerald
41 Remove, as a knot
43 Award for a knight: Abbr.
44 Neighbor of Vietnam
45 Like some kisses and bases
46 Novelist Hesse
48 Sentimentalists, maybe
49 Superlative ending
50 Subject of psychoanalysis
51 1962 Cary Grant/Doris Day movie

59 Actor Bruce of radio's "Sherlock Holmes"
60 Chess finale
61 "God's Little ___"
62 Lachrymose
63 Hardly any
64 Rural carriage

DOWN

1 Sheep's sound
2 Stats for eggheads
3 Egyptian boy king
4 Barber's obstruction
5 Cooking up
6 Change, as a motion
7 Swiped
8 Comic dog's bark
9 Split asunder
10 Jessica of 1976's "King Kong"
11 Prefix with cycle
12 ___ de vie
13 Insult, in slang
18 Pumpkin-colored
19 Food seller
22 Out-of-date: Abbr.
23 Last Beatles album
24 Gadabout
25 Jazzman "Fatha"
26 "The Taming of the Shrew" locale
27 Change names
28 Even smaller
29 "You bet!"
31 April ___ Day
34 Parachute material
35 Babbled

37 Shanty
38 Delay
39 Aah's partner
42 U.S.N. officer
44 Summing-up word
45 Flew alone
47 Olympic race unit
48 Conductor Zubin
50 "Get outta here!"
51 Explosive inits.

52 Hasten
53 ___ Khan
54 Thurman of "Pulp Fiction"
55 Mothers
56 "___ bin ein Berliner"
57 Gun enthusiast's grp.
58 Codebreaker's discovery

ACROSS

1 Farm structure
5 Kon-Tiki wood
10 Boutique
14 Rev. Roberts
15 From the East
16 Windex target
17 Conjointly
19 Killer whale film
20 Till bill
21 Plant part
22 Ham
24 Certain pints
25 Vessel
26 Novelist-screenwriter Eric
29 Person in need of salvation
32 Places to buy cold cuts
33 Dugout
34 Showtime rival
35 Greatly
36 Where Joan of Arc died
37 Wilde's "The Ballad of Reading ___"
38 Catty remark?
39 Vine fruit
40 Snorkeler's sight
41 "O Pioneers!" setting
43 Talkative
44 Joins the team?
45 Stable newborn
46 Insignia
48 Sheryl Crow's "___ Wanna Do"
49 Kind of story
52 Handyman Bob

53 Bobby Vinton hit
56 Word after pig or before horse
57 Burdened
58 Tittle
59 Ribald
60 Works in the cutting room
61 Midterm, e.g.

DOWN

1 Part of London or Manhattan
2 Teheran's land
3 Rural route
4 Like a centenarian
5 Back-and-forth
6 Grate expectations?
7 Actor Neeson
8 ___ Diego
9 "Father Knows Best" family name
10 Lampoons
11 Sidney Sheldon TV series
12 Some time ago
13 Fruit cocktail fruit
18 Tropical getaways
23 Pal, Down Under
24 Dismounted
25 "We'll go to ___, and eat bologna . . ."
26 Rhett's last words
27 Free-for-all
28 Detailed account
29 Singer Nyro or Branigan

Puzzle 56 by Gregory E. Paul

30 German sub
31 Candy on a stick, informally
33 Parts of wine bottles
36 Look like
37 Soccer score
39 Enter a Pillsbury contest
40 Mountain range
42 Hero of early French ballads

43 Punctuation marks
45 Armada
46 Like Satan
47 Bog
48 German auto
49 Gin flavor
50 Scoreboard stat
51 Cop's milieu
54 Youth
55 Bridle part

ACROSS

1 Meal at boot camp
5 Sell tickets illegally
10 Sam the ___ of 60's pop
14 "Beetle Bailey" dog
15 It's a no-no
16 Car with a meter
17 Lose one's nerve
19 Israeli guns
20 Tennis great Rosewall
21 Bohemian
22 "Gunsmoke" star James
24 Vulgar one
26 Tyke
27 70's–80's Yankee pitching ace
34 Imus's medium
37 Goods
38 "Blue" bird
39 Abba of Israel
40 Opera headliners
41 Stupor
42 ___ 'easter
43 Sheets, pillowcases, etc.
44 Put on the payroll
45 Old instrument of punishment
48 "Who ___ you?"
49 Sounded, as a bell
53 Prestige
56 Villa d' ___
58 Actress Gardner
59 Major league brothers' name
60 Quaint dance
63 "___ the Mood for Love"
64 Actress Samantha
65 Microwave, slangily
66 Grandmother, affectionately
67 Immunizations
68 ___ off (plenty mad)

DOWN

1 Treats cynically
2 Lucy's best friend
3 Children's author R. L. ___
4 League: Abbr.
5 Audiophile's setup
6 Quitter's word
7 "It's ___!" (proud parents' phrase)
8 Singer Rawls
9 Shepherd's pie ingredients
10 Publicity seekers' acts
11 Smog
12 X or Y, on a graph
13 Ole ___
18 Nonmusician's musical instrument
23 Flagmaker Betsy
25 Opposed to, in the backwoods
28 Playground equipment
29 Overhangs
30 Research money
31 Not quite shut
32 Stare, as at a crystal ball
33 Checked out

Puzzle 57 by Fred Piscop

34 Pull apart
35 "___ Ben Adhem"
36 Jeanne ___ (French saint)
40 Eating alcoves
41 Pickle flavoring
43 Italian money
44 Nonsense
46 Hawaiian medicine man
47 Frolicking animals
50 Lash ___ of old westerns

51 Call forth
52 Went out with
53 Old Testament murderer
54 ___ mater
55 Nickel or copper, but not tin
56 Therefore
57 Three-player card game
61 "Yecch!"
62 Blaster's need

ACROSS

1 Utters
5 Military plane acronym
10 Desertlike
14 Wyoming neighbor
15 Striped critter
16 Hurting
17 State of financial independence
19 CAT ___
20 Singer Lopez
21 Kett of old comics
22 Little guitars
23 Singer Cara
25 Guard
27 It's a stitch!
29 Mint and sage
32 Stadium sounds
35 Basketball hoop site, often
39 Acorn, in 2020?
40 "Surfin' ___" (Beach Boys hit)
41 Gandhi's title
42 Ryan's "Love Story" co-star
43 Russian space station
44 Puzzle
45 4:1, e.g.
46 Mubarak's predecessor
48 Recipe direction
50 Some Broadway shows
54 Overhead shot
57 Last name in spydom
59 "There ought to be ___!"
61 Suggest itself (to)
63 Thrift shop stipulation
64 "The Birdcage" co-star
66 Possess
67 Whitney Houston's "All the Man That ___"
68 Verve
69 Parrots
70 Chooses actors
71 E-mail command

DOWN

1 Winter bird food
2 Video arcade name
3 Arafat of the P.L.O.
4 Wallflower's characteristic
5 Much-publicized drug
6 Existed
7 Helps in dirty deeds
8 El Greco's birthplace
9 Underworld figure
10 Guarantee
11 Ice cream parlor order
12 "Dies ___"
13 TV rooms
18 ___ qua non
24 1991 Tony winner Daisy
26 "Take ___ Train"
28 When repeated, a fish
30 Like a worn tire
31 T-bar sights
32 Jamaican exports
33 Pacific Rim region

Puzzle 58 by Elizabeth C. Gorski

34 Computer part
36 Joplin piece
37 24-hr. conveniences
38 Certain exams, for short
41 Prefix with physical
45 The Scriptures
47 Gets up
49 "___ Fire" (Springsteen hit)
51 Wired, so to speak

52 "The George & ___ Show" (former talk show)
53 Fills up
55 Union rate
56 Chinese province
57 Joker's gibe
58 Rush job notation
60 Stimulate
62 Rip apart
65 Want ___

ACROSS

1 Prop up
6 Goddess pictured in Egyptian tombs
10 Fraud
14 Old autos
15 Short letter
16 Patriot Nathan
17 Feeling really good
20 Get-out-of-jail money
21 Hors d'oeuvre spread
22 Song for Aida
23 Chomped down
24 "___ cost to you!"
25 Novelist Waugh
27 Batter's goal
29 Frigid
30 "Turandot" slave girl
31 Moon-landing vehicle
32 ___ de Triomphe
33 "I ___ Grow Up" ("Peter Pan" song)
34 Heads of state get-together
38 "It can't be!"
39 Be in session
40 Nothing
41 Peas' holder
42 Pennies: Abbr.
43 Creeks
47 Storm warnings at sea
49 Clinton's #2
50 Wrestler's place
51 Site for a swing
52 Rikki-tikki-___ (Kipling mongoose)
53 Capable of
54 Little that's visible
57 Poker call
58 Mending site
59 Louis XIV, 1643–1715
60 Hawaii's state bird
61 Remove from office
62 Dunne of "I Remember Mama"

DOWN

1 Thick-trunked tropical tree
2 Italian soprano Scotto
3 Clarinetist Shaw and others
4 Refrigerate
5 One of Kreskin's claims
6 Wee one
7 ___ voce (almost in a whisper)
8 Spillane's "___ Jury"
9 Visualize
10 Beach
11 Set of bells
12 Relieving
13 Club ___
18 They expect the best
19 Undulating
24 "Um, excuse me"
25 Like a three-dollar bill
26 Cashew, e.g.
28 "Tickle me" doll
29 Anger
32 Quantity: Abbr.
33 Sly trick
34 Cable channel
35 Support

Puzzle 59 by Eileen Lexau

36 "___ the season . . ."
37 Radial, e.g.
38 Photo ___ (media events)
42 Musical sign
43 Bygone Russian group
44 Electrical unit
45 Female attendant
46 Cheap cigar

48 Sierra ___
49 Scottish Celts
52 10 C-notes
53 Opposite of unter, in German
54 Can's composition
55 Notwithstanding that, briefly
56 Biblical priest

ACROSS

1 27, to 3
5 Virgule
10 St. Nick accessory
14 The top
15 "Remember the ___!"
16 "Ars Amatoria" poet
17 Surgical site in the Beaver State?
19 Kid's phrase of request
20 Chang's Siamese twin
21 Itch
22 Full moon color
24 Commedia dell'___
25 Rapper who co-starred in "New Jack City"
26 Le Carre character George
29 Methodology
32 Estate papers
33 Gunk
34 Champagne Tony of golf
36 ___ vera
37 Middays
38 Money to tide one over
39 It's west of N.C.
40 Just
41 "What ___ I do?"
42 Nielsen stats
44 Comic Charles Nelson ___
45 Unpleasant task
46 Hospital unit
47 Declarer
50 Swiss river
51 "___ is me!"
54 Glitzy sign
55 Doc from the Old Line State?
58 Cartoonist Al
59 Chorus girls?
60 The first: Abbr.
61 Fashion's Klensch
62 1956 Four Lads hit "___ Much!"
63 It's just for openers

DOWN

1 Supergarb
2 "___ the housetop . . ." (Christmas lyric)
3 Arctic Ocean sighting
4 Phone line abbr.
5 ___-pants (wise guy)
6 Jessica of "Frances"
7 Right-hand person
8 ___-cone
9 Decorated officers
10 Driver's license in the Gem State?
11 Russian "John"
12 Engine knock
13 Actress McClurg
18 Fishing gear
23 ___ room
24 Sound system in the Keystone State?
25 Humor not for dummies
26 Quite a hit
27 Distance runner
28 Actress Massey

Puzzle 60 by Stephanie Spadaccini

29 Chlorinated waters
30 1988 Olympics site
31 Inconsequential
33 Pagoda sounds
35 "Handy" man
37 Rural
41 Goddess of agriculture
43 Suffix with elephant
44 Least cooked
46 "Yippee!"
47 Suffix with utter

48 ___ piccata
49 Kin of "Uh-oh!"
50 Envelope abbr.
51 Alert
52 Leave off
53 Periphery
56 "Strange Magic" rock band
57 1988 Dennis Quaid remake

ACROSS

1 Civil disorder
5 Urban haze
9 Diners
14 Workers' protection org.
15 Variety of fine cotton
16 Hold dear
17 Tizzy
18 The New Yorker cartoonist Peter
19 Chateau-Thierry's river
20 "Petticoat Junction" setting
23 Lyricist Rice
24 Granola grain
25 Copyists
27 Trim, as a tree
32 Arp's art
33 Military address: Abbr.
34 Fishing line
36 The "S" in WASP
39 State north of Ind.
41 Adventures
43 Battle of Normandy objective
44 Big news exclusive
46 Reading lights
48 Ames and Asner
49 Pub orders
51 Practice
53 Edmonton's province
56 Everything
57 Random number generator
58 "Father Knows Best" setting

64 Texas site to remember
66 Have ___ good authority
67 Sewing case
68 Georgia city, home of Mercer University
69 Color of linen
70 Final Four inits.
71 Pronunciation symbol
72 Make-believe
73 Eschew

DOWN

1 ___ ha-Shanah
2 "Money ___ object!"
3 Louisville's river
4 Dragon, perhaps
5 Big Ten team from East Lansing
6 Nuclear missile, briefly
7 Prefix meaning 56-Across
8 London lockups
9 Kodaks, e.g.
10 Nabokov novel
11 "The Phil Silvers Show" setting
12 Sgt. Bilko
13 Looks like
21 Prominent rabbit features
22 Digital readout, for short
26 Mrs. McKinley and others
27 Beavers' constructions
28 Kind of proportions

Puzzle 61 by Gregory E. Paul

29 "I Dream of Jeannie" setting
30 Marsh duck
31 "Pomp and Circumstance" composer
35 Shiny fabric
37 Auto pioneer Ransom
38 Victory margin, at times
40 Tunnel
42 Moss for potting plants
45 ___ non grata
47 Prefix with starter

50 Nascar sponsor
52 Little green men
53 Revolutionary leader Samuel
54 Light purple
55 Pisces's follower
59 Scratch it!
60 Nick and ___ Charles
61 Make an aquatint
62 Hilo feast
63 Primatologist Fossey
65 Cut the grass

ACROSS

1 Support
5 Hindu gentleman
9 Indonesian island
14 Nautical direction
15 Part of the eye
16 Mirror ___
17 Charlemagne's legacy
20 Lepidopterist's equipment
21 Corrida cries
22 Condemned
23 Marking float
24 Tiny memory measures
25 "Nothing ___!"
27 James Buchanan, notably
31 Reign noted for magnificent porcelain
33 Actress Hagen
34 Commentators' page
35 Cricket sides
36 Play start
37 German direction
38 Virginia's nickname
42 Farewells
44 Chips in?
45 Rara ___
46 Semicircles
47 Gene Kelly's activity in the 30-Down
50 Hammett pooch
51 Stage of history
54 Disney realm
57 Draw a bead on
58 Subsequently
59 Venom
60 Cache
61 Stitches
62 Charon's river

DOWN

1 Where to take a Volkswagen for a spin
2 Shampoo ingredient
3 Breton, for one
4 Crucial
5 What John Scopes taught
6 Former majority leader Dick
7 Partiality
8 Milit. branch
9 Coarse fodder grass
10 Levy
11 Impair
12 Bogeyman
13 Army surgeon Walter
18 Spherical
19 Pronouncement
23 Nickname for the Cowboys' hometown
24 One who sings the part of Boris Godunov
25 Boozehound
26 "And ___ grow on"
27 They were big in the 40's
28 "A Tale of Two Cities" heroine
29 Director Preminger et al.
30 See 47-Across
31 ___ synthesizer
32 Stem joints

Puzzle 62 by Jonathan Schmalzbach

36 Termites' kin
38 Render unnecessary
39 Fibbing
40 Forked-tail swallows
41 From early Peru
43 Buxom blonde of 50's TV
46 Crooked
47 B.&O. stops
48 "___ a New High" (1937 Lily Pons song)

49 Verne's captain
50 Lumbago, e.g.
51 Blue-pencil
52 ___-poly
53 Big Board's brother: Abbr.
55 "___ Not Unusual"
56 Literary monogram

ACROSS

1 Org. that safeguards pets
5 Prefix with port
9 Liability's opposite
14 Songwriter Gus
15 Plow animals
16 Marvy
17 "Yikes!"
18 Actress Hayworth
19 Mississippi ___
20 Lead singer with Dawn
23 Opposite of 42-Across
24 Alphabet trio
25 Reduced fare
26 ___ la Douce
28 What "hemi-" means
30 Odd
33 Popular record label
36 Cosmetician Elizabeth
37 Treaty
40 Seabees' motto
42 B or better
43 Impassive
45 Horses' home
47 Morning or afternoon travel
49 Vlad the Impaler, e.g.
53 Stallion's mate
54 Water, in Cadiz
56 "Do Ya" rock grp.
57 Kind of testing, in law enforcement
59 Los Angeles suburb
62 Sonata section
64 Mrs. Chaplin
65 Jazz performance
66 Dual conjunction
67 Men's business wear
68 Buster Brown's dog
69 Pirate's prize
70 Nobelist Wiesel
71 TV's "___ Three Lives"

DOWN

1 Artist's rendering
2 Chinese temple
3 Estee Lauder rival
4 Rooney of "60 Minutes"
5 Frightful
6 Banish
7 Free to attack
8 ___ instant (quickly)
9 Neighbor of Spain
10 Go out with
11 60's–70's A's third baseman
12 Ending with Henri
13 Wart-covered creature
21 Stench
22 Morse code click
27 Baseball owner Schott et al.
29 Bluebeard's last wife
30 Actress Thompson
31 Storm or Tracker, in the auto world
32 Finis
34 Postpaid encl.
35 It's a blast
37 Utilities watchdog grp.
38 From ___ Z
39 "Dirty Dozen" marauder

Puzzle 63 by Thomas W. Schier

41 Inflexible
44 Superficial, as a look
46 Emulate Pisa's tower
48 Tetley product
50 Cosmetics applicator
51 Senior years
52 Blew a horn

54 Run ___ of (violate)
55 Bottled spirits
57 Cheerless
58 Banned act
60 Bloodhound's sensor
61 ___ spumante
63 Complete an "i"

ACROSS

1 Indian title of respect
6 Love handles, essentially
10 Gad about
14 "Fur ___" (Beethoven dedication)
15 Clarence Thomas's garb
16 Second word of many limericks
17 It's not as threatening as it looks
19 Give up
20 Current strength
21 Antiaircraft fire
23 London lavatory
24 "Rocky ___"
25 ___ A Sketch (drawing toy)
26 Old age, in old times
27 Italian cheese
31 ___ Major (southern constellation)
35 Mat victory
36 River of Russia
37 Man ___ (famous race horse)
38 Jive talkin'
40 Running shoe name
41 Marquand's Mr. ___
42 Rotter
43 Does some lawn work
44 Disappear through camouflage
46 Mineral springs
48 Tended to the weeds
49 "High ___" (Anderson play)
50 Photo ___ (camera sessions)
53 Repudiate
56 Horrid
58 It's put off at the bakery
59 Shooter's target
61 Change for a C-note
62 Roof overhang
63 Homes for hatchlings
64 Philosopher
65 Exceeded the limit
66 Gaggle members

DOWN

1 Flower part
2 Bowie's last stand
3 Swimmer in the Congo
4 "Now it's clear!"
5 Additions to an ice cream sundae
6 North Pole-like
7 Theater section
8 Burrows of the theater
9 Chewing out
10 Geologist
11 ___-Day (vitamin brand)
12 Australian hard-rock band
13 Like a milquetoast
18 Party game pin-on
22 New Deal prog.
25 "___ go bragh"
28 Math subject

29 Money brought in
30 Pub quaffs
31 Toothed item
32 Roll call misser
33 Hoops great Archibald
34 Lou Gehrig nickname, with "the"
35 Seat cover
38 Arts' partner
39 Touch down
43 Bringing in
45 ___ Jones
46 Hung around

47 Splendor
50 Corpulent plus
51 Draws, as a line on a graph
52 Good judgment
53 Pencil-and-paper game
54 Brainstorm
55 Carol
56 Garroway of early TV
57 "The African Queen" scriptwriter
60 Drink like Fido

ACROSS

1 Musicians' copyright grp.
6 King with a golden touch
11 Business fraud monitoring agcy.
14 TV exec Arledge
15 "Be ___ . . ."
16 Spanish gold
17 Grant vs. Bragg, Nov. 1863
19 Tease
20 Sandwich choice
21 Parkers feed it downtown
23 ___-do-well
24 Black Sea port
25 Wakeful watches
28 Bush aide John
30 Neighborhood
31 Idiot
32 Chinese food additive
35 On, as a lamp
36 For fun
38 Place for a hole in a sock
39 Winter clock setting in Vt.
50 Union branch
41 Coal stratum
42 "Old ___" (1957 Disney film)
44 Lines of cliffs
46 Slugged
48 Salon job
49 Perth ___, N.J.

50 Unlike Mr. Spock of "Star Trek"
55 Brock or Costello
56 Rosecrans vs. Bragg, Sept. 1863
58 Continent north of Afr.
59 Eagle's nest
60 Listlessness
61 It follows a dot in many on-line addresses
62 Not our
63 Syria's Hafez al-___

DOWN

1 It may have fallen on a foot
2 Manhattan locale
3 Jacket
4 Cather novel "My ___"
5 Small sea bird
6 Millionaire's home
7 Elvis Presley, in the 50's and 60's
8 "I ___ it!" (cry of success)
9 H.S. math
10 Patrick Ewing specialty
11 Anderson vs. Beauregard, Apr. 1861
12 Attempts
13 Striking snake
18 Good blackjack holdings
22 Poet's dusk
24 ___ about (lawyer's phrase)

Puzzle 65 by Gene Newman

25 Caesar's farewell
26 Spring bloom
27 Meade vs. Lee, July 1863
28 Kind of energy or flare
29 ___ Mountains (edge of Asia)
31 Riot queller
33 Ivory, e.g.
34 Onyxes and opals
36 Night prowler
37 Auctioneer's last word
41 Pago Pago residents

43 D.D.E.'s command
44 ___ poor example
45 Sevastopol locale
46 Ancient: Prefix
47 Love affair
48 Fireplace rod
50 Dublin's land
51 1102, in dates
52 Women in habits
53 Tijuana water
54 Deposited
57 Sneaky laugh sound

ACROSS

1 Bid
6 Mesa dweller
10 Nod off
14 Site of Cnossus
15 Big name in cosmetics
16 German biographer ___ Ludwig
17 "___ looking at you, kid"
18 Lady's man
19 Movers
20 Quirky
21 Impressive achievement
24 Sorbonne, e.g.
26 Tire channel
27 Peer, to his servant
29 Plant with a medicinal root
33 More than peeved
34 Charles's domain
35 Hemispheric assn.
37 Ready to come off the stove
38 Examined, as before a robbery
39 Skip
40 Business mag
41 Lawn
42 "The Taming of the Shrew" setting
43 Spy's byword
45 Police datum
46 Assistance
47 Like toast
48 Final stroke
53 Fate

56 The "A" in A.D.
57 Film ___
58 Pan-fry
60 Harness part
61 Gusto
62 Greek satirist
63 These may be fine
64 On the main
65 Driving hazard

DOWN

1 Cuatro y cuatro
2 N.F.L. receiver Biletnikoff
3 Tropical viper
4 Bastille Day season
5 Give back
6 World Court site, with "The"
7 Finished
8 Thoreau subject
9 Confined, as in wartime
10 Give, as time
11 Gen. Bradley
12 Over-the-counter cold remedy
13 Otherwise
22 Aged
23 Ado
25 ___ d'Azur (French Riviera)
27 Certain skirt
28 Actor Jeremy
29 Long-winded
30 Nouvelle Caledonie and others

Puzzle 66 by Robert Zimmerman

31 Pseudonym
32 Julius Caesar's first name
34 W.W. II enlistee
36 Immediately, in the E.R.
38 Sideboard
39 Sculls
41 Part of a crossword
42 Clergymen
44 Poultry offerings

45 Compass tracing
47 Magna ___
48 Dear, as a signorina
49 Unique person
50 Military group
51 "Anything ___" (1934 or 1987 musical)
52 Levitate
54 Siouan tribe
55 Camp shelter
59 Be sick

ACROSS

1 Deep sleeps
6 Abbr. before an alias
9 Fragrant oil
14 ___-garde
15 Steal from
16 Push roughly
17 A Roosevelt
18 Afflicted with strabismus
20 Traffic tangle
21 The first "H" of H.H.S.
22 Quilting event
23 Cautious
24 Open a bit
28 Garbage barge
30 Come down
31 Clinton's veep
32 Sigma follower
33 Blue birds
34 Grown-ups
36 Snares
38 Shooting marble
39 Bill settlers
40 Coating metal
41 "Are we there ___?"
42 They're exchanged at weddings
43 Building block company
44 Goofs up
45 Of ships: Abbr.
46 Second-year student, for short
47 Not a beginner
48 Get down from a horse
50 Thesaurus compiler

53 Show with Richie and the Fonz
56 Dancer Astaire
57 Banish
58 Gun grp.
59 Brusque
60 "For ___ sake!"
61 Opposite NNE
62 Industrial city of Germany

DOWN

1 Long-running Broadway show
2 Turkey roaster
3 Paul Reiser/Helen Hunt series
4 President Jackson or Johnson
5 Do, as hair
6 Architectural frames
7 Ones with Seoul custody?
8 "All ___!" (conductor's cry)
9 Helper: Abbr.
10 Where Dutch royals live
11 Plaything
12 "___ Maria"
13 Like Time's border
19 Crafty
25 Pirate flags
26 More pretentious
27 Bowling alley buttons
28 Enter

Puzzle 67 by Shannon Burns

29 The Great White North
30 Swimmer's regimen
33 Place for pickles
34 ___ time (never)
35 Nov. follower
37 Fasten papers again
38 Visited tourist places
40 Gentle breezes
43 "___ Run" (1976 sci-fi film)

44 Wears away
46 Rock singer Vicious
47 Chatter
49 Caustic solutions
51 Otherwise
52 Adolescent
53 Wise, man
54 Chop
55 Orchestra's location

ACROSS

1 Stage between egg and pupa
6 "Durn it!"
10 Head of hair, slangily
13 "Silas Marner" author
14 Exploiters
16 Eggs
17 Teensy-weensy piece of beef?
19 Seat in St. Paul's
20 ___ Rosa, Calif.
21 1984 World Series champs
23 The sun
26 Johnnie Ray hit of the 50's
27 Biblical king
28 Sleazy
30 Sandlot sport
33 Cottonlike fiber
34 Without
35 Actress ___ Dawn Chong
36 Got 100 on
37 Dot on a monitor
38 Tiny bit
39 ___-de-France
40 Radius, ulna, etc.
41 U.C.L.A. player
42 Big North Carolina industry
44 "Dirty Rotten Scoundrels" actress ___ Headly
45 Kind of bean
46 Old French coin
47 ___ es Salaam
48 Tom Canty, in a Mark Twain book
50 Pedestals, e.g.
52 Mornings, for short
53 What stand-up comics do to keep their material shiny?
58 Soupy Sales missile
59 Long bout
60 Vicinities
61 Catalogue contents
62 Some P.T.A. members
63 Long (for)

DOWN

1 Moon craft, for short
2 Actress MacGraw
3 ___ Tin Tin
4 "Comment allez ___?"
5 Embassy worker
6 Name for a cowpoke
7 Movie pooch
8 Society page word
9 Like a proper rescuee
10 Ride an enginepowered bike?
11 Finished
12 Furry feet
15 Poodle and dirndl, e.g.
18 Professor 'iggins
22 Sailor
23 Sea route
24 Delphic shrine
25 "My gold dress isn't back from the cleaners yet" and others?

Puzzle 68 by Stephanie Spadaccini

27 Sharpens
29 Caesar of "Caesar's Hour"
30 At ___ and sevens
31 Chicana
32 Horseshoes shot
34 Sal of "Giant"
37 Instant picture
38 Anger
40 They're big in gyms
41 Colorful, crested bird
43 Strike lightly

44 "No kidding!"
46 MS. enclosures
48 Madonna's "___ Don't Preach"
49 In the center of
50 Dallas's nickname
51 Achy
54 Meadow
55 Mauna ___
56 It may be pulled in charades
57 ID digits

ACROSS

1 Throat-clearing sound
5 Fencing weapon
10 Actress Rowlands
14 Exploding star
15 Singer Page
16 Fairy tale's second word
17 St. Paul and Minneapolis
19 Require
20 Comedians Bob and Chris
21 In a wise manner
23 Lawyer's charge
24 "Gee!"
25 Sweatshirt part, perhaps
27 Flush beater
32 Writer Bellow and others
33 Place for a pimento
34 Not the swiftest horse
35 Posterior
36 "Death Be Not Proud" poet
37 Opera star
38 Dog breeder's org.
39 Imply
40 Doled (out)
41 Leaders of hives
43 Like some tea
44 Praise
45 Santa ___, Calif.
46 Refuse to acknowledge responsibility for
49 Post-marathon feeling
54 Quickly, in memos
55 Southern crop, from an economic standpoint
57 Writer Grey
58 Writer Zola
59 Humorist Bombeck
60 Got a good look at
61 Saw socially
62 Profound

DOWN

1 Pot starter
2 Loud laugh
3 More than devilish
4 Part of a car's exhaust system
5 Malice
6 Light bulb unit
7 Elevator inventor
8 Road map abbr.
9 Liquefy
10 Very enthusiastic
11 Fencing weapon
12 Christmas song
13 Raggedy Ann's friend
18 Some college students
22 Tennis great Arthur
24 Quick flashes of light
25 17-syllable poem
26 Precious metal unit of weight
27 Paid, as a bill
28 Arm bones
29 Come together
30 Backed up on disk
31 "Holy cow!"
32 The N.B.A.'s O'Neal, familiarly

Puzzle 69 by Peter Gordon

36 Exposed as false
37 Poured wine into another container
39 Chew
40 Actor Sal
42 Ran for one's wife?
45 Moved like a shooting star
46 Stun
47 British exclamation
48 Having all one's marbles
49 Tizzy
50 Leer at
51 To be, in Bordeaux
52 Not all
53 Jacket fastener
56 The Monkees' "___ Believer"

ACROSS

1 Neanderthal's weapon
5 Basketballer
10 Tramp
14 Sharpen, as a razor
15 Dateless
16 Finished
17 Touch up, as text
18 Repeated Chris O'Donnell movie role
19 Org. expanding into Eastern Europe
20 Healthy
23 Toward the stern
24 September bloom
28 Mother that can't be fooled
32 Much of kindergarten
35 Sports venue
36 Woeful word
37 The first X of X-X-X
38 Spotless
42 No longer working: Abbr.
43 Parts of bytes
44 "Frasier" character
45 Weaken
48 Ulcer cause, in popular belief
49 Emergency room supply
50 Cosmonauts' space station
51 Taut
59 Certain boxing blow
62 Send, as payment
63 Seldom seen

64 Mitch Miller's instrument
65 "Goodnight" girl of song
66 The dark side
67 Still sleeping
68 Copier powder
69 A.F.C. division

DOWN

1 Worker with an apron
2 New Jersey city south of Paramus
3 Army outfit
4 VHS alternative
5 Chianti container
6 Skyward
7 Mongolian desert
8 Camelot lady
9 Split
10 "I'm telling you the truth!"
11 Lab eggs
12 Craps action
13 Treasure of the Sierra Madre
21 See-through wrap
22 Minstrel's song
25 Y. A. of the Giants
26 Novelist Zola and others
27 Alcove
28 Mother-of-pearls
29 Longtime "What's My Line" panelist
30 Wobble
31 Spanish article

Puzzle 70 by Gregory E. Paul

1	2	3	4		5	6	7	8	9		10	11	12	13
14					15						16			
17					18						19			
20				21						22				
			23							24		25	26	27
28	29	30	31				32	33	34		35			
35					36							37		
38					39					40	41			
42					43					44				
45			46	47					48					
49							50							
			51		52	53	54				55	56	57	58
59	60	61			62						63			
64					65						66			
67					68						69			

32 Batter's position
33 Statutes
34 Baseball bat wood
36 "___ was in the beginning . . ."
39 Lawyers' org.
40 Prefix with venous
41 Madam's mate
46 Like a wagon trail
47 George Marshall's alma mater, briefly
48 Nun

50 Down East
52 Stick-to-itiveness
53 Submarine sandwich
54 Feds
55 Attracted
56 Strong thumbs-up review
57 "Mila 18" novelist
58 Liquefy, as ice cream
59 Mauna ___
60 Decline
61 Antagonist

ACROSS

1 One of 7-Down
6 Nicholas II, e.g.
10 Tattle
14 Kind of anesthetic
15 Roll call response
16 "I before E except after C," e.g.
17 Make amends
18 The witch's end in "Hansel and Gretel"
19 Where India is
20 Restorative
21 Clinton Attorney General Janet
22 Ollie's partner in slapstick
23 Popular oil additive
25 Tough as ___
27 One leads to Loch Lomond
31 Mounted again
35 Collection of anecdotes
36 One of 7-Down
38 Small drum
39 Signal for an act to end
41 Holy chalice of legend
43 Telephone sound
44 It increases by degrees
46 Make sense
48 The Red Baron was one
49 Curriculum vitae
51 Striped
53 Midsection, informally
55 It hangs next to 53-Across
56 "Hey, you!"
59 Growth on the north side of trees
61 Monastery staff
65 Reverberation
66 Satanic
67 1973 Broadway revival starring Debbie Reynolds
68 Pour
69 Singer Turner
70 Gypsy's deck
71 One of 7-Down
72 Midterm, e.g.
73 One of 7-Down

DOWN

1 Subdivision of land
2 ___-Rooter
3 It's clicked on a computer
4 Breakfast pastry for Hamlet?
5 Sophocles tragedy
6 God with a hammer
7 This puzzle's theme
8 "In the ___" (Nixon book)
9 Impressionist Pierre
10 High military muck-a-muck
11 One of 7-Down
12 Inter___
13 Noggin
24 Ping-___
26 Serve to be reserved
27 Cartoon Viking
28 Hole-___

Puzzle 71 by William Bernhardt

29 The Sharks and the Jets, e.g.
30 Taj Mahal site
32 German sub
33 Present
34 One of 7-Down
37 "___, Pagliaccio" (aria)
40 One of 7-Down
42 Moon goddess
45 Grounded bird
47 Drivers and hunters need them

50 Clown Kelly
52 Not concerned with right and wrong
54 Hollywood release
56 Dumas senior
57 Glance over
58 Thug's knife
60 Blinds piece
62 Peter or the Wolfe?
63 Half hitch, e.g.
64 Brother of Cain and Abel

ACROSS

1 Webster's, e.g.: Abbr.
5 Ones easily fooled
9 Afflictions
14 Jacob's twin
15 "Not guilty," e.g.
16 Dwelling place
17 Green shot
18 Bibliography, basically
19 Cheek cosmetic
20 Parts of lbs.
21 Diagonally
23 Put safely to bed, as a child
25 Peewee
26 Steal cattle
29 Actor Nielsen of "Airplane!"
33 Practices in the ring
35 Be jubilant
37 Octopus's defense
38 Cheryl of "Charlie's Angels"
39 Louvers
40 Lavish affection (on)
41 Lubricate
42 Taxonomic divisions
43 Clerics' confab
44 2 or 3, maybe, on the Richter scale
46 Macbeth and others
48 ___ Normandes (Channel Islands)
50 Tidbit
53 Dry bouquet item
58 ___ and cry
59 Poppy product
60 Stead

61 1995 porcine Oscar nominee
62 Not so good
63 Muscat's land
64 Rainless
65 Lip-curling smile
66 Telegraphed
67 Caddie supplies

DOWN

1 Train stop
2 Trooper on the highway
3 Children's string game
4 Syllable of reproach
5 Aid for a fracture
6 Dismounted
7 Buzzy one
8 Mythical goat/man
9 British sir
10 Cuts short, as a space flight
11 Verb accompanier
12 Advantage
13 Prophet
21 Smooch
22 Picks out
24 Northern Iraqi
27 "The Windsor Beauties" painter
28 Praise
30 Biggest portion
31 Absorbed by
32 Scraped (out)
33 Coin hole
34 Twosome
36 Great Salt Lake site

Puzzle 72 by Daniel Halfen

39 Nagger
40 One turning color?
42 Nylon, for one
43 Skiers' wish
45 Treat badly
47 Quantity
49 Missile pits
51 Jazz pianist Blake

52 City north of Sheffield
53 Some camp denizens, for short
54 "Once ___ a time . . ."
55 Beget
56 Margarita fruit
57 Like Jack Sprat's diet
61 Dracula, at times

ACROSS

1 Poker holding
5 Study for finals
9 Shaping machine
14 "Crimes & Misdemeanors" actor
15 Wife of Zeus
16 Flynn of "Captain Blood"
17 Fast
20 Land, as a big one
21 Late Chairman
22 Blood supplies
23 Long, long time
25 Hall-of-Famer Drysdale
27 Swift
35 Didn't face the enemy
36 Chow down
37 Like a Jaguar or Miata
38 Was in a play
41 Ms. alternative
43 ___ raving mad
44 Deutsch, here
46 Swiss peak
48 Society page word
49 Fleet
53 Fat farm
54 Pouting face
55 "Dance On Little Girl" singer
59 Piercing tool
61 Opera house cries
65 Quick
68 Non-earthling
69 Otherwise
70 ___ Stanley Gardner
71 Old-fashioned
72 Fate
73 Aussie hoppers

DOWN

1 Henry VIII's sixth
2 Not into the wind
3 Not in use
4 Criticize harshly
5 Hong Kong residents, now
6 ___ Speedwagon
7 Calla lily family
8 Symbol of Jewish resistance
9 Hawaiian garland
10 Fine or liberal follower
11 "How ___!"
12 Frost
13 Singer Fitzgerald
18 Best Picture of 1958
19 They may need coloring at a salon
24 Deception
26 Small bites
27 Fort ___, N.C.
28 Indy entrant
29 Prelim
30 Horse stall covering
31 Go bad
32 Neighbor of an Afghani
33 Sore throat cause, briefly
34 Little squirts, so to speak
39 Big bird
40 Drops bait
42 Brickbat

Puzzle 73 by Janet R. Bender

45 Like some stocks
47 Bit of math homework
50 Acted servilely
51 Hang ten or shoot the curl
52 Medicine man
55 In the distance
56 Aswan's river
57 Make an afghan

58 "Hard Hearted Hannah" composer
60 Composer Schifrin
62 ___ Beach, Fla.
63 Norse capital
64 Tom Jones's "___ a Lady"
66 Brian of rock music
67 Prefix with metric

ACROSS

1 Cleopatra's love ___ Antony
5 Dressed like Dracula
10 Frozen waffle brand
14 Controversial orchard spray
15 Open-mouthed
16 ___ of Arc
17 Coffee, slangily
18 Half note
19 Roof's edge
20 Post-Derby interview spot
23 Camel rival
24 L-1011, e.g.
25 Sign after Aquarius
28 Land bordered by the Mekong
30 Beanie
33 With 54-Across, a Revolutionary hero
34 Algebra or trig
35 Scarlett's estate
36 1965 Gary Lewis and the Playboys hit
39 Four-star review
40 Andy of the comics
41 Otherworldly
42 Neighbor of Wyo.
43 Reps.' opponents
44 Parts of acts
45 The "L" of L.A.
46 Dullsville
47 Flabbergast
53 Freq. quotation attribution
54 See 33-Across

55 Mormon state
57 ___-deaf
58 For rent
59 Recipe directive
60 Washstand vessel
61 Mild oath
62 Many millennia

DOWN

1 Capt.'s better
2 "There oughta be ___!"
3 Sitarist Shankar
4 Engine housing
5 Relief carvings
6 "If I Had ___ Like You" (1925 hit)
7 Opposites of a 39-Across
8 Many a Cecil B. De Mille film
9 Large bottle
10 Tape deck button
11 Hockey score
12 Contributed
13 "My ___ and Only"
21 Immensely
22 Legal matter
25 ___ dish (lab item)
26 "___ to Be You"
27 Hindu Trinity member
28 Reading lights
29 Sitting on
30 Stone mound
31 70's sitcom
32 Capitol Hill gofers
34 Sir's partner

Puzzle 74 by Joel D. Lafargue

35 Branch office?
37 Emulate Oksana Baiul
38 Stick-on
43 Bespectacled dwarf
44 Viewpoints
45 Hardly a partygoer
46 Animal variety
47 Comprehend

48 ___ of the above
49 Whip
50 Stewpot
51 Director Preminger
52 Excedrin target
53 Had a hero?
56 Action film "48 ___"

ACROSS

1 "Shoo!"
5 Bishop of old TV
10 Like some furs
14 Forbidden: Var.
15 Ballroom dance
16 Novelist ___ S. Connell Jr.
17 Gobs
18 Sharon of Israel
19 Behind schedule
20 Righteous Brothers' musical style
23 Cool fabric
24 Crisp fabric
28 Coda's place in a score
29 House of ___
33 Thingamajig
34 Think about
36 Old-time actor Wallace ___
37 1967 Van Morrison hit
41 Handel oratorio
42 Say again
43 Teamed up (with)
46 CD player maker
47 Corp. giant
50 They practice girth control
52 Less convincing, as an excuse
54 Popular Southern vegetable
58 Lima's locale
61 Sao ___
62 Touch down
63 1934 Pulitzer writer Herbert
64 Church officer
65 "Or ___!"
66 Big Apple section
67 Logician in space
68 Sunbeams

DOWN

1 Place to start a ride
2 Check voicemail, perhaps
3 Be plentiful
4 Student
5 Judge's order
6 Fabled fast starter
7 Oklahoma city
8 Discharge
9 Type of mutual fund
10 Took the bait
11 One of Frank's exes
12 Krazy ___
13 Opposite WSW
21 Fund
22 Sky light?
25 German river
26 Peacock's pride
27 Supplement
30 Bed-and-breakfast
31 River through Frankfurt
32 Juan Carlos and others
34 Former Kremlin hotshots
35 Property taken back
37 Hope-Crosby's "Road to ___"
38 Govern

Puzzle 75 by Elizabeth C. Gorski

39 Hideout
40 Singer Crystal
41 Down
44 Sushi bar order
45 Window treatments
47 African antelope
48 Wee
49 Swaps

51 Resell at a profit
53 Philosopher Mortimer
55 Bit of praise
56 Util. bill
57 Duchess of ___
58 Dads
59 Kind of maniac
60 "Go, team!"

ACROSS

1 Clinch, as a victory
6 R.B.I., e.g.
10 Keats, for one
14 Got out of bed
15 "Sock it ___!"
16 Fairy tale's first word
17 Super Bowl I champs
20 Slalom curve
21 New Jersey five
22 Kind of monkey
23 Anklebones
24 June 6, 1944
25 Yummy items
29 TV's "L.A. ___"
32 Waters: Lat.
33 "Xanadu" rock grp.
34 Remove from a manuscript
35 Sound of a cat or engine
36 Like Jack Benny, famously
38 More than a vogue
39 Pecan and pumpkin
40 Sought election
41 Had money in the bank
42 Sault ___ Marie
43 Football defensemen
46 It gets slapped around a lot
47 Skin cream ingredient
48 Book after Song of Solomon
51 Z ___ zebra
52 Hawaiian dish
55 On-line menaces
58 Nobelist Wiesel
59 Old Dodge
60 Artist's support
61 Bambi and others
62 When a factory whistle blows
63 Mink wrap

DOWN

1 Wise
2 Blows it
3 Trials and tribulations
4 Take advantage of
5 Mark Twain, for one
6 Kind of electricity
7 1992 Robin Williams movie
8 Sound stage equipment
9 Sign of sorrow
10 Hoosegow
11 Billfold bills
12 Light beige
13 "___ of the D'Urbervilles"
18 Dracula player Lugosi
19 Princely abbr.
23 Ivan and Nicholas
24 Boxer Oscar ___ Hoya
25 Northern Scandinavians
26 Phrase of resignation
27 Blender setting
28 Nancy Drew's creator
29 "Scram!"
30 Creator of the Ragged Dick books

Puzzle 76 by Randall J. Hartman

31 Garden intruders
34 Circumnavigator Sir Francis
36 "Jurassic Park" novelist
37 Length of yarn
41 Candle brackets
43 Hawaiian do
44 Smash, as a windshield
45 Inter ___

46 Flutist
48 Clinched, as a victory
49 ___ survivor
50 Parisian lady friend
51 Florence's river
52 Baja buck
53 Pitcher Hershiser
54 Bermuda, e.g.
56 Comic Philips
57 Kit ___ Club

ACROSS

1 Dateless
5 Chitchat
9 Chorus voice
14 Pasty
15 Prince William's school
16 Cancel
17 "___ me."
20 Stop working
21 Pull a con
22 Clear tables and such
23 Where le nez is
25 Door opener
27 Do film work
30 Pillow cover
32 Coercion
36 Bikini tops
38 Provo neighbor
40 Medicine for what ails you
41 "___ me!"
44 Lethargy
45 Second of three virtues
46 Where to see a hula
47 Draw
49 Dick Francis book "Dead ___"
51 Make a mistake
52 Unopened
54 Porn
56 Nothing's alternative
59 "Phooey!"
61 Gets used (to)
65 "___ me?"
68 Eskimo boat
69 Christen
70 Suffix with billion
71 Stately place
72 Barks
73 Pig food

DOWN

1 Practice with Rocky
2 Saga
3 Got down
4 "Understand?"
5 TV money-raiser
6 Gobbled up
7 Passing shots
8 New York hoopster
9 Disparage
10 Hard-working insect
11 Snooty one
12 "Star Trek" character
13 Auto maker Ransom E. ___
18 Very, in Valence
19 Currency, in Capetown
24 "Planet of the Apes" planet
26 Range choice
27 Gaping pit
28 Bo-peep's staff
29 Brownish gray
31 French wine district
33 Follow
34 Sound of the 60's
35 Scrub
37 Glaswegians, e.g.
39 Is gloomy
42 Former Austrian prince
43 Home wreckers
48 Affronted

Puzzle 77 by Stephanie Spadaccini

50 Star-Kist product
53 Lion-colored
55 Oompah instruments
56 Buzzing
57 Champagne Tony of golf
58 "___ Eyes" (Eagles hit)

60 Siamese, now
62 Stir up
63 Prefix with dollar or trash
64 Escalator part
66 ___-relief
67 Bit of electricity

ACROSS

1 Destine to disaster
5 Pepper's partner
9 Fix (in)
14 ___ Major
15 Pop singer Brickell
16 TV's "Kate & ___"
17 Word with land or critical
18 Score before 15
19 One who raises a stink?
20 Famous Wall Street panic
23 Reverse of WNW
24 De-squeaked
25 Travel far and wide
27 Make war
30 Modern refrigerators do it automatically
33 Prefix with cycle
34 Actor Davis
37 Field enclosure
38 Marksman of Swiss legend
40 Exodus mountain
42 Mideast's Gulf of ___
43 Spud
45 Skin: Suffix
47 Yucatan year
48 Well-read
50 Kind of piano
52 Deftness
53 Faint, as through ecstasy
55 Sit-ups firm these
57 1971 Steve McQueen film
62 Officer-to-be
64 Fountain drink
65 Overhang
66 Mannerism
67 Lackawanna's partner in railroading
68 Pavarotti piece
69 Final approval
70 Poetic contraction
71 Old Fords

DOWN

1 Slow-witted
2 Like some vaccines
3 Bones
4 Army's mule, e.g.
5 Concerned only with others
6 Idolize
7 Enraged
8 Ready to be hit, as a golf ball
9 Popular oven cleaner
10 Jan. 15 initials
11 1957 Fats Domino hit
12 One, to Hans
13 Astronaut Slayton
21 Narc's unit
22 "All the Things You ___"
26 Side squared, for a square
27 Montana city
28 Lend ___ (listen)
29 "Voices Carry" pop group
30 Honeybunch

Puzzle 78 by Gregory E. Paul

31 Happening place
32 Voice above baritone
35 Team
36 Suffix with elephant
39 Helen's mother, in Greek myth
41 Charlatan
44 Italian rice dish
46 Major League brothers' name
49 Half a score

51 Temper, as metal
53 Trap
54 Poet Elinor
55 ___ of the Apostles
56 Theda of Hollywood
58 "You said it, brother!"
59 Bull's-eye hitter
60 Ardent
61 Yes votes
63 Frozen Wasser

ACROSS

1 "Red" tree
6 Tues., for Tuesday
10 Poland's Walesa
14 24 sheets of paper
15 Peeved
16 First name in scat
17 Open, as a bottle
18 They produce a row on the farm
19 Swear
20 "Act your ___!"
21 Elated
24 Opera set in the time of the Pharaohs
25 Hershey brand
26 Elated
31 Handy
32 Large pitcher
33 Triangular sail
36 Fall cleanup need
37 Longed
39 Western writer Grey
40 P, in Greece
41 "Hi-___, Hi-Lo" (1953 film song)
42 Quarterback Brett
43 Elated
46 Countenance
49 Open
50 Elated
53 33 or 45, e.g.
56 It's taken out at the seams
57 Bucket
58 "Behold!"
60 Writer Lindbergh
61 Ever
62 Ballyhooed sitcom of 1997
63 Latvian
64 Lack
65 Chill, so to speak

DOWN

1 Shade of blue
2 It's breath-taking
3 Cut into cubes
4 Stat for Maddux
5 Dinosaur, e.g.
6 Depth charge, in slang
7 Engage, as an entertainer
8 Belgian songwriter Jacques
9 Not showing emotions
10 Ballet dancer, at times
11 Oft-cited sighting
12 Copy
13 Peddles
22 Uganda's Amin
23 Forest denizen
24 Competent
26 Extra-short haircut
27 Bryce Canyon locale
28 Anti-apartheid activist Steven
29 Magic wish granters
30 Be in debt
33 Cawfee
34 Letters for Jesus
35 Miller, for one
37 Join in a football heap
38 Kind
39 Wacky

Puzzle 79 by Alan Arbesfeld

41 Italy's ___ di Como
42 Eternally
43 Picture gallery site?
44 Threw out, as a runner
45 Word to end a card game
46 Song part
47 Hole-___

48 Meager
51 Scandinavian
52 Enjoyable
53 Brook
54 Emotional request
55 Domestic cat
59 Corrida cry

ACROSS

1 One of the Three B's of classical music
5 Milkshake conduit
10 Church recess
14 Field measure
15 Nile capital
16 Close, as an envelope
17 "Horse Feathers" stars
20 Put in stitches
21 Orders to plow horses
22 Eagle's nest
23 Pencil's innards
24 New York nine
26 Eastern philosophy
29 Scandalous gossip
30 Getty product
33 Broadcasts
34 Larger than quarto
35 9-to-5 grind
36 Genre of 17- and 56-Across
40 Vietnamese holiday
41 Picnic places
42 First murder victim
43 Gawk at
44 Prevaricates
45 Placid
47 Hairless
48 Stocking flaws
49 West Indies, e.g.
52 Connect, as girders
53 Where: Lat.
56 "The Outlaws Is Coming" stars
60 Jacket
61 Hot coal
62 Escape battle
63 "___ springs eternal"
64 Like many attics
65 Classify, as blood

DOWN

1 Cave dwellers
2 Feel sore
3 Rowing sport
4 Skirt's edge
5 Reaction on a roller coaster
6 Burdened
7 Barbecued dish slathered with sauce
8 Flightboard abbr.
9 Court
10 Cigar residue
11 Equal
12 Indian dress
13 "What ___ is new?"
18 Long, long time
19 Skin art
23 Speech problem
24 Dairy products
25 Newsman Sevareid
26 Flavor
27 Choreographer Alvin
28 Declaim
29 Links with a space station
30 Diving bird
31 Poet W. H. ___
32 Flair
34 Out of a job
37 Quite a display
38 Mermaid feature
39 Pathfinder's locale

Puzzle 80 by Robert Goldberg

45 Torrid
46 Inner: Prefix
47 Divine Miss M
48 Stopwatch button
49 Compulsive desire
50 "Begone!"
51 Quantum ___
52 Insect snares

53 Hideous
54 Pager sound
55 Expression of understanding
57 Claret color
58 Ostrich kin
59 Frequently

ACROSS

1 Fruit of the Loom rival
6 Where boys will be boys
10 Frost
14 Word with time or rights
15 Indian music
16 Some mutual fund accts.
17 Ingratiate oneself, e.g.
19 Dust busters, for short
20 Film critic Pauline
21 Cuckoo bird
22 Style
23 Original state
27 "Virginia Woolf" dramatist
29 1955 children's heroine
30 Ogle
32 Charged particle
33 Mail carriers have them: Abbr.
37 With 6-Down, operator of a 63-Down
38 Auction offering
40 Butterfly catcher
42 Pitcherful, maybe
43 Droops
45 Post-W.W. II grp.
47 "Shucks!"
49 La Scala productions
52 Shark watchers' protectors
53 Sherlock Holmes player
57 Way in
58 Sale item marking: Abbr.
59 Big exam
62 Pulitzer writer James
63 Words of wisdom
66 "Twittering Machine" artist
67 Gulf war missile
68 Al ___ (firm)
69 Does lawn work
70 Summer shirts
71 Lock of hair

DOWN

1 "Shucks!"
2 Water color
3 Famed trial venue
4 Before now
5 Like Wile E. Coyote
6 See 37-Across
7 Italian cheese or meat dish
8 Give it ___ (try)
9 Roof top
10 Rosie the ___
11 Khomeini, for one
12 Computer shortcut
13 German Pittsburgh
18 The 2% of 2%
22 Dogfaces, today
24 Patricia of "Hud"
25 Twelve ___
26 Ate fancily
27 Word of resignation
28 "Star Wars" princess
31 Radio station need
34 Cousin of an orange

Puzzle 81 by Elizabeth C. Gorski

35 Peace Nobelist Wiesel
36 Places for props
39 "Gone With the Wind" setting
41 Guacamole's place
44 Evening get-togethers
46 Rundown feeling
48 Hurried next door, e.g.
50 Thickness
51 Tears up
53 Prominent toucan features

54 The "A" of WASP
55 Riding horse
56 Stagewear for Madonna
60 Plays the part
61 Some popular jeans
63 See 37-Across
64 Serve like Sampras, e.g.
65 Banned pesticide

ACROSS

1 Amo, ___, amat (Latin practice)
5 College prep exam
9 Thin and bony
14 Singer-actress Lorna
15 "Picnic" playwright
16 Daddy Warbucks's little girl
17 Prefix with phobia
18 Years and years
19 Get together
20 Demonstrate affection like a plumber?
23 Saharalike
24 ___ Khan (ex of Rita Hayworth)
25 Place to park a car
29 French cheese
31 Krazy ___ of the comics
34 "Tiny" Albee character
35 Tugboat sound
36 Prefix with dynamic
37 What a plumber says to noisy kids?
40 Days before big events
41 Bands' bookings
42 Preferred invitees
43 TV room
44 Therefore
45 Vertebral columns
46 Exploit
47 Gloomy guy
48 Declines, as a plumber?
56 Where Leonardo was born

57 Oklahoma city
58 Atmosphere
59 Part of the pelvis
60 Sicilian blower
61 Ribald
62 "E pluribus unum," e.g.
63 Like a busybody
64 Dummies' replies

DOWN

1 "Woe is me!"
2 Lots of
3 60's hairdo
4 Put away
5 South Dakota's capital
6 Very white
7 Lambs: Lat.
8 Experiment
9 Charles de ___
10 Bother
11 Purdue, e.g.: Abbr.
12 Evening, informally
13 Golfer's gadget
21 Made a border
22 Port-au-Prince's land
25 Stared openly
26 Breathing
27 Get ready to be picked
28 One-spots
29 Beatnik's drum
30 Paddles
31 Enter, as computer data
32 Got up
33 Praises loudly

Puzzle 82 by Stephanie Spadaccini

35 Branch offshoot
36 "___ Wanna Do" (Sheryl Crow hit)
38 Monsters
39 Run out, as a subscription
44 Igloo dweller
45 Half a weekend
46 Not abridged
47 Procures

48 Where fodder is stored
49 Monogram unit: Abbr.
50 High schooler
51 "I'm ___ you!"
52 Voting district
53 Meal on Maui
54 Mezz. alternative
55 Paths
56 Energy

ACROSS
1 "Holy mackerel!"
5 Shady lady
9 Landscaper's tool
14 California wine valley
15 1847 South Seas adventure
16 Running bowline, e.g.
17 Desert mount
19 7–11 game
20 Full up
21 Aria, usually
23 "¡" topper
24 "Yuck!"
25 Place for marbles
29 Baby blues
31 Hillbilly TV fare
35 Strait of Dover port
37 Got some shuteye
38 Hightail it
40 New Zealand native
43 Executive: Abbr.
44 Bit of parsley
46 "You've got my support"
48 Settles bills
50 How many bouquets are made
53 Desperation football pass
56 Native: Suffix
57 Bad Ems, e.g.
60 School sports org.
61 Gave a ticket
63 Caterpillar, for one
65 Irish locale of song
68 Caper
69 Go ___ detail
70 "The Masque of Alfred" composer
71 Kind of answer
72 Kind of tide
73 Humorist Bill and others

DOWN
1 Finishes
2 Home annex
3 Rx purveyor
4 Woman of distinction
5 Physique, slangily
6 Physicians' grp.
7 "What's the ___ that could happen?"
8 "___ mind?"
9 They follow standing ovations
10 Golden, in France
11 Spur
12 Hockey great Phil, familiarly
13 Take five
18 1957 Ford debut
22 ___-di-dah
26 Bygone London transport
27 Part of SEATO
28 Barker
30 Reverend's responsibility
32 Like many titles
33 "Tarzan" extra
34 Lb. and kg.
36 ___-distant (self-styled): Fr.

Puzzle 83 by Christopher Page

38 Recipe amt.
39 Emissions tester: Abbr.
41 Pro ___
42 Operatic prince
45 Camel's cousin
47 Rolls's partner
49 Paparazzo's prize
51 Ev'rlasting
52 Goes brunette this time
54 "E pluribus unum," e.g.

55 Bath's state
57 Leave laughing
58 Glazier's unit
59 Theater, opera, etc.
62 Tabriz's land
64 Bordeaux, e.g.
66 Educ. group
67 Top 40 music

ACROSS

1 Separate, as flour or ashes
5 Forum language
10 Paul Bunyan's ox
14 Doughnut's middle
15 Primitive calculators
16 Military no-show
17 Bit of physics
18 "Dear friend!"
19 Door sound
20 Overjoyed
23 April 15 initials
24 Paper purchases
28 Egg-rolling time
32 Reddish-brown horse
35 Copper, e.g.
36 Greeting at sea
37 Hush-hush govt. group
38 Highly pleased with oneself
42 Afternoon hour on a sundial
43 Info
44 Country singer Crystal
45 Garbage-marauding critters
48 Present and future, e.g.
49 Borden's cow
50 Forbid
51 Bonkers
59 Opposite of all
62 Perch
63 "___ to leap tall buildings . . ."
64 Skunk's defense
65 TV duo Kate and ___
66 Carbonated drink
67 Overhaul
68 Bread maker
69 Trial balloon

DOWN

1 Mideast ruler of years past
2 Small amount
3 Dud
4 Office fill-in
5 Actress Hedy
6 Vast chasm
7 Novelist Janowitz
8 Suffix with poet
9 One of Columbus's ships
10 Two-pointer
11 Cobbler's tool
12 Feathered stole
13 Shade tree
21 Submit
22 Four Monopoly properties: Abbr.
25 Pesters
26 Biceps, e.g.
27 Belmont ___
28 Sovereign's domain
29 Antenna
30 Zeno and others
31 Fraternity "T"
32 Cowboy's wear
33 Aspiration
34 Hurricane's center
36 "Unto us ___ is given"
39 Fuss
40 60's rocket stage
41 Soup container

Puzzle 84 by Gregory E. Paul

46 Roman orator
47 Poet's preposition
48 Sampler
50 Count of jazz
52 Lebanese, e.g.
53 Defender of Dreyfus
54 Egg part
55 Wear well

56 Mitch Miller's instrument
57 The "O" in R.E.O.
58 Peachy-keen
59 Neither's partner
60 "___ to a Nightingale"
61 Doze (off)

ACROSS

1 Catherine who survived Henry VIII
5 Eden dweller
9 ___-ski
14 Theater award
15 Timber wolf
16 Fit to be tied
17 Dieter's credo?
19 One of Lear's daughters
20 French farewell
21 Program airing
23 State of high alarm
26 Praiseful poem
27 Dieter's credo?
32 Pitcher's pride
35 First name in scat
36 Flood embankment
37 Hi-jinks in a stolen car
40 Determines limits in advance
42 Had title to
43 Regarding
45 Realize
46 Dieter's credo?
50 Calamity
51 Comic musical work
55 Mt. Rainier's site, with "the"
59 "___ Pretty" (song for Maria)
60 Anticipate
61 Dieter's credo?
64 It results from work well done
65 Gamblers' mecca
66 This, in Mexico
67 Polk's predecessor
68 Dutch cheese
69 Bygone Tunisian V.I.P.'s

DOWN

1 Kind of bear
2 Stand for
3 Unbending
4 Fix, as leftovers
5 Draught, maybe
6 Mafia boss
7 Act of touching
8 Wear a long face
9 Terrier type
10 Comes before
11 Indian music style
12 Greek H's
13 On its way, as a message
18 Noted site of ancient Mexican ruins
22 British john
24 Managed, with "out"
25 Take the reins again
28 Portable PC
29 Place to broil
30 Lavish party
31 Suffix with gab or slug
32 "Get ___" (1958 hit)
33 English poet laureate Nicholas
34 Popular pet bird
38 Killing of a king
39 Blind worshiper
41 Banned Pete
44 Stinko

Puzzle 85 by Nancy Salomon

47 Like the gray mare
48 Actor Estrada
49 Officiated a game
52 Rib
53 Irascible
54 Choir voices
55 Nemo, e.g.: Abbr.
56 Not straight
57 Leave dock
58 To be, in France
62 One-million link
63 ___ de guerre

ACROSS

1 Response to an insult
5 Tibetan monk
9 Snack chip
14 Prefix with dynamic
15 Pastoral poem
16 "Not you ___!"
17 Expressway access
18 Big bag
19 Saltine brand
20 Attractions near the Nile
23 Doorway
24 Elderly
25 Orthodontist's org.
28 Sights around road repairs
33 "Quiet!"
36 Fishing equipment
37 ___ Ababa
38 Rural outing
41 Fine gold and enamelware
43 Viper
44 Swiss peak
45 Question's opposite: Abbr.
46 1, 8, 27, 64, etc.
51 That: Sp.
52 It's 21% oxygen
53 Stallone title role
57 Components of some auto engines
62 Screen symbols
64 Grand Dragon's group
65 Barely passing grades
66 "___ and Punishment"
67 Table of contents, e.g.

68 ___ spumante (wine)
69 18 on a golf course
70 Canyon effect
71 Distribute, with "out"

DOWN

1 "Beetle Bailey" character
2 Gain knowledge
3 Medieval helmet
4 Warhol's genre
5 Have trouble with esses
6 "An apple ___ . . ."
7 Sherlock Holmes's brother
8 Acid neutralizer
9 "Schindler's List" villain
10 Elderly
11 Prophetess of Greek myth
12 Strike
13 "Put ___ Happy Face"
21 Scandinavian war god
22 1600, to Cato
26 Condescend
27 Biblical beasts of burden
29 Common conjunction
30 Finder's ___
31 Taxi
32 "___ to the West Wind"
33 Mold
34 Devil's domain
35 Swift watercraft
39 Third man in the ring

40 Anger
41 Winter bug
42 Police alert, for short
44 Kind of paint
47 Convertible or coupe, e.g.
48 Amuse
49 White-tailed eagle
50 Iraq's Hussein
54 Reagan Attorney General Edwin

55 Royals great George
56 Actor Davis
58 "This one's ___"
59 Applies
60 Whip
61 "What's gotten ___ you?"
62 German "I"
63 ___-Magnon

ACROSS

1 Follower of Mary
5 Return to base before proceeding
10 Hot springs
13 Resort town near Santa Barbara
14 "You ___ Beautiful" (1975 Joe Cocker hit)
15 Hard to comprehend
16 Sneaky thief
18 Flying-related
19 Mined metal
20 Real howler
21 In shreds
23 Dagger handle
24 Close
25 In ___ (intrinsically)
28 Comedy brothers of 60's-70's TV
32 Satirist Mort
33 Set in "Die Fledermaus"
34 Prez's stand-in
35 Skater's maneuver
36 ___ Carlo
37 Spanish general Duke of ___
38 A very good pair
39 Egyptian cross
40 Cherished
41 Bargain with the prosecutor
43 Jumpy
45 Signals at Sotheby's
46 Item on a cowboy boot
47 Slightly bounce

50 "Pardon me"
51 Draft org.
54 Double-reed instrument
55 Theme of this puzzle
58 Ship's spine
59 Chrissie of tennis
60 Jai ___
61 U.F.O. crew
62 Old yet new again
63 Toasty

DOWN

1 Nuts or crackers
2 Slightly open
3 Aussie buddy
4 It's usually served with lobster
5 Import duty
6 Shoptalk
7 Moolah
8 It's a free country
9 Window onto the ocean
10 Caught sight of
11 Lima's land
12 Each
15 Luke Skywalker's father
17 Russia's ___ Mountains
22 Not at home
23 Member of a notorious biker gang
24 Will of 55-Across
25 Writer Asimov
26 Tourist mecca near Mexico City
27 Blind followers

Puzzle 87 by Nancy Schuster

28 The daddy of decafs
29 Went congering
30 Pack again, as groceries
31 Fifth wheel
33 Tommy Lee of 55-Across
36 Seagoer's woe
42 Campaigner, for short
43 Not rejecting out of hand
44 Not feeling

46 Bake, as eggs
47 Speechmaker's opening
48 "Yeah, sure!"
49 Proceeds
50 Work without ___ (be daring)
51 Hacienda room
52 Wound reminder
53 Dairy-case choice
56 Adam's mate
57 Jurisprudence

ACROSS

1 The Bee Gees brothers
6 Subside
9 Big hit, in Variety slang
14 Journalist ___ Rogers St. Johns
15 Inlet
16 Zhou ___
17 Classic film duo
20 Andean animals
21 Entrance
22 Villa d' ___
23 Old card game
26 Film ___
27 Sirs' counterparts
32 "Catcher in the Rye" author
37 "My Three Sons" son
38 Classic film duo
40 The "A" in RAM
41 Vanquished
42 Nearby things
43 Go over 212 degrees
44 Bird on a U.S. coin
45 Weaving machine
49 Actor Emilio
54 Old-time actress Ina
56 Classic film duo
59 Stradivari's mentor
60 Help
61 Itsy-bitsy
62 Without face value, as stock
63 Numbered hwy.
64 Swashbuckling Flynn

DOWN

1 Bit of Gothic architecture
2 False gods
3 Fathered, biblical-style
4 Hold responsible
5 F.D.R.'s mother
6 Cenozoic, e.g.
7 Coal container
8 Nag, nag, nag
9 Vanquished
10 A single time
11 Imperfection
12 F.D.R.'s pooch
13 Unctuous
18 Former Presidential aspirant Paul
19 Tollbooth part
24 Popular brand of faucet
25 Spaniel, for one
27 Look dejected
28 With 49-Down, former Israeli statesman
29 Border
30 Bog
31 FedEx, e.g.
32 Suffix with thermo-
33 Part of the foot
34 Shoestring
35 Boardwalk coolers
36 Where bulls and bears run: Abbr.
37 Mirror
39 Greeting to Hitler
43 Charity event
44 Poet's period after dusk

Puzzle 88 by Barbara Campitelli

45 Cake part
46 Long-spouted can
47 University of Maine town
48 Streep of "Out of Africa"
49 See 28-Down

50 Japanese wrestling
51 Golf hazard
52 Jazz singer ___ James
53 To see, in Marseille
55 Overdue
57 Small point to criticize
58 J.F.K.'s predecessor

ACROSS

1 Kind of layer
6 Applaud
10 Locking device
14 Of neap and ebb
15 Overconfident racer of fable
16 Charles Lamb pseudonym
17 Raise
18 Quickly, quickly
19 Charitable donation
20 Start of a Daniel Webster quote
22 "Act now!"
23 New England's Cape ___
24 Generally
26 Turn to cinders
29 Sentry's cry
32 Prevent from acting
33 Chicken ___
34 Syrup brand
35 Radical college org.
36 Middle of the quote
42 California's Fort ___
43 Cover for a diamond
44 Theater sign
45 Élève's place
48 Janet of Justice
49 Latin love
50 Whom Reagan beat in 1984
52 Tanner's tub
54 Tweed, for one
55 End of the quote
61 Related
62 Andes land
63 Sporty Toyota
64 Rudner of comedy
65 Protection: Var.
66 Diet guru Jenny
67 Hang onto
68 Gusto
69 Refuges, old-style

DOWN

1 Roman emperor after Galba
2 Utah national park
3 Garfield's foil
4 Racing org.
5 Singer John
6 Honolulu-based detective
7 Survive
8 Noah's landfall
9 English diarist Samuel
10 Whiplash preventer
11 Total
12 Cousin of a metaphor
13 Scrapbook user
21 "___ me, villain!"
25 Total
26 Navy noncom
27 Sweetie
28 It's swung in forests
30 "___ longa, vita brevis"
31 Singer Lenya
34 "M*A*S*H" setting
35 Endeavored
37 Sudden arrival of fall weather
38 Author Fleming

Puzzle 89 by Richard Hughes

39 Belief
40 Spanish gold
41 Negative joiner
45 Set sail
46 Gingersnap, e.g.
47 Kind of inspection
48 Go back on a promise
49 Rose oils

51 "If I Had a Hammer" singer
53 Pet protection org.
56 Goddess of discord
57 Problem for Sneezy?
58 "Do as ___, . . ."
59 Buzz's moonmate
60 Eastern discipline

ACROSS

1 One-named supermodel
5 Ready and willing's partner
9 One praised in Mecca
14 Clinton Attorney General Janet
15 Paris's Rue de la ___
16 French valley
17 Tiny tunnelers
18 Ingrid's "Casablanca" role
19 Not evenly padded, as a mattress
20 Like an animal . . .
23 Historical period
24 Use a crowbar
25 Cream puff, for one
29 Miles per hour, e.g.
31 At the present
34 In the future
35 O. Henry's "The Gift of the ___"
36 ___ Gigio (frequent Ed Sullivan guest)
37 . . . vegetable . . .
40 Pulled to pieces
41 Ontario tribe
42 Blabs
43 Muddy home
44 The former Mrs. Bono
45 Better than better
46 Texas patriot Houston
47 Buddy
48 . . . or mineral
55 Assign, as a portion
57 Polly, to Tom Sawyer
58 "The Andy Griffith Show" role
59 River by the Louvre
60 Manuscript encl.
61 What a cowboy calls a lady
62 Flute player
63 New World abbr.
64 Alka-Seltzer sound

DOWN

1 Mideast hot spot
2 Bill of fare
3 The "A" of ABM
4 Pinocchio's giveaway
5 Bee colony
6 Light wood
7 One of "The Simpsons"
8 Test
9 Magnetism
10 Stinky
11 7-Up ingredient
12 Dadaist Hans
13 "Yo!"
21 ___ cotta
22 Of the eye
25 Treaties
26 "The game is ___": Holmes
27 Tale
28 Prefix with photo or phone
29 Indy entrant
30 Tropical fever
31 Lofty

Puzzle 90 by Stephanie Spadaccini

32 Foreign-made General Motors cars
33 Deserving the booby prize
35 Stallion's mate
36 Federal agents, informally
38 Noodlehead
39 New York city
44 Reagan's predecessor
45 Speed demon's cry
46 Precious ___
47 Parson's home
48 Accident on ice
49 "The Right Stuff" org.
50 U.S. Pacific territory
51 Frolic
52 October gem
53 "See you," in Sorrento
54 1996 running mate
55 Nile viper
56 Maui garland

ACROSS

1 Slam-dunks
5 Stiller and ___
10 Prefix with business
14 Like Nash's lama
15 Waters of song
16 Amorphous mass
17 1935 Cole Porter song
20 Pundit
21 Olio
22 Disney's" ___ and the Detectives"
25 Vietnam's Ngo ___ Diem
26 No longer hold up
29 F. Scott Fitzgerald had one: Abbr.
31 New York's ___ Island
35 Swellhead's problem
36 Number of mousquetaires
38 Invited
39 Unofficial Australian "anthem"
43 Anon's partner
44 ___ objection (go along)
45 Nurse's bag
46 Lax
49 Garden tool
50 Molly Bloom's last word in "Ulysses"
51 Pot builder
53 Torture chamber item
55 Well-to-do
59 Gut-wrenching feeling
63 1939 Andrews Sisters hit

66 ___ ideal (perfect model)
67 "Camelot" tunesmith
68 Mariner Ericson
69 Memo abbr.
70 Winter hazard
71 Advanced

DOWN

1 Steven of Apple computers
2 Once more
3 Prefix with phone
4 Ooze
5 Encountered
6 Biblical verb ending
7 "Beg your pardon"
8 Bridge action
9 One of the Carringtons, on "Dynasty"
10 Largest of the United Arab Emirates
11 Fluent
12 Author Jaffe
13 "___ to differ!"
18 Pacific Fleet admiral of W.W. II
19 Lady's partner
23 Letters from Calvary
24 Den fathers
26 Drain
27 Century plant
28 Automaton
30 Go-getter
32 Loquacious
33 Jockey Arcaro
34 ___-foot oil

Puzzle 91 by Arthur S. Verdesca

37 Daub
40 Demonstration test
41 Singer Paul
42 Cobbler's tip
47 Slight
48 Base runner's stat
52 Register
54 Small hill
55 "Dancing Queen" pop group

56 Podiatrists' concerns
57 Potential Guinness Book entry
58 Shade giver
60 Open delight
61 Scrape, as the knee
62 Electee of 1908
64 Female with a wool coat
65 Tennis call

ACROSS

1 The Hatfields or the McCoys
5 Trip to Mecca
9 Quench
14 Any one of three English rivers
15 "Summertime," e.g., in "Porgy and Bess"
16 Jazzman's cue
17 Woolen wear
20 Bizarre
21 Small ball
22 Makes certain
25 Long, long time
26 Toyota model
28 Govt. agent
32 Fortify, as a town
37 Brit's reply in agreement
38 Spot in a supermarket
41 Cowboys' entertainment
42 Said again
43 Not new
44 Scold
46 Court
47 Riddles
53 Names
58 A lot of Shakespeare's writing
59 Ambassador's stand-in
62 You can dig it
63 Island near Kauai
64 Touches lightly, as with a hanky
65 Soccer shoe
66 Ending with cable or candy
67 Command to Fido

DOWN

1 Drink served with marshmallows
2 Hawaiian feasts
3 Aides-de-camp: Abbr.
4 India's first P.M.
5 "Scots Wha ___" (Burns poem)
6 Sheet music abbr.
7 Goes kaput
8 Quartz variety
9 Oft-televised bishop
10 Polygraph flunker
11 Westernmost Aleutian
12 Canal to the Baltic
13 Raison d'___
18 Debussy's "La ___"
19 Rider's "Stop!"
23 "What's this, Pedro?"
24 "Star Trek" helmsman
27 Kind of lab dish
28 Melt ingredient
29 Catcher's catcher
30 Suit to ___
31 Taped eyeglasses wearer
32 Very light brown
33 Conductance units
34 "Venerable" English writer
35 Passed with flying colors
36 Bout outcome, in brief

Puzzle 92 by Fred Piscop

37 "___ Sera, Sera"
39 Give up
40 Begin bidding
44 Baskin-Robbins purchase
45 Show off on the slopes
46 Isle of ___
48 Sweet-as-apple-cider girl
49 Diagrams
50 French Revolution figure Jean Paul

51 Microscopic creature
52 Giving a little lip
53 Electrical letters
54 Sen. Gramm
55 Noggin
56 Killer whale
57 Coal-rich European region
60 Home-financing org.
61 "Fe fi fo ___!"

ACROSS

1 "Othello" villain
5 Flat-topped hills
10 Colonel Mustard's game
14 Eschew
15 Some of the Pennsylvania Dutch
16 Feed bag contents
17 Filly's mother
18 "Truly!"
19 Takes advantage of
20 Jalopy
23 Poker starter
24 "Roses ___ red . . ."
25 Like a lot
28 Fawn's mother
31 Necklace units
35 Come about
37 Department of Justice div.
39 Tiny
40 Autumn 1940 aerial war
44 Prior to, poetically
45 Mao ___-tung
46 Tenor Caruso
47 Council of Trent, e.g.
50 Flower holder
52 Spud
53 Lawyer's thing
55 Texas Western, today: Abbr.
57 Mule, e.g.
63 Kind of purse
64 Sidestep
65 Norse Zeus
67 Five-time Wimbledon champ, 1976–80
68 Vintner Ernest or Julio
69 Girl-watch or boy-watch
70 ___-Ball (arcade game)
71 Church officer
72 Marsh plant

DOWN

1 Doctrine: Suffix
2 Captain obsessed
3 Maven
4 Like some diamonds, sizewise
5 "Luncheon on the Grass" painter Edouard
6 Chewed the scenery
7 Fodder storage site
8 "___ I cared!"
9 Yemen, once
10 Grand ___ Dam
11 Word before laugh or straw
12 Salt Lake City students
13 Feminine suffix
21 Toll
22 Regalia item
25 French clerics
26 Hon
27 Time after time
29 Bid
30 Retrocede
32 Lie in store for

Puzzle 93 by Gregory E. Paul

33 Winter windshield setting
34 Sir, in Seville
36 What may be followed by improved service?
38 Dander
41 Buckeyes' sch.
42 The "I" in ICBM
43 Cause of an unexpected fall
48 Jellybean flavor
49 ___ Plaines, Ill.
51 Marriageable

54 Old Wells Fargo transport
56 Elizabeth I was the last one
57 Library unit
58 Dublin's land
59 Elliptical
60 Quit, in poker
61 Winning margin
62 Longest river in the world
63 "60 Minutes" network
66 TV's "___ and Stacey"

ACROSS

1 "Woe is me!"
5 A wanted man, maybe
9 Miss in the comics
14 ___ Le Pew
15 Oldsmobile, e.g.
16 Sound during hay fever season
17 47-stringed instrument
18 Flair
19 "Jurassic Park" sound
20 Parental advice, part 1
23 ___ Moines
24 "O Sole ___"
25 Antislavery leader Turner
26 Call to Bo-peep
27 Once more, country-style
29 Name
32 See-through wrap
35 Scandinavian capital
36 "The Official Preppy Handbook" author Birnbach
37 Advice, part 2
40 ___ Major
41 Economist Smith
42 Listens to
43 "See ya!"
44 Utopia
45 Served with a meal
46 Choice of sizes: Abbr.
47 Not their
48 Twaddle
51 End of the advice
57 "Silas Marner" author
58 Derby distance, maybe
59 Small field
60 Training group
61 "Zip-___-Doo-Dah"
62 Wedding wear
63 Injured sneakily
64 Back talk
65 Mesozoic and others

DOWN

1 Garden pest
2 What all partygoers eventually take
3 After, in Avignon
4 Fall mo.
5 Flier Earhart
6 "Where's ___?"
7 "Sure, why not?"
8 Letterman rival
9 Hit game of 1980
10 Showy display
11 Call to a mate
12 Search, as a beach
13 Long (for)
21 Mideasterner
22 Merger
26 Where Bear Bryant coached, informally
27 Oriental
28 Grab (onto)
29 ___-a-minute (call rate)
30 Previously owned
31 Chorale part
32 The short end
33 Wrong
34 Floral gift
35 Ye ___ Tea Shoppe
36 Told a whopper

Puzzle 94 by Stephanie Spadaccini

38 Soup scoop
39 "Ta-da!"
44 Hammed it up
45 90's group with the hit
   "Killing Me Softly,"
   with "the"
46 Boutique
47 Looks at boldly
48 Track car

49 Open-air rooms
50 Skins
51 Isthmus
52 Pearl Buck heroine
53 Coastal flooding factor
54 Holiday season, for
   short
55 Verdi heroine
56 90's party

ACROSS

1 Tarzan's love
5 Bungle
10 Tickled
14 Johnny Cash's "___ Named Sue"
15 Before the due date
16 Singer McEntire
17 Formative Picasso phase
19 Terrible czar
20 It picks up readings
21 Hustler's tool, maybe
23 Religious council
25 Actor Davis
26 Assail
30 Football Hall-of-Famer Merlin
32 Newspaper publisher Adolph
33 Year, south of the border
34 Wouldn't proceed
39 Center of a 1994 chase
42 Apollo 13 commander
43 Holds
44 Tennis champ Bjorn
45 Cleaner/disinfectant brand
47 Connection
48 Octagon or oval
52 One of "The Honeymooners"
54 "Carnival of Venice" violinist
56 Tough
61 Jai ___

62 Sophie Tucker was the "last"
64 Opposite of ja
65 Writer Asimov
66 General's command
67 "Auld Lang ___"
68 Tailor
69 Bean counters, for short

DOWN

1 Quick punches
2 Up to the task
3 Verb preceder
4 Potato parts
5 Drunken
6 Paddle
7 July 14, in France
8 Sun blockers
9 F.D.R.'s ___ Park
10 Southern breakfast dish
11 Popular pants since 1850
12 Old-style calculators
13 "Thanks, Gerhard"
18 Hitching ___
22 Sub's "ears"
24 Taboo
26 New Year's Day game
27 22-Down reply
28 Hood's knife
29 Villa d'___
31 Trails off
33 Be ___ in the ointment
35 Earring locale
36 Fort ___ (gold depository site)

Puzzle 95 by Mark Elliot Skolsky

37 Stocking shade
38 Labradors and Yorkshires
40 Comedienne DeGeneres
41 Flamboyant Surrealist
46 Most mentally sound
47 Not masc. or fem.
48 Crosses over
49 Alex who wrote "Roots"
50 One more time

51 "Common Sense" pamphleteer
53 "Time in a Bottle" singer Jim
55 Pupil locale
57 Detroit financing co.
58 "The World According to ___"
59 Austen heroine
60 From nine to five, in the classifieds
63 Kubrick's "2001" mainframe

ACROSS

1 Top piece of a two-piece
4 Italian seaport
11 Timber wood
14 "Alley ___"
15 Zoom-in shot
16 Chinese principle
17 Sex determinant
19 ___ rampage
20 Ready to go
21 Taste test label
23 200 milligrams, to a jeweler
25 Funnyman Philips
28 Not have ___ in the world
29 Spinks defeater, 1978
30 Parallel bar exercises
32 Not nude
33 Complicated situations
37 Debussy contemporary
39 Treasure hunter's declaration
43 Pen
44 Parti-colored
46 Quite the expert
49 Having conflicting allegiances
51 ___ du Diable
52 Kind of fool
54 Wood splitter
55 Quite the expert
57 For adults only
59 Tickle one's fancy
61 Play (with)
62 Twenty-somethings
67 Jargon suffix
68 Earth, wind or fire
69 Squid secretion
70 Texas-Oklahoma boundary river
71 Tennis volleys
72 Gypsy Rose ___

DOWN

1 Word with band or sand
2 Dutton's sitcom role
3 "Art is long, life is short," e.g.
4 Astronaut Carpenter
5 Soprano Gluck
6 Blotto
7 Suffix with lion
8 Rock's ___ Speedwagon
9 Feeling the effects of Novocaine
10 "Don Giovanni," for one
11 Like Schoenberg's music
12 Bullock of "Speed"
13 Took in, in a way
18 Genetic stuff
22 Say "yes" to
23 Auto shaft, slangily
24 "Family Ties" boy
26 Anonymous man
27 Moonfish
31 Fruit/tree connector
34 Deemed appropriate
35 Miscalculate

Puzzle 96 by Frank Longo

36 "Saturday Night Live" segment
38 Prefix with propyl
40 Greek portico
41 Salad dressing ingredient
42 Boob tube, in Britain: Var.
45 Hankering
46 Bandleader Les
47 Revolted
48 Not neat at the ends

50 More imminent
53 Pioneer in Cubism
55 Fido and friends
56 "___ recall . . ."
58 Take out
60 "Buddenbrooks" novelist Thomas
63 Surfing site
64 Big bird
65 Opposite SSW
66 Classic Jaguar

ACROSS

1 Cleopatra's love ___ Antony
5 Scrabble play
9 Cosmetician Lauder
14 On the briny
15 Verdi's "D'amor sull'ali rosee," e.g.
16 Con man
17 List component
18 Datum
19 Bronco catcher
20 Good-time Charlie
23 Norway's capital
24 Embarrassing sound, maybe
25 Mouse catcher
28 Airedale, for one
31 Volcanic fallout
34 Playing marble
36 Building wing
37 Forearm bone
38 Best
42 Mishmash
43 Coach Parseghian
44 Kingdom
45 Fishing gear
46 Chicago newspaper
49 "Treasure Island" monogram
50 Wilt
51 Use Western Union, e.g.
53 Noble one
60 Diamond weight
61 Bit of thatching
62 Like hen's teeth
63 Martini garnish
64 ___ Spencer, brother of Princess Diana
65 Stadium section
66 Passover meal
67 "If all ___ fails . . ."
68 Child's Christmas gift

DOWN

1 Pony Express load
2 ___ spumante
3 Coral ridge
4 Alfred Hitchcock film appearance, e.g.
5 Breakfast dish made on an iron
6 Patrick Henry, for one
7 Rolling in dough
8 Whom one goes out with
9 Cream-filled pastry
10 Astute
11 Dry run
12 "No problem"
13 Ike's W.W. II command
21 Bone: Prefix
22 Suave competitor
25 Dinner rooster
26 Like a gymnast
27 Implied
29 Recovery clinic
30 Suffix with percent
31 Where "I do's" are exchanged
32 Tackle box item
33 Injures
35 Ring result, briefly

Puzzle 97 by Gregory E. Paul

37 Indian with a sun dance
39 North Dakota's largest city
40 The first "T" of TNT
41 "Goodnight" girl of song
46 Make ragged
47 Wedding workers
48 Pine leaf
50 Spartacus, e.g.

52 Pub game
53 December 26 event
54 Rainless
55 At no cost
56 Dabbling duck
57 Banister
58 Arbor Day honoree
59 Group of cattle
60 Comedian Bill, to friends

ACROSS

1 "Quite contrary" nursery rhyme girl
5 Sudden outpouring
10 June 6, 1944
14 Pinza of "South Pacific"
15 "Here ___ trouble!"
16 Straight line
17 Chest organ
18 Make amends (for)
19 Goat's-milk cheese
20 60's TV medical drama
22 Detective Lord ___ Wimsey
23 Guinness suffix
24 Shooting stars
26 World Wildlife Fund's symbol
30 "The Hairy Ape" playwright
32 Gets educated
34 Finale
35 Deep cut
39 Saharan
40 Writer Bret
42 Butter alternative
43 ___ contendere (court plea)
44 Kind of "vu" in a classified
45 Colossus of ___
47 Hardy's partner
50 Get used (to)
51 Medicine injector
54 Neighbor of Syr.
56 Enough to sink one's teeth into
57 Pasternak hero
63 "___ just me or . . . ?"
64 Indian corn
65 Not theirs
66 Rat (on)
67 TV's "Kate & ___
68 Romance lang.
69 In___ (actually)
70 She had "the face that launched a thousand ships"
71 Fuddy-duddy

DOWN

1 Blend
2 Cote d'___
3 N.H.L. venue
4 Cartoon bear
5 Oodles
6 Latke ingredient
7 Cupid
8 Rent-controlled building, maybe
9 WNW's opposite
10 British rock group since the mid-70's
11 Because of
12 Take up, as a hem
13 Sophomore and junior, e.g.
21 Low-fat
22 ___ Club (onetime TV group)
25 Downy duck
26 Scheme

Puzzle 98 by Gregory E. Paul

27 Prefix with dynamic
28 It gets hit on the head
29 1967 Rex Harrison film role
31 Moxie
33 Shoulder motion
36 Actor Alan
37 Trickle
38 Party thrower
41 Wiry dog
46 Spy Mata ___
48 Unspecified one

49 Tin ___
51 Wallop
52 O.K.'s
53 Train tracks
55 Luster
58 Streamlet
59 Empty
60 Garage occupant
61 Alum
62 Sonja Henie's birthplace
64 ___-jongg

ACROSS

1 N.B.A.'s O'Neal, familiarly
5 Nicklaus's org.
8 Orbital point
13 Cape Canaveral grp.
14 E.T. vehicles
15 The Beatles' "You Won't ___"
16 Santa checks it twice
17 Popular adhesive
19 Facility
21 Egg ___ yung
22 And others: Abbr.
23 Canasta relative
26 Cash register key
28 ___ trick (three goals)
29 It kept a princess up
30 Dallas player, for short
31 Small island
32 "Oh, ___ kind of guy . . ."
34 Score in horseshoes
37 New Orleans hot spot
41 Edits
42 Overindulgent parent, e.g.
44 "Meet the Press" network
47 Actress Sue ___ Langdon
48 Feather source
50 ___-Magnon
51 Conditioning, as leather
53 Ham holder
55 Golfer's pocketful
56 Cool ___ cucumber

58 Future atty.'s exam
59 1777 battle site
62 Worst possible score
65 Role player
66 Athlete with a statue in Richmond, Va.
67 Hydrox rival
68 Villa ___ (Italian site)
69 Hair goo
70 Highway entrance

DOWN

1 Variety show since 1975, briefly
2 "Bali ___"
3 O.K.
4 Persian Gulf nation
5 Army rank E-3
6 Disney star
7 Regarding
8 Campfire remnant
9 "For ___ sake!"
10 Washington State airport
11 Relative of a gazelle
12 Old vaudeville actress Blossom
14 1972 Bill Withers hit
18 Longtime Harvard president James Bryant ___
20 Second-biggest movie hit of 1978
23 Touch-tone 4
24 Poetic foot
25 "Cheers" bar owner Sam

27 Recording studio add-ins

30 Raymond of "East of Eden"

33 Shade

35 Tackle's neighbor

36 Custom Royale of old autodom

38 Popular pain relief cream

39 And so on

40 Trillion: Prefix

43 Engine part

44 So-so

45 Writer Ambrose

46 Footballer's footwear

49 Free-for-all

52 "Once ___ Enough"

53 Pay boost

54 Shadow eliminator?

57 Booty

60 Rap's Dr. ___

61 Devils' org.

63 Dream period, for short

64 Alley ___

ACROSS

1 "If I ___ the World" (pop hit)
6 Boutique
10 Kind of carpet
14 Glue
15 Carbonated canful
16 Scarlett's plantation
17 Run to the altar
18 Brother of Cain
19 N.M. neighbor
20 Accounting principle, for short
21 Comic strip witch
23 ___ Steamer (early auto)
25 Land west of Britain
26 Brain wave reading: Abbr.
27 Track records?
29 Sine ___ non
32 Journalist Alexander
35 Isn't on the street?
36 Phoenix fivesome
37 Defeat decisively
40 "Ball!" callers
41 Scolds ceaselessly
42 Birchbark boat
43 Toothpaste type
44 Days of long ago
45 Inclined (to)
46 Feldman role in "Young Frankenstein"
48 Mill in 1848 news
52 Seal tightly, as a coffee can
56 Cleveland's lake
57 Memorable periods
58 Tiny bit
59 Area of corporate investment, briefly
60 1996 Broadway hit
61 Walked (on)
62 Popular watch brand
63 Plumb loco
64 Slangy assents
65 German industrial city

DOWN

1 Movie units
2 Illuminated from below
3 Bath sponge: Var.
4 Square numbers?
5 Hair coloring
6 Hair-raising
7 Traveling tramp
8 Bogus butter
9 Tree with fan-shaped leaves
10 Flight of steps
11 Clown
12 Dry, as a desert
13 Disputed Mideast strip
21 Entreat
22 Towel inscription
24 One of Jacob's wives
27 Unwelcome water on a ship
28 Seth's son
30 Next-to-last word of the golden rule
31 Tennis's Arthur
32 Self-satisfied
33 "Fourth base"
34 Resume submitter

Puzzle 100 by Patrick Jordan

35 From a distance
36 Specialized police units
38 Outrageousness
39 Sales slip: Abbr.
44 Last word of the golden rule
45 Northern diving bird
47 Bursts of wind
48 Gazillions

49 Sea eagles
50 Chain of hills
51 Alternative to a convertible
52 Sink or swim, e.g.
53 Vicinity
54 Skin opening
55 On the peak of
59 ___ v. Wade (landmark decision)

ACROSS

1 "___ Network" (1980's comedy series)
5 False god
9 Phillips head item
14 ___ vera
15 Austen's Woodhouse
16 Mild cigar
17 Unload, as stock
18 Ruler's length
19 Hammerin' Hank
20 "Just one gosh-darn minute!"
23 Rebel (against)
24 Vim
25 Part of the Dept. of Trans.
28 Like a taxi
31 Scrooge's cry
34 The "A" in James A. Garfield
36 Tire fill
37 Inter ___
38 "Be polite!"
42 Actress McClurg
43 Handyman's vehicle
44 Detail map
45 Poor grade
46 Preschooler's auto accessory
49 Opposite NNW
50 Hockey's Bobby
51 Farm unit
53 "Hush!"
60 Stocking stuffer
61 Singer Guthrie

62 Russia's Itar-___ news agency
63 Musical eightsome
64 Peter the Great, e.g.
65 Nights before
66 Beach spot
67 Chumps
68 Start all over

DOWN

1 Window frame
2 Nile queen, informally
3 Tunnel fee
4 South African expanse
5 "Age ___ beauty"
6 Add up (to)
7 Love, to Livy
8 Builder's backing
9 With knees knocking
10 Purse part
11 Scarce
12 February 14 figure
13 Triumphed
21 Scrumptious
22 "La Bohème," e.g.
25 Widely known
26 Put up with
27 Golfer with an "army"
29 Takes home, as salary
30 Basketball blackboard attachment
31 Hallow
32 Buenos ___
33 Waste maker
35 Fruit drink
37 Landers with advice
39 Egg maker

Puzzle 101 by Gregory E. Paul

40 Former Mideast inits.
41 Explosive, informally
46 Devise
47 Part of a cold-weather cap
48 The "A" in S.A.G.
50 Playful water animal
52 "Come in!"
53 "Brandenburg Concertos" composer

54 "___ each life some . . ."
55 Horse's mouthful
56 Celestial bear
57 Donated
58 Not new
59 Sinclair rival
60 "Send help!"

ACROSS

1 Struck, old-style
5 Uneven hairdo
9 Winery in Modesto, Calif.
14 Yesterday's dinner today
15 Smog
16 To no ___ (futilely)
17 Actor John, once married to Shirley Temple
18 Appliance on a board
19 Greene of "Bonanza"
20 "The Lone Ranger" catch phrase
23 Carryall
24 "Eureka!"
25 "The Honeymooners" catch phrase
32 Monte ___
33 Filleted fish
34 One with filling work?: Abbr.
35 Woodwind
36 Ground grain
38 Big elephant features
39 Announcer Pardo
40 Chimney duct
41 "God bless" preceder
42 "The Goldbergs" catch phrase
46 Spanish gold
47 Rebellious one, maybe
48 "Star Trek" catch phrase
55 In concealment
56 Report cards' stats
57 Pained look

58 Writer Nin
59 Needle case
60 College in New Rochelle
61 Whom Jason jilted
62 Part to play
63 Hatfields or McCoys, e.g.

DOWN

1 ___ of Iran
2 Travelers to Bethlehem
3 "___, old chap!"
4 Choke
5 Many an Iranian
6 Home of poet Langston Hughes
7 Asia's Sea of ___
8 Trait carrier
9 Lancelot's son
10 Promise
11 Zhivago's love
12 Streaked
13 Matador's cheer
21 It borders Regent Street
22 Charged
25 Pork, to a Jew, e.g.
26 Maine campus town
27 Willow
28 Circus cries
29 Popular potato
30 Modern "book"
31 Where an Edsel filled up, maybe
32 Wild West Show star
36 Despondency
37 ___ and Coke

Puzzle 102 by Robert Malinow

38 Business-related
40 Where Taipei is
41 One of the Baldwins
43 Grinder
44 State capital on the Mississippi
45 Singer Smith
48 Rib, for one

49 "Heavens to Betsy!"
50 Elbe tributary
51 ___ no good
52 Cat's-paw
53 Cape Cod catch
54 Bear young, as sheep
55 Beaver's work

ACROSS

1 Frosts, as a cake
5 Give off an odor
10 "Iliad" or "Aeneid," e.g.
14 Trig ratio
15 No-no
16 Warrior princess of TV
17 Declare with confidence
18 TV-top antenna
20 1996 Michael Crichton novel
22 Confidential matter
23 Skeleton's place?
24 Broad valleys
26 "So there!"
28 Sprinted
29 Dripping
32 Town square
36 Genesis garden
38 Jazzy talk
39 Nutty thought
42 Tennis great Lendl
43 Humor columnist Bombeck
44 Harbingers
45 Physicist's workplace
46 Mensa members have high ones
47 ___-fi (book genre)
49 Rockne of Notre Dame
51 Once a year
56 Set of advantages
59 Generosity
61 Beginners' skiing area
63 Price
64 Actor Estrada
65 Uses a Smith-Corona
66 Competed
67 There are 435 in Cong.
68 Sesames, e.g.
69 Makes mistakes

DOWN

1 Stern that works with a bow
2 Kind of engineer or service
3 Month after diciembre
4 Feudal workers
5 Layers
6 Sir's counterpart
7 Receded
8 Arcing shot
9 Perry White was her boss
10 Company V.I.P.'s
11 Prickly ___
12 Legal memo starter
13 It's made of plaster of paris
19 Selective Service registrant, agewise
21 Post-op period
25 Sports venues
27 Cosmopolitan publisher
29 Broad
30 Like left-hand page numbers
31 Lipton products
32 Comedian Hartman
33 Volcano output

Puzzle 103 by Peter Gordon

34 United ___ Emirates
35 Kind of Buddhist
37 Not too intelligent
38 "Huckleberry Finn" character
40 Bands take them
41 Performing
46 Annual Memorial Day event
48 Gentle stroke
49 Difficulties to be worked out

50 Run off to the chapel
52 Chutzpah
53 Pan Am rival, formerly
54 Daisylike bloom
55 Yorkshire city
56 "Deutschland ___ Alles"
57 Undiluted
58 Scissors cut
60 Mimicked
62 Soapmaker's solution

ACROSS

1 Like fine wine
5 Revival shouts
10 Impertinent one
14 Where the Vatican is
15 Newspapers, TV, etc.
16 Actress Petty
17 Suffix with psych- or neur-
18 Like a snake-oil salesman
19 Components of elevens
20 Aristocratic types
23 Berlioz's "Les nuits d'___"
24 Contained, with "up"
25 Packs down
28 Isn't feeling good
29 Dolt
31 Brink
33 Conquistador's haul
34 E or G, e.g.
35 Self-righteously virtuous types
40 Work unit
41 Start of many naval vessel names
42 Subject to breezes
43 Phrase in a new way, as a question
46 Throw hard
48 Farm mudholes
49 Salespeople, informally
50 Sheepish reply
53 Pompous types
57 Deep laugh
59 Vassal
60 Mata ___
61 Nondairy topping
62 Get-go
63 Former sneaker brand
64 Something to do
65 Uproots?
66 Campus figure

DOWN

1 Stood
2 "I understand!"
3 Classic Rousseau novel
4 Clobber
5 Popular brew from Holland
6 Cantaloupes
7 Proclamation
8 Shaving cut
9 Noted short-story writer
10 "Just say no," for instance
11 Favorable life insurance category
12 Miff
13 Detectives, for short
21 Used binoculars, maybe
22 To the ___ degree
26 Where "e'en" is seen
27 Heaven
28 Long ___
29 Full house sign
30 Beloved comic's nickname
31 White heron
32 Small sharks

Puzzle 104 by Elizabeth C. Gorski

33 Cries of pain
36 "Tasty!"
37 Mao ___-tung
38 Draconian
39 Van Gogh's "Irises," e.g.
40 Hesitant sounds
44 Shot again, as a photo
45 Tempe sch.
46 Didn't give a definite answer

47 Unexpected wins
49 Singer Della
50 Intrepid
51 Courtyards
52 Kind of flu
54 Move like lava
55 Better than good
56 "___ the Craziest Dream" (1942 song)
57 Steamy
58 Ending with schnozz

ACROSS

1. "Gee whillikers!"
5. Like a good lounge chair
10. Go steady with
14. Follow, as orders
15. ". . . like a big pizza pie, that's ___" (old song lyric)
16. Russian river or mountain
17. "St. Elmo's Fire" actor Rob
18. Sinks one's teeth into
19. Is sick
20. 60's sitcom/90's movie
23. Aardvark's tidbit
24. Lumberjack's tool
25. Possesses
28. Shirt or dress
32. Monet supply?
35. What to make a dep. into
37. Dweeb
38. Allude (to)
40. 60's sitcom/90's movie
43. Individually owned apartment
44. Opposite of a thinker
45. Airport conveyance
46. Sweltering
47. Invisible troublemaker
50. Where the iris is
51. Knot
52. "Hold on a ___!"
54. 60's sitcom/90's movie

63. Artist's work
64. Flip out
65. Jazz lingo
66. Location
67. ___ Dame
68. Preowned
69. Kilt wearer
70. Kills, as a dragon
71. Emperor with a burning ambition?

DOWN

1. Credit card color
2. Clarinet cousin
3. Stitched
4. Laughing ___
5. Where to get a taxi
6. Exclude
7. Butterfly's cousin
8. Liberate
9. Flunky
10. One of the Allman Brothers
11. Operatic solo
12. Baby powder ingredient
13. Otherwise
21. Gerund's end
22. Bonus
25. "Down the ___!" (drinker's toast)
26. Sound before "Gesundheit!"
27. Bloodhound's trail
29. English author Charles
30. 1983 Michael Keaton comedy

Puzzle 105 by Mark Gottlieb

31 Ford flop
32 Flaming
33 Pass-the-baton race
34 Product sample's invitation
36 Little bit
39 CPR practitioner
41 Calf, to a cowboy
42 Flying toys
48 Acts as king
49 Born as
51 Den appliance

53 New Orleans cooking style
54 Any Buffalo Bills Super Bowl result
55 Grand, as an adventure
56 Car
57 Hammer or sickle, e.g.
58 "Toodle-oo"
59 Grand Ole ___
60 Workbench clamp
61 At any time
62 Start over

ACROSS

1 Lots
5 Desert streambed
9 Tennis great Rod
14 "Are you some kind of ___?"
15 Black
16 "___ at the office"
17 Vidal's Breckinridge
18 Roar at the shore
19 Count with an orchestra
20 1989 Madonna hit
23 Churchill's sign
24 Basic college degrees
25 Summit
29 ___-Jo (1988 Olympics name)
31 Mosque V.I.P.
35 Live, in a TV studio
36 Like Britain
38 Poetic palindrome
39 It may be used in minor surgery
42 Quattro minus uno
43 Freshman, sophomore, etc.
44 Revolving machine part
45 Reply to "Are not!"
47 I-80, e.g.: Abbr.
48 Item in a Mexican fiesta
49 Luau dish
51 Sound from Sandy
52 Bibliophile's treasures
61 Belief in sorcery and magic

62 Pre-tractor farmer's need
63 Plummet
64 "A votre ___!"
65 Grp. affecting gas prices
66 Go gently (into)
67 More correct
68 Brood
69 "Jeopardy!" host Trebek

DOWN

1 Charades, e.g.
2 Cameo stone
3 Pat on the back, as a baby
4 Asterisk
5 Setting for Thomas Hardy novels
6 Maltreatment
7 Boat with oars
8 Data
9 Astrologically, the thoughtful, diplomatic type
10 Tennis great Andre
11 Bouquet site
12 Satanicalness
13 Sailor's peril
21 Don or Phil of 50's–60's pop
22 W.W. II menace
25 Physicist Alessandro
26 Vast, old-style
27 Regattas
28 Spanish aunt

Puzzle 106 by Bernice Gordon

29 French brother
30 Minus
32 Acclaimed "Hostess with the Mostes' "
33 Unrestrained
34 Stiller's comedy partner
36 Buzzing pest
37 Savings and loan
40 Condor's home
41 Long time
46 Narcotic
48 William or Harry, e.g.

50 Word with woman or worldly
51 Take ___ breath
52 Bewildered
53 Construction support
54 Maître d's offering
55 Condemn
56 Montreal player
57 Bright thought
58 Spoken
59 Winning margin, maybe
60 Glasses, in ads

ACROSS

1 Freight
6 Watering holes
10 "Puttin' on the ___" (Berlin classic)
14 Completely foreign
15 Early part of the day
16 "Toreador Song," e.g., in "Carmen"
17 River to the Rhône
18 Italian man
19 Rope material
20 Parlors
23 Metal refuse
24 Hwy.
25 Stovetop item
28 Mailing ctrs.
31 "Damn Yankees" temptress
33 Predicament
35 Official proceedings
37 Cartoonist Gross
39 ___ diem (seize the day)
40 Applause, plus
43 Chili con ___
44 Vasco da ___
45 Back talk
46 Where some shoes are made
48 Bring home the bacon
50 "Yo!"
51 Martial arts expert Bruce
52 ___ Cruces, N.M.
54 Spanish rivers
56 Cane
61 Graduation month

64 Poi ingredient
65 Artist Matisse
66 Marco Polo crossed it
67 Catchall abbr.
68 Like certain seals
69 An American, to a Brit
70 Ownership document
71 Gobs

DOWN

1 Elliot, of the Mamas and the Papas
2 Jai ___
3 Uproar
4 Men's room sign
5 "Mourning Becomes Electra" playwright
6 Customs officer's concern
7 Opposite of rich
8 Knight's protection
9 High-hats
10 Cheerleaders' cheers
11 Anger
12 Director Burton or Robbins
13 Knock out, as with a remote
21 Supermodel Campbell
22 Muslim's destination
25 Outcast
26 Go up against
27 Wee
28 French mathematician Blaise
29 87 or 93 at the pump
30 Go on a hunger strike

Puzzle 107 by Stephanie Spadaccini

32 Pond covering
34 "Fudge!"
36 Years, in old Rome
38 Roseanne's ex
41 Singer Reese
42 Brazilian airline
47 Stored, with "away"
49 Snacks
53 Use Rollerblades
55 Pilfer

56 Lacking strength
57 "Dies ___" (hymn)
58 Concerning
59 Ship's staff
60 Joshes
61 First Chief Justice John
62 Red, white and blue team
63 Writer Anaïs

ACROSS

1 Shopaholic's hangout
5 Out-and-out
10 Way to go
14 Pacific Rim locale
15 Shoe material
16 As a result
17 Part of a popular song lyric
20 Actress-skater Sonja
21 Chinese restaurant flowers
22 Suffix with idiom
25 Open, as an envelope
26 Old-fashioned illumination
30 Monticello, for one
34 1970's discipline
35 Bête ___
37 Book after Gen.
38 More of the song's lyric
42 Do-well starter
43 Anteater's feature
44 Actress Peeples
45 Not asea
48 Supporters of Ivan and Nicholas
50 Sells (for)
52 Onetime Spanish queen and namesakes
53 Draws
57 Midafternoon
61 Statement describing the subject of the song
64 Nectar flavor
65 Microwave brand
66 Gave the boot
67 Censor's target
68 Where Durban is
69 Baseball's Sandberg

DOWN

1 It takes figuring
2 U.S. Open stadium name
3 Property encumbrance
4 Of the lips
5 G.I. entertainment grp.
6 Large cask
7 Sermon basis
8 Newswoman Magnus et al.
9 Secondhand transaction
10 Did a horticulturist's job
11 Planets and such
12 Malarial fever
13 Children's connectibles
18 Eye layer
19 "Trinity" author
23 "___ a Name" (Jim Croce hit)
24 Debt markers
26 "I can't ___ satisfaction" (1965 lyric)
27 Visibly frightened
28 Shipment to Detroit
29 E. C. Bentley detective
31 Impulse transmitters
32 Namely
33 Author Ferber and others
36 Jagged

Puzzle 108 by Thomas W. Schier

39 Exaggerator
40 Chinese dollar
41 Geologic layers
46 One noted for bringing couples together
47 Abase
49 Babylonian love goddess
51 1965 march site
53 Rewards for waiting

54 News bit
55 Son of Rebekah
56 Mattress support
58 Classic theater name
59 Gershwin biographer David
60 "Momo" author Michael
62 Actress Merkel
63 Actor Kilmer

ACROSS

1 Milky-white gem
5 Turned white
10 Inclusion with a MS.
14 Trucking rig
15 French love
16 Drug ___ (Washington pooh-bah)
17 Patronizing person
18 Sparkling headwear
19 Ladder step
20 Start of a quip
23 Son of Aphrodite
24 Fencing blade
25 Harmony
28 On the up-and-up
31 Rioter's take
32 Joins
34 Hen's pride
37 Middle of the quip
40 Adriatic, e.g.
41 Ryan and Tatum of filmdom
42 Verdi's slave girl
43 Tête-à-têtes
44 Awry
45 Feedback of a sort
47 Like auto shop floors
49 End of the quip
55 ___ and tell
56 Scarlett, for one
57 Snug
59 Sped
60 Heavy volumes
61 Lamb's sobriquet
62 Took advantage of
63 Kasparov's game
64 Red light directive

DOWN

1 C.I.A. predecessor
2 Await judgment
3 To me, in Paris
4 It kept Bizet busy
5 Outdoor lounging area
6 Faulty
7 Temporary use
8 Currency that replaced the mark, franc, lira, etc.
9 "Phooey!"
10 Actor's "homework"
11 Sky-blue
12 "À votre ___!"
13 Work unit
21 Word repeated before "again," in a saying
22 Jefferson, religiously
25 Priests' garments
26 Grimace
27 Smidgen
28 Beans in a stew
29 List-ending abbr.
30 Catches on
32 Forearm bone
33 Boris's refusal
34 Actor Estrada
35 1947 Literature Nobelist André
36 Eat beaver-style
38 Not at all
39 Classic 30's–40's radio comedy
43 Reprimanded, with "out"
44 100%
45 Group character

Puzzle 109 by Grace Fabbroni

46 Taking out the garbage, e.g.
47 Fairy tale villains
48 Bridge declaration
50 University mil. group
51 "Oops!"
52 Reputation
53 Revolver inventor
54 Pinza of the Met
55 Trio after R
58 Prattle

ACROSS

1 ___ de Boulogne (Paris park)
5 Constant complainer
9 Excite, as interest
14 Ancient inscription
15 Daughter of Cronus
16 Pluck
17 Start with boy or girl
18 "The jig ___!"
19 Much-played part of a 45
20 Led Zeppelin hit, 1969
23 English ___
24 Rocker Garcia, informally
25 Big Blue
26 "___ Yes!" (old political placard)
28 Jewel
30 Classic clown
32 It comes after Mardi
33 Gagging cry
35 Actor Beatty
36 Make out
37 Midgame broadcasts
42 Inch, e.g.
43 "Pish posh!"
44 Part of an academic yr.
45 Sicilian spouter
46 McDonald's founder Ray
48 Dance version of a pop song, e.g.
52 "Comprende?"
53 Clump
54 Make sense, with "up"
56 British verb ending
57 Alternative to a Whopper
61 Deceit
62 Engagement gift
63 Waters: Fr.
64 Part of a furniture joint
65 Pins and needles holder
66 Fair distance
67 Works with words
68 Do carbon-testing on
69 Table scraps

DOWN

1 Barroom fights
2 Do better than at bat
3 Altogether
4 Whiskered circus animal
5 Its capital is Santiago
6 Soak up again
7 In ___ (stuck)
8 Saint John, for one
9 Sacred song
10 ___ facto
11 Shaker
12 Just walk through a role, say
13 Stretch, with "out"
21 Cassette deck button
22 Homes
27 Questions
29 First-term Clinton victory
31 ". . . and ___ grow on"

Puzzle 110 by Brendan Emmett Quigley

32 Treasure-hoarding dwarf
34 Popular candy bar
37 Tinted
38 Artificially made to look old
39 Pasta favorite
40 Trounced, in sports
41 Hidden
47 Screw backer
49 Any point in a trapeze artist's routine

50 Tristram's love
51 Persian king who destroyed Athens
53 Brown songbirds
55 Cowboy's stray
58 Tons
59 Meter maid of song
60 Verne captain
61 AT&T competitor

ACROSS

1 Walk, trot or canter
5 Cheese served with crackers
9 Cavort
13 Speak without notes
15 Loaf about
16 Race track
17 Girl in a children's story
19 Dried up
20 Go on and off, as a traffic light
21 Spain and Portugal
23 Polluted
26 Having round protuberances
27 Hammed it up
28 Irish accent
29 Foremost's partner
30 Try, as a case
31 Go out with
34 Liturgical vestment
35 Mocked
38 Clear (of)
39 Shirts for golfers?
41 Opposite of include
42 Mellowing, as cheese
44 Long-legged shorebird
46 90's music or fashion
47 These can be winning or losing
49 Scarlet bird
50 Readies, as a pool cue
51 Harold who wrote "Stormy Weather"
52 Harangue
53 Worse than awful
58 Fairy tale's opening word
59 They crisscross Paris
60 Grafting shoot
61 Bambi and kin
62 They may be loose or split
63 Burden

DOWN

1 Joke
2 Commotion
3 State west of Ind.
4 Choice morsels
5 Flaxen-haired
6 Boulder
7 Variety
8 Hamlet's home
9 Citizen Kane's last word
10 Domineering
11 Nobelist Curie
12 Beg
14 Military lodgings
18 Stretched the truth, so to speak
22 Peat locale
23 Trim, as a roast
24 Author Zola
25 Restraint
26 Velveeta maker
28 Comport with
30 Development developments
32 Touch of color
33 Landscaping tool
36 Overconfident

Puzzle 111 by Holden Baker

37 Sock menders
40 More slender and graceful
43 Wild llama
45 Acorn tree
46 Joyous celebration
47 Seafood order
48 Macbeth, for one

49 Lady's keepsake to a soldier, once
51 Not up yet
54 Convent dweller
55 Storage container
56 Costello or Grant
57 Printer's widths

ACROSS

1 Golf hazard
5 Abound
9 A few
13 ___ law (old Germanic legal code)
15 Lunchbox treat
16 Opposite of unter
17 Having feet pointing inward
19 Physics calculation
20 "Tender ___" (1983 Robert Duvall film)
21 "Holy smokes!"
23 Surfing site
24 Dutch airline
25 Not much for mixing
27 Attire
29 Onetime Yugoslav chief
30 The time of one's life
31 Brenda of the comics
32 Markets
33 Bewitch
34 Having keen vision
37 Baby beagle
40 Nonliteral humor
41 Dusk to dawn
45 34th Prez
46 New Jersey hoopsters
47 Indian homes
48 Soup dishes
50 PC alternative
51 Home planet in a 1978–82 sitcom
52 One of the McCartneys
53 Dairy workers

55 Cinergy Field team
56 Like one's fun house mirror image, maybe
59 Baseball's Moises
60 Salinger dedicatee
61 Lace place mat
62 Journalist Hamill
63 Arousing
64 Protected

DOWN

1 Recipe amt.
2 Attire
3 Search for the unknown?
4 Jetty
5 Pole on a reservation
6 God of love
7 Very wide, shoewise
8 In a humble way
9 Poison ___
10 Book after Amos
11 Bit of E-mail
12 Hosp. areas
14 Foolish
18 Cairo's river
22 Flexible, like some lamp shafts
23 "Scream" director Craven
25 Choreographer Alvin
26 Big Apple subway stop, for short
28 Mine metal
29 Rebellious time
32 Casino machines
35 Soldiers' "pineapples"

Puzzle 112 by Peter Gordon

36 Quick swim
37 Raucous card game
38 Tiny Tim's instrument
39 August birthstone
42 Where Athens is
43 Feminine pronoun
44 "Naughty, naughty!"
47 Like most N.B.A. players

49 Follow
50 Boy in Life cereal ads
53 1910, on cornerstones
54 Stars have big ones
55 Hip-hop
57 Put to work
58 Hair coloring

ACROSS

1 Catches in the act
5 Composer Franz
10 R.N.'s "touch"
13 Singer Guthrie
14 Kind of daisy
15 Where the Mets play
16 1934 Shirley Temple musical
19 Volcano spew
20 Protest that gets out of hand
21 Bizarre
22 Striped fish
23 Uses to achieve later success
25 Infuriate
28 Place to get all steamed up
29 Hideaway
30 Mode
31 President Lincoln
34 Take time out
38 Hearty mugful
39 Batter's position
40 Battering wind
41 Mailman's beat
42 Plant reproductive bodies
44 One just let out of jail
47 Couples
48 Perfect
49 Bushels
50 "So that's what you meant!"
53 Goldbrick
57 Not so much
58 Kareem ___-Jabbar
59 Back of the neck
60 Take to court
61 Social position
62 Mandated safety sign

DOWN

1 Mars Pathfinder launcher
2 Partner of crafts
3 Ho-hum
4 Prodigal ___
5 1991 buddy film "Thelma & ___"
6 Montréal team
7 Miami team
8 Writer Rand
9 Deeply blushing
10 Eta follower
11 Skeptical
12 Gives a hoot
15 Six-time Super Bowl coach Don
17 Downer
18 Safe place in the ring
22 Fishhook's end
23 "Band of Gold" singer Freda
24 "___ Lang Syne"
25 "Born Free" lioness
26 It gets hit on the head
27 ___ of passage
28 Condition
30 Rink need
31 Outlawed spray
32 Cotton bundle
33 "First Wives Club" members

Puzzle 113 by Alex K. Justin

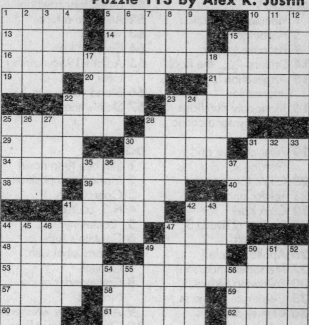

35 Moon-landing program
36 Tip-off
37 Subjects of psychoanalysis
41 Highways and byways
42 Nonobvious
43 Deluxe
44 Multivitamins, e.g.
45 Goodbye

46 Shortstop Pee Wee
47 Glazed food item
49 Olympus dwellers
50 Rival of Bon Ami
51 Southwest Indian
52 Help in a heist
54 Servicewoman, briefly
55 Hawks' and Bucks' org.
56 Opposite WSW

ACROSS

1 Handle the situation
5 Harbinger
9 Pancake topper
14 Drifters' "___ the Roof"
15 Application form information
16 Monopoly purchase
17 Alex Raymond comic strip
19 Peter of Peter and Gordon
20 C.I.A. forerunner
21 Tokyo, once
22 Coin side
24 Feature of five U.S. Presidents
26 Apollo vehicle
27 Manager Anderson
30 Following orders
35 Corporate emblems
36 Clumsy dancer's problems
37 The Magi, e.g.
38 Christie or Quindlen
39 Things to crack
40 Part of E.M.T.: Abbr.
41 Kind of tea
42 Pearl Buck heroine
43 Sacred song
44 Western Hemisphere
46 Sliding dance step
47 The Red Baron, for one
48 Curtain fabric
50 Musicians
54 Electric swimmer
55 Telephonic 3
58 Kind of board
59 Legendary cowboy
62 Attach to a lapel
63 Wicked
64 Come in last
65 Adlai's 1956 running mate
66 Broad valley
67 Sloth's home

DOWN

1 Stephen King novel
2 Musical composition
3 Operatic Lily
4 H.S. course
5 "Sometime . . ."
6 Captain's superior
7 Record label with Capitol
8 Commander of the Nautilus
9 Attacked the whiskers
10 Ornery Warner Bros. cartoon character
11 Essen's river
12 Manipulates
13 Father, in France
18 Vichyssoise ingredients
23 Give a benediction
24 Namath's nickname
25 Gadgets
27 Done in
28 Puerto Rican port city
29 1973 resigner
31 Existed
32 Humorist Bombeck et al.
33 Physicist Bohr

Puzzle 114 by Gregory E. Paul

34 The Velvet Fog
36 Bridge fee
39 Kitchen utensil
43 Collins and Donahue
45 Seas
46 Louisiana lingo
49 Heavy-hitting Fielder
50 "Essay on Man" author
51 San ___ Obispo, Calif.

52 "You ___ seen nothin' yet!"
53 Raced
55 New Look designer
56 If not
57 Head for the hills
60 Stowe girl
61 Lunch order, briefly

ACROSS

1 Fill in at the office
5 Manias
9 Dressed
13 L.A.-based petroleum giant
14 "Dies ___" (hymn)
15 Salty
16 Corner square in Monopoly
17 Lounge
18 Suddenly leap (at)
19 Second of two pieces of fire truck equipment
22 Take for granted
25 Paragons
26 More drenched minister, at times
30 One who's out of this world?
31 Pays attention to
32 Pie holder
35 Ranges of knowledge
36 Smutty
37 Ending with Cine- or cyclo-
38 Superlative suffix
39 Count ___ & His Orchestra
40 Motive questioner
41 Resentful auctiongoer
43 ___-Lorraine (French region)
46 "Relax, soldiers!"
47 Murmur "a good bad-weather race horse"
51 Thrown for ___
52 Footnote abbr.
53 Morsel for Miss Muffet
57 Former Sen. Sam and family
58 Highway hauler
59 Manipulator
60 Enzyme suffixes
61 Mahogany or maple
62 Prepare, as the way

DOWN

1 ___ Mahal
2 Period in history
3 AT&T alternative
4 Harms the environment
5 Aquarium purifier
6 "I smell ___!"
7 Stun
8 Clairvoyant
9 Less refined
10 Actress Hamilton or Hunt
11 Heavenly host?
12 Salon professionals
15 In-line skates, for short
20 Prayer closer
21 Nixon staffer G. Gordon ___
22 Conscious
23 Tennis star with a palindromic name
24 Limited work assignment
27 Bridge precursor
28 Strange
29 Discourage from acting

Puzzle 115 by Mark Danna

32 Bear that's not really a bear
33 Gallic girlfriends
34 Mother-of-pearl
36 Library gizmo
37 International golf competition
39 Bodybuilder's bulges
40 Commend officially
41 Majorettes twirl them
42 Villain, slangily
43 Major oven maker
44 Doozies
45 Rock
48 Morning haze
49 Over, in Österreich
50 Bygone phone call cost
54 Olympics chant
55 Gun, as an engine
56 Rap's Dr. ___

ACROSS

1 Half of a 60's quartet
6 Small farm spread
10 Explorer Vasco da ___
14 Necklace fastener
15 Linseed oil source
16 Caboose
17 Alaska's first capital
18 Freeway exit
19 ___ the Red
20 Start of a quote by Lily Tomlin
23 Twosome
24 Chimney accumulation
25 "What ___ the odds?"
26 Graze
29 Moo
31 Engaged in swordplay
33 Part 2 of the quote
37 Overfill
38 Swift bird
39 Verdi heroine
43 Part 3 of the quote
48 Slug but good
51 Dandy
52 Select, with "for"
53 Coach Parseghian
54 Tabularize
57 Dorothy Parker quality
59 End of the quote
64 Fishing item
65 A beret covers it
66 Garden bulb
68 Sailing
69 "Symphonie espagnole" composer
70 $C_4H_8O_2$, e.g.
71 Canine cry
72 Utopia
73 "Hansel and Gretel," for one

DOWN

1 Compaq products
2 Came down to earth
3 Way
4 Popped a question
5 Flipper?
6 60's haircut
7 North Pole name
8 Stallone title role
9 Detonate
10 Matured
11 Kind of photo
12 ___ d'hôtel
13 Like a gateway, often
21 2, to 4, or 8
22 Needle case
26 U.F.O. crew
27 "Yes, I see!"
28 ___ offensive
30 Birdhouse resident
32 Jacob's twin
34 Lively old dance
35 Paris associate
36 Sleeve's end
40 ___ Jima
41 Immerse
42 Tiny worker
44 Mouselike animal
45 Letter
46 Cry of pain
47 Tranquilizers
48 Attack en route
49 Impassion

Puzzle 116 by Alan Olschwang

50 Victor's prize
55 Ending with farm or home
56 Library info
58 Kind of account
60 Harvest
61 Revolutionary Trotsky
62 Countertenor
63 Stadium section
67 Meddle

ACROSS

1 "I give up!"
6 Does and bucks
10 Writer Hunter
14 Environment-friendly energy choice
15 Gather leaves
16 It's full of shafts
17 French love affair
18 Products of a 16-Across
19 Customer
20 Hatfield-McCoy affair
21 Place of bliss
23 Stick-on
25 "Here's to you!" and others
26 Hotelier Hilton
28 Make drunk
30 Prefix with cycle
31 Cut into cubes
33 Electrical pioneer Nikola
37 Billions of years
39 House of the Seven Gables site
41 Exhibition
42 Gloomy, in poetry
44 "All sales ___"
46 Playwright Burrows
47 Flood embankment
49 Displayed ennui
51 Entertain, as with stories
54 1924 Ferber novel
55 Place of bliss
58 Irish offshoot
61 ___-mutuel
62 Worker protection org.
63 From Mars, say
64 Margin
65 Airline to Tel Aviv
66 Sat and did nothing
67 Requisite
68 Specks
69 Pre-1917 Russian rulers

DOWN

1 It has its academy in Colo. Spr.
2 Alaskan outpost
3 Place of bliss
4 Cosmetician Estee
5 Flub
6 Openly salivate
7 Make, as money
8 Managed, with "out"
9 Adjusts, as a clock
10 Copies
11 Travel papers
12 Regarding
13 Hardly hipsters
21 African waterbeds
22 Plant anchorer
24 No-goodnik
26 Prompted
27 ___ about (circa)
28 Contradict
29 Paradise
32 Eatery
34 Place of bliss
35 Earring site
36 In wonderment
38 On the payroll

Puzzle 117 by Mary E. Brindamour

40 Giuliani, e.g.
43 Depend (on)
45 Inventor's workplace
48 Said no to
50 Exercises, as authority
51 Come of age
52 Get around

53 Stuff to the gills
54 Flippered animals
56 Nobel Peace Prize city
57 One of the five W's
59 Séance holder
60 Quashes
63 River islet

ACROSS

1 "___ the Horrible"
6 Challenge to a gunslinger
10 Out-of-focus picture
14 Wonderland girl
15 Relaxation
16 Country road
17 Evasive answer #1
20 Have a feeling
21 Prefix with linear
22 Swiss peak
25 Twain's "The Gilded ___"
26 Wailing woman, in folklore
28 Tell
30 Insertion symbol
31 Race track shape
32 Haying machine
33 Droop
36 Evasive answer #2
40 ___ gratia artis
41 Nonsecular types
42 Jason's ship
43 Members of a chess line
44 Rough, as terrain
46 "Thank you for ___ . . ."
49 Author Rand
50 Golfer Ernie
51 Founder of the Soviet Union
52 Plot of land
54 Evasive answer #3
60 Capri, e.g.
61 Detroit products
62 Florida city
63 ___-do-well
64 Overpublicize
65 "I understand!"

DOWN

1 "Bali ___"
2 Entirely
3 TV actor Gerard
4 Does film work
5 Warm up, as food
6 Thick
7 Garden tool
8 White ___ ghost
9 Internet
10 Deepest azure
11 Gate holder
12 Knot
13 Knot again
18 "Picnic" planner
19 Obstinate
22 Scent
23 TV actor Burton
24 "Hamlet" and "Macbeth"
26 Mild, as weather
27 Neighborhood
29 Priestly garb
30 Playbill listings
32 Existence
33 Suit material
34 Broadway backer
35 Merchandise
37 "Seinfeld" lady
38 Open wide
39 Base in baseball
43 First-grade book

Puzzle 118 by Stephanie Spadaccini

44 Pitcher Nolan
45 Clear, as a drain
46 Killed
47 German Hermann
48 Leg joint
49 Get up
52 Canvas cover

53 Mexican sandwich
55 Oh, in Heidelberg
56 ___ Men's Health
Crisis
57 Tit for ___
58 Yalie
59 Stinker

ACROSS

1 They welcome people at the door
5 Gymnast Korbut
9 Lariat
14 Carrier to Jerusalem
15 News "items"
16 ___ Island (immigrants' spot)
17 Turkish title
18 "Inventions of the Monsters" artist
19 German currency, informally
20 Mother of country music
22 "___ Johnny!"
23 Takes care of
24 River to the Fulda
26 Alpine transport
29 Not just
33 Cousin of a stogie
37 Colorless
39 Arm bone
40 Prefix with mechanics
41 Tasmanian ___
42 Bonkers
43 Caroled
44 "Got you"
45 Fernando's farewell
46 Famous last words?
48 Garage job
50 Cheer (for)
52 Lawrence's land
57 Eastern mystic
60 Melville hero
63 "The Rebel" essayist
64 Romantic interlude
65 Out of port
66 Positive pole
67 Singer Horne
68 Cross-check
69 Types wearing pocket protectors
70 Extend credit
71 Point on Columbus's compass

DOWN

1 Stands for
2 Lake life
3 Western resort
4 Shuts vehemently
5 Handyman's assignment
6 Molokai meal
7 Like some charge cards
8 "All kidding ___ . . ."
9 "Little" storybook character
10 Cartoon character with a big gun
11 Agricultural chemical
12 Enervate
13 Entreats
21 "Tell ___ the Marines!"
25 One-on-one
27 Copies
28 Get tangled up
30 Jai ___
31 Data
32 Lab runners
33 Ski resort legwear?
34 Wife of Jacob

Puzzle 119 by Elizabeth C. Gorski

35 Composer Thomas
36 Onetime CBS anchor
38 Stead
41 Purcell's "___ and Aeneas"
45 Hawk's home: Var.
47 Boom and zoom
49 "Ode to Billie Joe," e.g.
51 Govt. security

53 Drop off
54 Double-deckers, e.g.
55 That is
56 "___ which will live in infamy": F.D.R.
57 Glance over
58 Drop off
59 Love overseas
61 Concept for Claudette
62 Newswoman Sherr

ACROSS

1 Capital of Azerbaijan
5 ___ Kett of early comics
9 Confronts
14 X ___ xylophone
15 Statutes
16 Nonsensical
17 Leave in, editorially
18 Explorer called "the Red"
19 Kind of orange
20 With 34-, 43- and 58-Across, message on a tourist's postcard
23 Chou En-___
24 Bout outcome, briefly
25 River at Ghent
26 Strike caller
29 After
32 Truck track
34 See 20-Across
39 Composer Stravinsky
40 Moray, e.g.
41 Lendl of tennis
43 See 20-Across
48 Ordinal suffix
49 Card game start
50 Born: Fr.
51 Airline with the old slogan "Up, up and away"
54 Broadcast
56 Oversized
58 See 20-Across
65 Put ___ to (end)
66 Surrealist Salvador
67 Gym socks may have one
68 India's first P.M.
69 "Holy moly!"
70 What's holding things up
71 Like Gatsby
72 Actress Russo
73 Root in Hawaiian cookery

DOWN

1 Wingding
2 Nick and Nora's dog
3 Chicken ___ (deep-fried dish)
4 "Don't open ___ Christmas!"
5 Mournful
6 Scarlett's home
7 Baby branch
8 Broad necktie
9 Discover
10 Med. course
11 Carp
12 Hostile force
13 Tennis champ Monica
21 Back of the neck
22 Gumbo
26 A.P. rival
27 Prefix with bucks or phone
28 Ship's front
30 Part of a rose
31 Preppy's fabric
33 Significantly underweight

Puzzle 120 by Arthur S. Verdesca

35 At liberty
36 "What ___ can I say?"
37 Uniform
38 Lightly cooked
42 Actress Carrie
44 "Don't move!"
45 Toledo's home
46 Trip to the airport, say
47 Nobelist Wiesel
51 Nasal tone
52 More prudent

53 "___ World Turns"
55 Less polite
57 Basic Halloween costume
59 Jewish wedding dance
60 Carry on
61 Vivacity
62 ___ St. Vincent Millay
63 Din
64 Hence

ACROSS

1 Islands west of Portugal
7 Third place
11 Southern ___
14 Barrio grocery
15 Hardly believable
16 "You ___ here"
17 Diane Keaton, to Woody Allen, often
18 Author Turgenev
19 Arrangement of masts
20 Lots, pricewise
23 H. H. Munro, pseudonymously
26 Velvet finish
27 Effortless
28 Ike of the O.K. Corral
31 Priestly garb
34 Josh
35 The Four Seasons' "Walk Like ___"
37 Coffee shop emanations
41 Lots, lovewise
44 Make some after-the-whistle contact
45 Dutch portraitist Frans
46 Fri. preceder
47 Sabbath activity
49 Deck out
51 Jump out of one's skin?
54 Dine
56 Chess castle
57 Lots, timewise
62 Boxers' letters?
63 Bowser's bowlful
64 Ducks

68 Brain scan, for short
69 Boo-boo
70 Chewy confection
71 High-pH substance
72 Dog's breath
73 Cleopatra's love

DOWN

1 "20/20" network
2 Where to do some petting
3 Takes too much
4 Hire, as counsel
5 Richard of "A Summer Place"
6 Franklin D.'s mother
7 Gunk
8 Harbor where the Maine blew up
9 Mideast land
10 Proceed
11 "Cheers" waitress
12 80's Dodge
13 Having attractive gams
21 Of the kidneys
22 Ancient moralist
23 Dump into a Dumpster
24 "I ran out of gas," e.g.
25 Afghan capital
29 Sierra Nevada lake
30 Future signs
32 Serve, as stew
33 Chutzpah
36 Slangy refusal
38 Copycat's words
39 Allergy season sound
40 ___ cabbage

42 Sealy rival
43 1993 treaty, briefly
48 Tough pickup for some bowlers
50 Audition
51 Old-time actress Normand
52 Hand-wringer's words
53 Rock shelf
55 Vote to accept
58 Heavy file

59 Milan's Teatro ___ Scala
60 "Two Years Before the Mast" writer
61 (Ding-dong) "___ calling"
65 Billy Joel's "___ to Extremes"
66 Dapper fellow?
67 Piggery

ACROSS

1 With gold trim
5 Jewish text
10 Breakfast restaurant chain
14 Dr. Frankenstein's assistant
15 Scent
16 Taboo
17 "Psycho" setting
19 Buttonhole
20 Elvis's Graceland, e.g.
21 In dire ___
23 Sudden swelling
26 Contents of a playground box
27 Radio tube gas
30 Aardvark's nibble
32 Razz
35 Used
36 Winslow Homer, e.g.
38 Day in Jerusalem
39 Nabokov heroine
40 Hooey
41 Bachelor's last words
42 Stimpy's pal
43 Emissary
44 Winged pest
45 Jump out of the way
47 Opposite WSW
48 Pick up on
49 Replaceable shoe part
51 Snares
53 Dagwood's lady
56 Rag
60 Item often kept on hand?

61 Title setting for a Neil Simon play
64 Hurler Hershiser
65 Egg on
66 Tear up
67 Yarborough of the Daytona 500
68 "Lorna ___" (1869 novel)
69 Slices of history

DOWN

1 Taunt
2 Certain supermarkets, for short
3 Sen. Trent ___
4 Benedict Arnold's crime
5 Bronco buster
6 Aztec treasure
7 Go bad
8 Iowa State University site
9 Puts a stop to
10 Loony
11 "White Christmas" setting, 1942
12 "Put a lid ___!"
13 Partner of pans
18 Flabbergast
22 Threadbare
24 Auto repair shop
25 Contest contestant
27 Obie, for one
28 Calgary Stampede, e.g.

Puzzle 122 by Gregory E. Paul

29 Title setting for a 1932 Oscar film
31 Hairdresser, at times
33 Fountain treats
34 Ham it up
36 London libation
37 Envision
40 Run in the wash
44 Signal with the hands
46 Not rough
48 Hot tubs
50 Biochemical compound

52 Swift's "___ of a Tub"
53 Univ. hotshot
54 Money in Milan
55 "Sesame Street" Muppet
57 Bleacher feature
58 Sicilian rumbler
59 Zinfandels
62 Sgt.'s mail drop
63 Buddhist sect

ACROSS

1 Teeny amounts
5 ___ nova
10 Japanese middle managers?
14 Metallurgists' studies
15 Perfume
16 Zippo
17 Meanie
18 Old TV comic
20 Blonde's secret, maybe
21 Ladies' man
22 Memorable name
24 Holier-than-thou type
28 Set boundaries
31 Some soda pops
32 Compunction
36 Lyric poem
37 "The Dunciad" writer
41 Latin lady: Abbr.
42 Keeps from escaping
43 Zhou ___
46 They show the way
50 Hip characters
54 "___ nous . . ."
55 Got off track
58 "There you are!"
59 1967 Pulitzer poet
62 Sign of healing
63 Kind of jet
64 "___ say more?"
65 In this place
66 Test venues
67 Supplemented
68 Jekyll's counterpart

DOWN

1 Dingus
2 Sock pattern
3 "Get with it!"
4 Atlanta-to-Tampa dir.
5 California peninsula
6 Western Indians
7 Energy for Fulton
8 Decline
9 Leafy shelter
10 Discounted
11 Scrooge's cry
12 Yes, at the altar
13 Dupe
19 "Terrible" czar
21 One of the financial markets, for short
23 Bog
25 Hwy. eatery
26 A or B, on a cassette
27 Literary monogram
29 "___ helpless as a kitten up a tree . . ."
30 Dial sound
33 Vitamin bottle abbr.
34 Actress Ward
35 Once, once
37 Florentine river
38 "Le Roi d'Ys" composer
39 Stacked
40 ___ even keel
41 Brief time
44 Trees with catkins
45 Italian refreshments
47 English travel writer Thomas
48 Founder of est

Puzzle 123 by Elizabeth C. Gorski

49 U.S. Navy builder
51 Stadium
52 Levied
53 Located
56 Locale of riches
57 Oklahoma city
59 Whole shebang
60 Teachers' org.
61 Collar
62 "No whispering!"

ACROSS

1 Birthplace of Columbus
6 Doesn't exist
10 Dog-paddle, say
14 Baking chambers
15 Headline
16 "___ you don't!"
17 What the jury does after deliberating
20 Poker starter
21 Small and weak
22 Swearing to tell the truth, and others
23 The highest degree
24 Perjured oneself
25 Facility
26 Sleuth, informally
27 Not real
29 Michael Douglas, to Kirk
32 Heavenly hunter
35 Passes easily
36 Knight's wife, in olden times
37 Legal reach, metaphorically
40 Actress Lanchester
41 "___ Misbehavin' "
42 Siskel's partner
43 Wreak vengeance on
44 Chicken style
45 Big blast maker
46 Biblical garden
48 Cash substitutes
50 Test-___ treaty
53 A Beatle
55 It's clicked on a computer
56 Vigor
57 Judge's cry
60 Thirteen popes
61 Toward shelter, nautically
62 Word with ear or peace
63 Dict. items
64 Antidrinking org.
65 + end

DOWN

1 Tennis star Ivanisevic
2 News basis
3 Under, in poetry
4 A single time
5 Baseball bat wood
6 Philately offering
7 Awaits sentencing
8 Dark blue
9 Number of coins in an Italian fountain
10 Ice cream drinks
11 January store happening
12 Distance between belt notches, maybe
13 Witty sayings
18 Like the "Iliad" and "Odyssey"
19 Wander
24 Songstress Horne
25 Sunrise direction
26 Ceremonial gown
28 Bulk
30 "Rubáiyát" poet
31 Salamander

Puzzle 124 by Mark Moldowsky

32 Designer Cassini
33 Part to play
34 Rather than
35 Gallic girlfriend
36 Money owed
38 Reason for postponement
39 Egg producers
44 Critic Walter
45 Composer's output
47 Chemise
49 Marveled aloud
50 Shoe designer Magli

51 Broadcast
52 ___ Dame
53 Auctioned off
54 Shade giver
55 "To Live and Die ___" ('85 film)
56 West German capital
58 "___ shocked!"
59 Spy org.

ACROSS

1 Prelude to a duel
5 Not hearing
9 Competitor for a Clio
14 Seat of Allen County, Kan.
15 Unattractive fruit that sounds that way
16 Upright, e.g.
17 Taking radical action
20 Kiss mark
21 Lamb's kin
22 Wonderment
23 "Bye!"
24 Much too bright
27 Romulus's brother
29 Rundown in appearance
33 Words of woe
37 "Buddy"
38 "23 ___": Var.
39 Holing up
42 Expired
43 Princess of operetta
44 "___ boy!"
45 One who can't go home
46 Give quarters to
48 Laotians, e.g.
50 Mowed strip
55 Breakfast staple
58 Have some tea
59 Sound investment?
60 Civil War story
64 Disconcert
65 Theater award
66 Peak in the "Odyssey"
67 "Same here!"
68 Fishing area
69 Lack

DOWN

1 Lovers' sounds
2 Sarge's boss
3 Restaurant owner of song
4 Hanky-___
5 Scout's pledge word
6 I, to Claudius
7 Inn drink
8 Repairmen
9 Like some mountain lodge activities
10 Conk out
11 Nursery call
12 Freshly
13 It smells a lot
18 Equipment
19 Prefix with light
24 Dillinger fighter
25 Setting for this puzzle's theme
26 Alpine heroine
28 Give off, as light
30 Redo, as text
31 Puts on
32 Eastern discipline
33 Grimm character
34 Martian invasion report, e.g.
35 60's dress style
36 ___ Gay (W.W. II plane)
38 Mass of hair
40 Caller's playful request

Puzzle 125 by Manny Nosowsky

41 3:1, 5:2, etc.
46 Portable computer
47 Renaissance name of fame
49 Certain grandson
51 Champions' cry
52 Get up
53 Edgy

54 Nonsurfer at the beach
55 "Omigosh!"
56 Mongolian desert
57 Flying pest
59 Tool repository
61 N.C. and S.C. zone
62 Cable channel
63 Type of type

ACROSS

1 "Chapter Two" star James
5 Provide for, as a party
10 Sacred bird of the Pharaohs
14 Tough-guy actor Ray
15 Skylit courts
16 Fisherman's offering?
17 "The Twilight Zone" host
19 Lily Pons specialty
20 Small bill
21 Dec. holiday
22 New Haven Line stop
24 Scolds
26 Newswoman Shriver
27 Sing Sing inhabitant
28 Machine part fastener
31 Where to pin a pin
34 "Olympia" painter
35 Sis's sib
36 Una década has 10
37 More rational
38 ___ slaw
39 Docs
40 Ellington and Wellington
41 Parts of apples
42 Venomous snake
44 Swab
45 Backpacker
46 Defensive wall
50 Wall Street type
52 Gang's area
53 Pierre's friend
54 Stockings
55 Armed robber

58 "It's ___ you!"
59 The "p" of 6p
60 ___ in a poke
61 Turns right
62 P.L.O.'s Arafat
63 Cowboy Roy's better half

DOWN

1 Chocolate substitute
2 "___ at last!"
3 Cousin of 42-Across
4 Refusals
5 Bizet heroine
6 Hammond product
7 Hall-of-Famer Speaker
8 Strauss's "___ Heldenleben"
9 High-quality writing medium
10 Slanted type
11 Maine resort
12 Hipbones
13 Baseball feature
18 Laud
23 Once, once
25 Tops
26 Flowing tresses
28 Porch chair craftsman
29 ___ Stanley Gardner
30 Troubles
31 Aladdin's treasure
32 "The King ___"
33 Quickly
34 Manufacturer
37 James Bond, e.g.
38 Nightclub of song

Puzzle 126 by Ed Early

40 Place for a finger?
41 Where Prince Philip was born
43 MTV fare
44 Promissory note in a casino
46 Designer Emilio
47 Argentine expanse

48 Cybermessages
49 Bit of color
50 55-Across, maybe
51 1948 Hitchcock thriller
52 Cans
56 Sri Lanka export
57 Expand unnecessarily

ACROSS

1 Electrical overload protector
5 Surrealist Salvador
9 Fodder holder
13 Where to see "E.R." or "Ellen"
14 Archeological site
15 "Star Wars" director George
16 Oklahoma Indian
17 ___'acte (intermission)
18 Portly plus
19 Like dentists?
22 Org. overseeing quadrennial games
23 Neighbor of Syr.
24 Like trampolinists?
30 Bleats
34 Friendly Islands, formally
35 Mandolin's ancestor
36 551, in Latium
37 Bind, as a chicken for roasting
38 Gilbert and Sullivan princess
39 Pre-entree course
41 Martians and Venusians, for short
42 Esposito of hockey
43 Irish county north of Limerick
44 Film unit
46 Like tree surgeons?
48 Advice-giving Landers
50 German spa
51 Like fencers?

59 "It was the ___ I could do"
60 Lifeless
61 "Whoops!"
62 Otherworldly
63 Money drawer
64 It's nothing to Agassi
65 Bikini, e.g.
66 Exclusive
67 Bridge

DOWN

1 Eat it
2 "___ us a son is given"
3 Put in an overhead bin, say
4 Prime time times
5 Dump water on
6 Jemima, e.g.
7 Art print: Abbr.
8 About
9 Evanston, to Chicago
10 "Original Gangster" rapper
11 Whip
12 Sugar suffix
15 Novelist Anita
20 Smidgens
21 Deep mud
24 Out-and-out
25 ___-cochere (carriage entrance)
26 Occupied
27 Statesman Root
28 Check for embezzlement, perhaps
29 Author Calvino

Puzzle 127 by John Greenman

31 Dwight's opponent in '52 and '56
32 Car security device
33 Part of a cassette tape
39 Rapscallion
40 ___ Day (November 2)
42 Duck's home
45 Timmy's dog
47 What CD players don't require
49 Nick at ___

51 Hive dwellers
52 Nobleman
53 Beanery sign
54 Beethoven piano piece
55 Capitol site, with "the"
56 Restaurant with waffles and such
57 ___ Scotia
58 "What happened next . . ."
59 Blooming neckwear?

ACROSS

1 Setting for the lingo in today's theme
6 Brick material
10 Cutting remark
14 Titlark
15 Bonheur or Parks
16 Birthplace of seven Presidents
17 NASA satellite launcher
18 Thomas Moore's land
19 Indicates assent
20 Begin's peace partner
21 [.][.]
23 Oral Roberts University site
25 Tarzan portrayer
26 Request sweetener
29 Entertained
33 Physics unit
34 Elephant Boy of 30's film
37 Hippodrome
38 [::][::]
42 Contemptuous look
43 Certain Ford, for short
44 Call ___ day
45 Saw-toothed
47 Reduce
50 Midafternoon on a sundial
51 Luxurious
53 [.] [.:]
57 Cassettes
61 Concert halls
62 Trick
63 R-rated or higher
64 Large bell sound
65 Writer Bagnold
66 T, in physics
67 Otherwise
68 Pixels
69 Calvin Trillin piece

DOWN

1 Auditors
2 Baltic port
3 Copied
4 It may be beaten at a party
5 Prestige
6 Salad greenery
7 "___ Doone"
8 Where the Gobi is
9 New Englander
10 Cemetery, informally
11 Hail, on the briny
12 Carnival attraction
13 Supervisor
22 "Pomp and Circumstance" composer
24 "___ we forget . . ."
26 Iron
27 Frankie who sang "Moonlight Gambler"
28 Gardening tool
29 German industrial region
30 Union leader John L. ___
31 Growing outward
32 Six-Day War leader
35 "Sigh!"
36 Spell-off

Puzzle 128 by Stanley B. Whitten

39 Birthright
40 Hiker's spot
41 Org. that defends the
 Bill of Rights
46 Layered
48 Manor
49 Sunglasses
51 Propose

52 City on the Aire
53 Ear part
54 Person with fans
55 Counting method
56 Jupiter's wife
58 Cat
59 Scat lady
60 "Don't move!"

ACROSS

1 Opera house box
5 Geography book
10 Golfer's alert
14 Gung-ho
15 Aplomb
16 Missing from the Marines, say
17 Trio in Bethlehem
18 Kindergarten adhesive
19 Onionlike plant
20 Noël Coward play
23 Dobbin's nibble
24 Postsurgical program
28 "Total ___" (1990 film)
32 Set free
35 Internet messages
36 "You'd ___ Nice to Come Home To"
37 Trouble
38 "Ho, ho, ho" sayer
42 Ike's W.W. II command
43 Flunky
44 Disney mermaid
45 Arts and crafts class
48 Garb
49 Secret rendezvous
50 Sold-out sign
51 Nickname for Hubert Humphrey, with "the"
59 On ___(without commitment)
62 Knight's wear
63 Not working
64 Prefix with bucks
65 Drink served with marshmallows
66 Grain for farm animals
67 Atop
68 Get used (to)
69 Town NNE of Santa Fe

DOWN

1 Gentle one
2 Skating rink, e.g.
3 Lerner and Loewe musical
4 Rewrite
5 Sex ___
6 Wedding offering to the bride and groom
7 Daffy Duck's impediment
8 Italian wine region
9 Psychic
10 Stumble
11 Be in arrears
12 Future flounder
13 Big game animal
21 Christmas decoration
22 Indignation
25 Michener novel
26 Penitent
27 Ladybug, e.g.
28 Veto
29 Ham
30 Dieter's unit: Var.
31 Be bedridden
32 Yorkshire city
33 "Uh-huh"
34 Rock's ___ Jovi
36 ___-a-brac
39 Moo goo ___ pan

Puzzle 129 by Gregory E. Paul

40 University of Florida student
41 N.Y.C. subway
46 Waste receptacle
47 N.Y.C. subway overseer
48 Genesis mountain
50 Hawk's descent
52 White-spotted rodent
53 Egg on
54 Community org. with a gym

55 Break in friendly relations
56 Notion
57 Parkay product
58 Cincinnati nine
59 Home of the Mustangs, for short
60 Oomph
61 It may need massaging

ACROSS

1 Put one's foot down
6 Not stiff
10 Without: Fr.
14 Prefix with anthropology
15 Eye part
16 "Here comes trouble!"
17 Arctic or Indian, e.g.
18 Flees
19 Noose material
20 "Yes!"
22 Ogled
23 Name for many a theater
24 Totally absorbed (in)
26 Bright and bouncy
29 "Get ___ of yourself!"
33 Easter bloom
37 Managed
38 Often-welcomed part of the week
39 Suffix with switch
40 Bara of the silents
42 Lymph ___
43 Interstellar cloud
45 Diamond ___
46 Alum
47 Southwestern home material
48 "___ of Two Cities"
50 Atlantic Seaboard, with "the"
52 Egyptian's tongue
57 Quick
60 "Yes!"
63 Prez

64 So long, in Soho
65 Utter fear
66 Engineer's school
67 Western Indians
68 Court TV coverage
69 Nick and Nora's dog
70 Attention-getter
71 Because

DOWN

1 Mar
2 Tasteless
3 Kind of acid
4 Civil War general
5 Pay
6 One of a kind
7 "Terrible" czar
8 Computer capacity
9 Ziti, e.g.
10 "Yes!"
11 Hey there, at sea
12 Nah
13 Outbuilding
21 Mafioso's code of silence
25 Golfer's goal
27 Cheerleader's cry
28 Genuflected
30 Aroma
31 Terhune's "___ Dog"
32 Like Easter eggs
33 Songstress Horne
34 Enraged
35 Gray wolf
36 "Yes!"
38 Bit of finery

Puzzle 130 by Eileen Lexau

41 A day in Spain
44 Lowing herd's place
48 Baseball stat
49 Gives way to rage
51 ___ and took notice
53 Early name in video games
54 African republic

55 Ending with sacro-
56 Rinse or dry, in a dishwasher
57 Goat cheese
58 Gives the heave-ho
59 Splinter group
61 Holy Fr. ladies
62 Malt kiln

SOLUTIONS

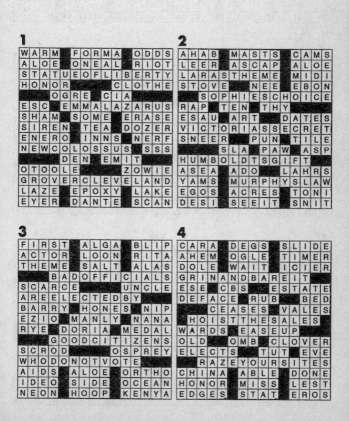

1

W	A	R	M		F	O	R	M	A		O	D	D	S
A	L	O	E		O	N	E	A	L		R	I	O	T
S	T	A	T	U	E	O	F	L	I	B	E	R	T	Y
H	O	N	O	R			C	L	O	T	H	E		
			O	G	R	E		C	I	A				
E	S	C		E	M	M	A	L	A	Z	A	R	U	S
S	H	A	M		S	O	M	E		E	R	A	S	E
S	I	R	E	N		T	E	A		D	O	Z	E	R
E	N	E	R	O		I	N	N	S		N	E	R	F
N	E	W	C	O	L	O	S	S	U	S		S	S	S
			D	E	N		E	M	I	T				
O	T	O	O	L	E			Z	O	W	I	E		
G	R	O	V	E	R	C	L	E	V	E	L	A	N	D
L	A	Z	E		E	P	O	X	Y		L	A	K	E
E	Y	E	R		D	A	N	T	E		S	C	A	N

2

A	H	A	B		M	A	S	T	S		C	A	M	S
L	E	E	R		A	S	C	A	P		A	L	O	E
L	A	R	A	S	T	H	E	M	E		M	I	D	I
S	T	O	V	E		N	E	E		E	B	O	N	
		S	O	P	H	I	E	S	C	H	O	I	C	E
R	A	P		T	E	N		T	H	Y				
E	S	A	U		A	R	T		D	A	T	E	S	
V	I	C	T	O	R	I	A	S	S	E	C	R	E	T
S	N	E	E	R		P	U	N		T	I	L	E	
			S	L	A		P	A	W		A	S	P	
H	U	M	B	O	L	D	T	S	G	I	F	T		
A	S	E	A		A	D	O		L	A	H	R	S	
Y	A	M	S		M	U	R	P	H	Y	S	L	A	W
E	G	O	S		A	C	R	E	S		T	O	N	I
D	E	S	I		S	E	E	I	T		S	N	I	T

3

F	I	R	S	T		A	L	G	A		B	L	I	P
A	C	T	O	R		L	O	O	N		R	I	T	A
T	H	E	M	E		S	A	L	T		A	L	A	S
			B	A	D	O	F	F	I	C	I	A	L	S
S	C	A	R	C	E			U	N	C	L	E		
A	R	E	E	L	E	C	T	E	D	B	Y			
B	A	R	R	Y		H	O	N	E	S		N	I	P
E	Z	I	O		M	A	N	L	Y		N	A	N	A
R	Y	E		D	O	R	I	A		M	E	D	A	L
			G	O	O	D	C	I	T	I	Z	E	N	S
S	C	R	O	D			O	S	P	R	E	Y		
W	H	O	D	O	N	O	T	V	O	T	E			
A	I	D	S		A	L	O	E		O	R	T	H	O
I	D	E	O		S	I	D	E		O	C	E	A	N
N	E	O	N		H	O	O	P		K	E	N	Y	A

4

C	A	R	A		D	E	G	S		S	L	I	D	E
A	H	E	M		O	G	L	E		T	I	M	E	R
D	O	L	E		W	A	I	T		I	C	I	E	R
G	R	I	N	A	N	D	B	A	R	E	I	T		
E	S	E		C	B	S		E	S	T	A	T	E	
D	E	F	A	C	E		R	U	B		B	E	D	
			C	E	A	S	E	S		V	A	L	E	S
	H	O	I	S	T	T	H	E	S	A	L	E	S	
W	A	R	D	S		E	A	S	E	U	P			
O	L	D		O	M	B		C	L	O	V	E	R	
E	L	E	C	T	S		T	U	T		E	V	E	
	R	A	Z	E	Y	O	U	R	S	I	T	E	S	
C	H	I	N	A		A	B	L	E		D	O	N	E
H	O	N	O	R		M	I	S	S		L	E	S	T
E	D	G	E	S		S	T	A	T		E	R	O	S

5

```
S C O W   I L S A   C H I T S
A R L O   L O A D   R I C H E
W E E W I L L I E W I N K I E
N E G   G I L D   A T T E N D
    W A N E   A R I   S K Y
V E N I V I D I V I C I
E X I L E   D O N   N Y E T
T A L L   T H I N G   F O T O
S M E E   O O O   M A G O O
    M A K E M I N E M I N K
W E D   L I S   G O R Y
A N I M A L   I N R E   B U S
L O V E S L A B O R S L O S T
S L E E K   P E R I   I D E A
H A S T A   E X E S   D E R N
```

6

```
A V E R   B R E D     A D A M
C O R E   L I E U   S C O N E
T W I C E T O L D   E Q U A L
A S C O T     S C R U B
    R A T I O   A V I L A
O D D L O T S   B I R E M E
D A I S   R A T S   L E T O N
E X T   V I L L A G E   A L Y
P A T T I   Y E L L   F L E A
S C O R N S   R E E B O K S
  A M A T I   S M E A R
    A N N E S     J A U N T
F O R C E   T W O B A G G E R
I N K E R   U R D U   E L L E
B O S S   B Y E S   S I L K
```

7

```
P A P A   L E A S H   I S N T
I L L S   A L B E E   S T I R
C L A S S C L O W N   L U N A
T E N E T   A M E N   A D A M
S N O R E D   B R A W N Y
    T R O T   A D H O C
L A D S   N O S H E R   A D O
I C E   A N A T O M Y   L I T
A L A   N A T U R E   K L E E
R U N O N   A N D A
    S C A R F S   D E R A I L
L O L A   I O U S   L A S S O
A V I S   G Y M T E A C H E R
L E S E   O L M O S   H E R R
A R T Y   R E A P S   I S E E
```

8

```
A B E T   T A M P A   O L L A
L A V A   E M I L Y   N E A R
T R I X   N O L A N   B A T E
O N L I B E R T Y   O R R I N
      E T A   M A D O N N A
S P O O N   L U A N D A
H O R N E T   S T A   D R A B
A L L Y   E T H E R   W I L E
Y O Y O   M A E   M E A N I E
    U M P I R E   T Y K E S
Q U A R R E L   S T U
U N I T S   O N T H I N I C E
I T S O   B R A H E   O N L Y
T I L E   R E N E S   S T A R
O L E S   A D O R E   H O P E
```

9

```
H A S H   B L O T   S H R E W
A G H A   L O A N   T O O T H
P R I N C E O F T H E C I T Y
P E R S I A N S   A N K L E S
Y E T   C R Y   T W O S
    P A Y   B E A S   C A B
S T E E D   A L A I   S O S O
A S T R A N G E R I N T O W N
L A N K   E E N Y   O A K E N
E R A   S E N D   B R R
S O D A   R A M   L A S
P O S T A L   C I A A G E N T
I T T A K E S A V I L L A G E
S T O L E   O P E N   I S L E
H O P E D   B E R G   B E E P
```

10

```
  S E M   D I S C   E A R N S
G E R E   I S L E   U B O A T
A U R A   M E A D   G E T T Y
F R A N K I E V A L E T
F A N T A N   R A N   U G H
E T D   P I C T   D E B B I E
  P U S H E S   R E L Y
M A R T H A S T E W A R D
S A L E   S T A T I C
P I M P L E   A B C S   S R I
A D A   I L E   H E S T E R
    A L I S T A I R C O O K
U H U R A   S I N N   R O P E
M U S I C   A G O G   A G E D
A R E A S   Y E N S   P E N
```

11

T	O	R	E		A	R	B	O	R		S	A	N	S
A	P	E	S		D	I	A	N	A		C	L	A	P
B	E	S	T	W	I	S	H	E	S		A	L	M	A
O	R	E		O	D	E	S		C	A	L	M	E	R
O	A	T	B	R	A	N		C	A	G	E	Y		
		E	M	S		C	O	L	E	S	L	A	W	
C	A	S	A	S		G	A	Y	L	E		O	L	E
A	R	I	D		C	O	N	E	Y		I	V	A	N
P	E	N		G	A	T	O	R		B	R	E	S	T
P	A	C	K	I	T	I	N		P	E	A			
	E	I	G	H	T		H	U	G	S	A	N	D	
P	E	R	S	I	A		S	A	R	A		Z	O	O
A	L	E	S		Y	O	U	R	S	T	R	U	L	Y
R	I	L	E		A	D	I	E	U		O	R	A	L
K	E	Y	S		N	O	T	M	E		B	E	N	E

12

A	D	E	P	T		S	T	O	A	S		A	L	B
R	O	M	E	O		H	E	A	R	T		Z	O	O
C	L	I	N	T	W	A	L	K	E	R		T	U	X
H	E	R	N	I	A		L	E	N	A		E	S	E
	I	N	D	I	A	N	A	P	A	C	E	R		
S	T	E		G	E	M		S	P	A				
H	U	E	S		D	A	N	A		E	R	R	O	L
I	N	L	A	W		G	A	L		D	O	O	N	E
P	A	S	H	A		E	G	O	S		N	O	T	E
	I	T	S		F	I	R		F	O	R			
G	L	O	B	E	T	R	O	T	T	E	R			
L	A	X		R	E	E	L		A	T	E	A	S	E
A	M	I		B	L	A	D	E	R	U	N	N	E	R
Z	E	D		E	L	C	I	D		R	E	T	R	O
E	R	E		D	A	T	E	S		N	E	S	T	S

13

A	N	O	N		S	A	L	T		S	W	I	S	S
L	E	N	O		W	E	A	R		P	A	S	T	A
T	H	E	G	O	O	D	H	U	M	O	R	M	A	N
O	R	O		D	O	E	R		A	I	D	E	R	S
S	U	N	L	E	S	S		P	Y	L	E			
		A	S	H		G	L	A	S	N	O	S	T	
I	T	E	M	S		I	R	O	N		L	I	E	
T	H	E	B	A	D	N	E	W	S	B	E	A	R	S
C	O	L		R	A	G	S		A	B	Y	S	S	
H	U	S	T	L	I	N	G		B	I	B			
	H	A	V	E		A	L	L	S	T	A	R		
A	S	H	O	R	E		F	R	E	E		A	B	E
T	H	E	U	G	L	Y	A	M	E	R	I	C	A	N
N	O	R	G	E		A	C	E	D		T	E	T	E
O	P	A	H	S		W	E	D	S		S	T	E	W

14

O	L	A	N	D		Q	E	D		B	A	J	E	R
B	O	R	E	R		U	S	A		E	N	E	M	Y
J	U	M	B	O	J	E	T	S		A	D	A	T	E
	G	A	E	A		S	T	E	N					
S	O	J	O	U	R	N		V	I	S	A	V	I	S
A	C	U	T	E	S		M	A	R	I	N	A	D	E
S	E	M	I	S		C	A	P	E	T		L	E	A
S	A	P	S		J	A	S	O	N		A	J	A	B
I	N	I		S	E	N	O	R		C	R	E	T	E
E	I	N	S	T	E	I	N		T	O	G	A	E	D
R	A	G	T	O	P	S		S	E	C	O	N	D	S
			J	U	G	S		P	E	N	H			
A	B	A	C	I		J	O	L	T	I	N	J	O	E
B	O	C	C	E		R	P	M		S	H	E	I	K
M	A	K	O	S		S	E	A		E	L	U	D	E

15

A	F	R	O		S	T	A	R	R		A	B	B	A
S	L	E	D		L	E	V	E	E		L	A	I	R
H	E	A	D	T	O	H	E	A	D		M	C	L	I
E	E	L		A	P	E	R		E	V	O	K	E	D
		E	P	E	E		B	E	A	S	T			
A	L	F	R	E	D		S	E	M	I	T	O	N	E
M	E	A	N	S		H	O	V	E	L		B	I	N
I	N	C	A		S	A	N	E	R		T	A	C	T
S	T	E		R	I	V	A	L		C	A	C	H	E
H	O	T	C	I	D	E	R		H	A	N	K	E	R
	O	A	T	E	S		B	A	R	K				
R	I	F	L	E	S		G	A	L	L		T	A	E
S	L	A	M		H	A	N	D	T	O	H	A	N	D
V	I	C	E		O	S	A	G	E		O	B	O	E
P	E	E	R		W	A	T	E	R		G	U	N	N

16

L	E	A	P		A	T	T	I	C		B	A	B	A
I	T	E	R		C	H	I	N	O		E	M	I	R
A	C	R	E		H	E	L	L	O		A	I	R	E
R	H	O	D	E	I	S	L	A	N	D	R	E	D	S
	A	L	E	E		S	O	U						
H	A	T	T	E	R		B	I	K	E	P	A	T	H
A	P	R	O	N		S	E	M	I		L	O	Y	
F	L	O	R	I	D	A	S	U	N	S	H	I	N	E
T	E	L		I	S	T	S		C	O	N	A	N	
S	A	L	T	I	N	E	S		P	A	M	E	L	A
	U	N	O		R	O	L	E						
T	E	N	N	E	S	S	E	E	W	A	L	K	E	R
R	Y	A	N		A	I	S	L	E		A	N	T	I
A	R	N	E		U	P	P	E	R		N	E	A	P
M	E	A	L		R	E	S	T	S		D	E	L	E

17

B	E	T	A		H	A	C	K		C	A	C	T	I
A	M	A	S		O	B	I	E		O	C	H	E	R
R	E	B	A		L	O	S	E		S	T	O	R	E
C	R	O	P	C	I	R	C	L	E	S		P	I	S
A	G	O		A	S	T	O		L	A	M	S		
R	E	S	O	R	T		A	L	C	O	H	O	L	
		N	A	I	L	E	D		K	R	O	N	E	
P	A	C	T		C	U	T	I	N		A	P	E	D
E	L	L	A	S		V	E	N	O	M	S			
S	L	I	P	U	P	S		B	A	S	T	E	R	
P	E	P	E		S	P	O	T		R	A	E		
E	N	C		P	R	U	N	E	D	A	N	I	S	H
V	A	L	S	E		L	A	N	I		E	S	T	E
I	N	O	U	R		N	I	N	E		S	H	E	A
L	O	P	E	S		A	L	E	S		T	A	R	T

18

L	A	T	H	E		A	R	O	M	A		B	A	S
A	R	I	E	L		D	O	R	A	L		R	N	A
D	R	O	P	T	H	E	B	A	L	L		E	A	T
			R	O	L	E		R	E	T	A	K	E	N
A	P	P	E	A	S	E		R	E	T	A	K	E	N
M	E	A	N	I	E		H	O	B	A	R	T		
O	R	S	O	N		T	A	T	A	R		H	B	O
R	O	S	S		B	A	R	O	N		B	E	A	N
E	N	T		G	A	P	E	R		B	R	I	C	E
		H	A	R	L	E	M		B	E	A	C	O	N
A	T	E	L	I	E	R		B	A	R	T	E	N	D
L	O	B	E	S			B	A	T	S				
E	M	U		T	A	K	E	T	H	E	C	A	K	E
R	E	C		L	I	E	T	O		R	U	N	A	T
T	S	K		E	D	G	A	R		K	E	N	Y	A

19

A	T	R	I	A		C	O	U	P		A	R	C	H
N	O	O	N	S		E	A	S	E		C	O	L	O
K	N	O	C	K	E	D	F	O	R	A	L	O	O	P
A	S	T	A	I	R	E	S		R	U	S	S	O	
			N	E	D		F	A	G		T	E	N	
G	U	L	A	G			A	L	L	Y				
A	R	A	B		S	A	M	U	E	L		A	P	E
D	I	S	C	O	M	B	O	B	U	L	A	T	E	D
S	S	T		R	O	B	U	S	T		T	O	R	I
		I	G	O	R		K	A	P	U	T			
W	A	S		E	S	T		I	R	A				
A	G	A	I	N		S	T	A	R	T	R	E	K	
F	R	U	S	T	R	A	T	E	D	N	O	E	N	D
T	E	N	N		A	T	O	M		A	T	A	C	K
S	E	A	T		P	E	W	S		K	O	R	E	A

20

Z	I	P	S		P	I	L	E	D		T	A	M	S
O	M	I	T		E	N	E	R	O		I	L	I	E
L	O	T	U	S	E	A	T	E	R		C	O	R	E
A	N	T		E	D	N	A		M	A	T	T	E	D
			T	R	E	E		I	O	N	A			
N	U	M	B	E	R	C	R	U	N	C	H	E	R	
P	O	R	E	S		H	O	S	E		A	L	Y	
C	H	A	N		A	L	I	N	E		N	U	D	E
T	O	N		E	B	A	N		P	E	T	E	S	
S	W	O	R	D	S	W	A	L	L	O	W	E	R	
			E	G	O	S		A	U	N	T			
F	E	E	D	E	R		C	O	L	T		S	M	U
L	A	T	H		B	O	O	T	L	I	C	K	E	R
A	R	N	O		E	R	A	S	E		A	Y	E	S
P	S	A	T		D	A	T	E	D		B	E	T	A

21

W	A	N	T		O	M	A	H	A		T	O	U	T
A	R	E	A		R	O	S	A	S		W	I	S	E
D	I	A	L		P	R	A	T	T		E	L	A	N
E	A	R	L	T	H	E	P	E	A	R	L			
			O	A	S		E	V	A	D	E			
C	A	V	E	R	N		A	T	H	L	E	T	E	S
A	V	E	R	S		A	T	E	E		T	I	S	
D	E	N	N	I	S	T	H	E	M	E	N	A	C	E
E	N	D		E	T	O	N		C	H	I	E	N	
T	U	E	S	D	A	Y	S		G	R	A	N	D	E
S	E	E	T	O		S	O	U						
		W	I	L	T	T	H	E	S	T	I	L	T	
Y	O	G	I		A	H	O	O	T		O	D	O	R
A	P	O	S		S	A	R	A	H		A	L	O	E
K	E	P	T		S	T	O	L	E		D	Y	N	E

22

E	W	E	R	S		S	C	R	A	P		B	E	G
L	A	M	A	R		E	L	O	P	E		R	N	A
E	Y	E	S	O	F	L	A	U	R	A		M	A	R	S
C	O	R	P		H	E	R	E		N	O	N	O	S
T	U	G		B	A	S	K		S	U	B	D	U	E
S	T	E	A	L		J	E	T		I	T	S		
		H	O	U	S	T	O	N		A	S	E		
	D	O	W	N	T	O	E	A	R	T	H			
S	O	Y		T	I	N	Y	T	I	M				
T	E	N		F	I	R		T	E	M	P	I		
A	V	E	N	U	E		U	S	D	A		E	E	R
C	E	D	A	R		E	S	T	E		H	A	R	I
O	N	E	T	O	U	C	H	O	F	V	E	N	U	S
M	T	A		R	A	T	E	R		A	R	I	S	E
A	O	L		S	W	O	R	E		T	R	E	E	S

23

C	A	P	E		B	O	M	B	E		S	P	E	C
A	R	L	O		E	L	I	O	T		L	E	V	I
G	O	O	S	E	F	L	E	S	H		E	T	A	T
E	N	D		L	O	I	N	S		S	W	E	D	E
		S	A	G	E		I	G	N	O	R	E		
M	A	C	O	N		S	H	E	R	I	F	F		
A	V	O	I	D	S		I	S	I	T		I	E	R
M	I	L	L		P	A	R	T	S		O	N	C	E
A	D	D		B	A	L	E		T	O	U	C	H	E
		T	O	O	T	E	R	S		A	T	H	O	S
		M	U	S	T	E	R		P	C	T	S		
P	E	R	C	H		T	A	H	O	E		T	H	O
I	L	K	A		P	I	G	E	O	N	T	O	E	D
U	B	E	R		I	N	E	R	T		E	L	L	A
S	A	Y	S		A	G	R	E	E		A	L	L	Y

24

L	E	C	H		S	T	R	A	D		M	A	I	N
A	S	H	E		C	O	U	P	E		O	S	L	O
S	T	A	Y		A	B	L	E	B	O	D	I	E	D
E	E	R		A	L	E	E		A	R	E			
R	E	L	A	Y	E	D		A	C	E	R	B	I	C
		I	C	E	R		F	U	L	L	N	A	M	E
S	L	E	D		S	L	I	D	E	S		K	I	N
C	I	R	C	A		I	F	I		E	V	E	N	T
A	L	I		U	P	S	E	T	S		I	R	E	S
B	A	C	K	R	O	A	D		A	I	D	S		
S	C	H	O	O	L	S		J	U	J	I	T	S	U
		W	R	Y		P	O	R	K		R	O	N	
D	E	L	T	A	B	U	R	K	E		M	E	L	D
O	L	E	O		U	R	I	E	L		P	E	T	E
C	L	A	W		S	U	E	R	S		S	T	I	R

25

C	A	C	T	I		T	R	A	D	E		A	B	S
A	L	I	E	N		R	U	L	E	R		T	A	P
B	L	O	C	K	B	U	S	T	E	R		O	B	I
			N	A	S	H		A	D	M	A	N		
B	A	B	O	O	N	S		M	A	T	I	S	S	E
A	D	A	P	T	S		S	A	D	I	S	M		
S	E	C	T	S		A	T	T	I	C		A	R	C
E	L	K	S		S	I	R	E	N		I	S	E	E
D	A	B		M	A	L	A	Y		S	C	H	E	D
		R	O	O	N	E	Y		C	H	E	E	S	E
C	L	E	A	V	E	D		C	H	A	R	R	E	D
L	E	A	S	E		P	O	E	M					
I	N	K		S	A	F	E	C	R	A	C	K	E	R
O	N	E		U	M	I	A	K		N	O	O	S	E
S	Y	R		P	I	N	K	Y		S	O	P	P	Y

26

G	A	S		G	A	P	S		A	R	C	A	D	E
A	C	T		A	R	E	A		P	A	U	S	E	S
G	R	E	E	N	M	E	N		O	L	D	H	A	T
A	I	L	E	D		P	E	A	L	E		E	R	E
D	A	C	H	A		F	L	I	P					
		I	N	D	I	G	O	G	I	R	L	S		
S	L	A	P		D	I	S	H		H	O	O	E	Y
L	O	N	I		I	S	A	A	C		U	M	A	S
O	C	T	E	T		M	I	N	E		S	E	P	T
		W	H	I	T	E	L	A	D	I	E	S		
C	A	D		E	A	S	E	S		R	O	B	O	T
A	B	O	A	R	D		B	L	U	E	B	O	Y	S
S	U	N	D	A	E		B	I	K	E		N	E	A
A	T	T	E	N	D		S	T	E	S		E	R	R

27

P	A	S	T	A		R	T	E	S		T	S	A	R
A	C	E	R	B		E	I	R	E		I	T	T	O
S	E	M	I	S		S	N	A	I	L	M	A	I	L
T	R	A	V	E	S	T	Y		N	I	B	B	L	E
		P	I	N	E	S		R	E	T	E	S	T	S
I	T	H	A	C	A		S	E	D	E	R			
O	R	O		E	T	H	I	C		R	E	M	E	T
N	E	R	D		S	A	L	U	T		D	O	R	A
S	K	E	I	N		T	A	T	E	R		R	S	T
		S	I	D	E	S		N	O	I	S	E	S	
C	H	A	R	T	E	D		D	O	O	N	E		
A	U	B	U	R	N		S	U	R	F	A	C	E	S
G	R	A	P	E	V	I	N	E		E	R	O	D	E
E	R	S	T		E	D	I	T		R	O	D	I	N
D	Y	E	S		R	O	T	O		S	W	E	E	T

28

J	A	R		I	N	E	R	T		V	O	G	U	E
E	V	E		C	E	S	A	R		I	R	A	T	E
T	I	P	P	E	D	T	H	E	S	C	A	L	E	S
S	A	L	A	D	S		A	T	A	L	L			
E	T	A	L		U	D	D	E	R		E	P	A	
T	E	N		W	I	S	E	S	T		F	R	A	Y
		S	O	R	E	S		A	L	I	C	E		
R	O	C	K	E	D	T	H	E	B	O	A	T		
S	O	F	A	S		R	E	N	E	W				
R	I	F	T		C	L	O	S	E	D		P	C	S
O	L	E		S	L	A	Y	S		A	L	O	E	
		R	I	P	U	P		M	O	D	E	R	N	
S	P	I	L	L	E	D	T	H	E	B	E	A	N	S
T	I	N	E	A		O	R	A	T	E		T	E	E
A	N	G	S	T		G	Y	P	S	Y		S	A	N

29

```
F A C T | P A R A | S P A R K
A L O E | E V E R | H E M A N
I A N S | D O D O | A Z U R E
L I T T L E W O M E N | S E E
| R Y E S | A R G U E R S |
J A I | S T E P | A H S | |
A L V A | A L A S | A I S L E
W E E W I L L I E W I N K I E
S E D A N | A R C H | G I R L
| I V E | S T O W | N A Y |
T E X T I L E | D E A F | |
I M A | T I N Y B U B B L E S
P I X I E | R U I N | B I D E
S L I C E | O M N I | I N I T
Y E S E S | L A S T | E T T A
```

30

```
J A G S | B A S I S | C E D E
O G R E | E R I C A | A X E L
I R O N M A I D E N | S P A M
S E P T E T | E D I T I O N S
T E E | N I A | T A N S | |
| | P U T T E R A R O U N D
A D D I S | T R U R O | R O Y
L I O N | D E R B Y | F E T E
P E W | M A N O R | R O S E S
S U N D A Y D R I V E R | |
| | G O L D | C I A | E S C
S O R C E R E R | S C A M P I
T H A T | E L I J A H W O O D
U N D O | A L O N G | E T R E
B O E R | M E T R E | S E E R
```

31

```
D E L I | E L L A S | A F E W
E L O N | M E A D E | C O L A
J A C K S O N K E N T U C K Y
A N I S E T T E | A M I E S |
| | T I E | S A X E | | |
M A D I S O N I L L I N O I S
I R O N O N | D O A | | K O A
M O R A N | Z I P | A P I N G
I L S | M A O | A S O N I A |
C L I N T O N M I C H I G A N
| | O H M Y | L E I | | |
A L O N E | N O T E P A D S
J E F F E R S O N O R E G O N
A N N A | P A G A N | A U R A
R O O T | M O O S E | L A M P
```

32

```
G O A L S | B A E R | T H U S
R I V E T | O U S E | W A N E
A L O N E | C L A D | I B I D
D Y N A M I C D U O | N I T E
| | M R E | L I T T E R |
A N D E S | A C E T O | | |
C R E E D | S L A N T W I S E
O A H U | G R I S T | E N T O
S P I C E R A C K | U R G E S
| | E R A S E | I N S E T |
L A R S E N | U L M | | |
A V O W | D O U B L E P L A Y
K I W I | A R N O | A L E V E
E L A L | M A T A | N O V E L
S A N D | S L O T | T W I R L
```

33

```
F D I C | B A R D S | A S P S
L U N A | U B O A T | N E A L
E R I C | R O U S E | T R I O
D O T H E R I G H T T H I N G
| | E C O L E | H E F T S |
A L E P H | | W H A M | | |
D A D O O R O N R O N | A L P
A S I T | O N A I R | I D E A
M E T | M O U N T A I N D E W
| | C O T S | B A S K S |
S L O A N | A S P I C | | |
P O S T A G E D U E S T A M P
O N C E | N A M E R | I C E R
R E A R | A V E R S | V I N E
E R R S | T E N S E | E D D Y
```

34

```
P I E S | T E M P E | C H E R
A N A T | E V E R Y | R A T E
S P R Y | R E N E E | I R A N
T U T | V E N U S D E M I L O
A T H E I S T | | R A E | |
| | A N N A | C R O S S S E A
M O N D E | E R U P T | A R C
E G G S | A R I E S | S T A R
A G E | A B I E S | M O U S E
L I L A B N E R | C A R R |
| | C O O | B A N A N A S |
M E R C U R Y L Y N X | N R A
O L E O | M A I N E | D I E T
O M A R | A L T E R | A N N O
G O L D | L E E R S | D E A N
```

35

C	A	R	L		S	H	O	A	L		A	U	N	T
A	B	I	E		E	A	R	L	E		G	N	A	W
S	U	G	G	E	S	T	I	V	E		O	B	I	E
S	T	A	I	R	S		O	A	R	S		A	V	E
			O	N	I	O	N		E	A	G	L	E	T
	B	U	N	I	O	N		E	D	I	N	A		
D	A	N		E	N	E	M	Y		D	U	N	C	E
E	S	P	Y		S	W	E	E	T		S	C	O	W
B	E	R	E	T		A	L	L	E	S		E	T	E
		E	A	R	L	Y		E	L	A	N	D	S	
S	O	P	H	I	A		S	T	E	V	E			
A	L	A		P	U	P	U		F	E	E	L	E	R
F	I	R	E		D	I	S	C	O	R	D	A	N	T
E	V	E	N		E	T	H	A	N		L	I	T	E
R	E	D	D		R	H	I	N	O		E	N	O	S

36

C	M	O	N		E	L	L	A		S	A	C	R	E
R	O	P	E		D	U	E	T		A	C	R	E	S
A	N	E	W		M	A	S	T		M	E	A	N	T
M	A	D	A	B	O	U	T	Y	O	U		C	E	E
			R	O	N		S	T	R	I	K	E	S	
B	A	C	K	S	T	O	P		C	A	N	E		
O	U	R		C	O	M	A	S		I	N	D	I	A
A	R	A	B		N	I	N	E	S		S	I	B	S
R	A	Z	E	S		T	E	P	E	E		C	A	P
		Y	A	N	G		S	T	A	R	T	E	R	S
	S	E	Q	U	I	N	S		C	I	O			
A	S	U		C	U	C	K	O	O	C	L	O	C	K
S	T	I	C	K		A	L	K	A		E	L	L	E
H	A	L	L	E		M	E	L	S		D	E	A	N
A	S	T	I	R		P	E	A	T		O	O	P	S

37

A	L	A	S		T	R	E	N	T		D	R	A	B
R	O	S	A		R	U	L	E	R		A	O	N	E
M	A	I	N		E	N	L	A	I		N	O	T	E
	D	A	D	D	Y	W	A	R	B	U	C	K	S	
			W	A	S	A		E	S	E				
R	E	S	I	N		Y	O	M		E	R	N	I	E
E	R	E	C	T	S		T	A	P		O	N	S	
F	A	T	H	E	R	C	H	R	I	S	T	M	A	S
	I	T	T		O	R	E		E	T	H	A	N	E
T	O	O	T	S		I	R	S		A	R	D	E	N
			O	P	S		H	U	G	O				
	P	A	P	A	H	E	M	I	N	G	W	A	Y	
T	A	M	P		A	V	A	I	L		O	N	E	S
L	I	M	E		C	A	R	T	E		U	T	A	H
C	L	O	D		K	N	E	E	D		T	I	R	E

38

S	W	A	G	S		S	C	U	P		C	R	O	C
A	P	L	E	A		E	R	N	E		H	E	R	O
M	A	L	T	L	I	Q	U	O	R		I	T	E	M
	U	N	T	R	U	E		M	E	N	A	G	E	
D	E	V	O		M	E	L	T	I	N	G	P	O	T
A	R	I		B	A	L		O	T	T		E	N	O
G	A	U	Z	E		E	M	M	E	T				
		M	I	L	T	O	N	B	E	R	L	E		
				P	A	R	E	D		E	C	L	A	T
I	R	E		T	A	I		A	D	D		O	L	E
M	O	L	T	E	N	L	A	V	A		U	N	I	T
	B	O	U	N	D	S		B	A	L	I	N	G	
I	N	D	O		M	U	L	T	I	G	R	A	I	N
B	E	E	T		I	D	E	A		O	U	T	R	E
E	Y	R	E		T	E	R	R		R	H	E	T	T

39

S	A	L	A	D		B	A	S	K		N	E	S	T
I	M	A	G	E		A	N	T	I		O	V	E	R
N	A	V	A	L		A	G	E	S		M	O	V	E
		P	U	L	L	U	P	S	T	A	K	E	S	
S	E	C	E	D	E		S	P	E	E	D	E	R	S
H	M	O		E	T	C		E	R	A				
A	C	N	E		G	A	S		C	A	F	F	E	
H	E	A	D	F	O	R	T	H	E	H	I	L	L	S
	S	E	N	S	E		Y	E	N		M	O	A	T
			T	S	P		P	I	E		O	R	E	
P	R	E	A	C	H	E	D		A	S	I	D	E	S
	H	I	T	T	H	E	B	R	I	C	K	S		
O	P	A	L		I	B	I	S		I	L	I	A	D
T	O	G	A		K	L	E	E		M	E	N	S	A
O	N	E	S		S	E	R	E		O	S	C	A	R

40

C	H	I	C		M	I	N	U	S		D	O	T	
H	A	L	O		A	T	O	N	E	S		E	V	E
E	L	K	S		N	E	T	H	E	R		T	A	X
F	E	A	S	T	O	R	F	A	M	I	N	E		
			E	A	R		A	M	S		O	R	A	L
G	E	S	T	E		S	I	P		T	E	R	R	A
R	A	H	S		M	O	R	E	O	R	L	E	S	S
I	T	O		M	O	M		R	A	Y		N	O	S
N	O	W	O	R	N	E	V	E	R		A	C	N	E
D	U	C	T	S		W	E	D		P	R	E	S	S
S	T	A	T		S	H	E		U	A	R			
	S	O	O	N	E	R	O	R	L	A	T	E	R	
L	E	I		R	A	R	I	N	G		Y	A	L	E
O	W	N		G	R	E	E	C	E		E	C	O	N
B	E	G		E	S	S	E	S		D	O	N	T	

41

G	T	O		A	B	R	I	L		R	A	J	A	H
R	A	P		W	E	A	R	Y		E	R	O	S	E
E	L	I	A	K	A	Z	A	N		D	I	N	T	Y
C	O	N	N		G	E	E	N	A	D	A	V	I	S
O	N	E	I	L	L			N	O	N	O			
			L	E	E	G	R	A	N	T		I	S	M
T	A	P	I	N		L	A	L	A		O	G	L	E
R	I	A	N	T		E	N	O		I	N	H	O	T
A	D	U	E		B	A	C	H		L	E	T	G	O
M	A	L		T	O	M	H	A	N	K	S			
		L	O	A	N			O	A	T	E	R	S	
P	A	U	L	N	E	W	M	A	N		A	R	E	A
A	S	K	I	N		A	R	T	C	A	R	N	E	Y
L	E	A	V	E		D	E	M	O	N		I	V	E
L	A	S	E	R		E	D	E	M	A		E	E	R

42

T	A	X	I		S	P	A	C	E		H	U	M	E
O	X	E	N		O	R	S	O	N		A	Z	O	V
N	E	R	D		L	A	I	R	D		Y	I	P	E
G	L	O	O	M	A	N	D	D	O	O	M			
			L	O	C	K	E			A	O	R	T	A
S	T	P	E	T	E		A	W	K	W	A	R	D	
P	A	I	N	E		M	A	N	E			T	A	D
H	U	S	T	L	E	A	N	D	B	U	S	T	L	E
E	R	A		X	R	A	Y		P	A	L	E	R	
R	U	N	B	A	C	K		R	E	N	E	E	S	
E	S	S	E	S			B	L	I	N	D			
			S	H	A	K	E	A	N	D	B	A	K	E
C	H	A	T		B	E	L	T	S		A	V	I	D
A	U	T	O		C	N	O	T	E		N	O	T	I
P	H	E	W		S	O	W	E	D		K	N	E	E

43

B	O	N	U	S		O	M	A	N	I		C	S	A
A	V	A	N	T		F	I	X	E	R		R	U	B
B	U	T	T	E	R	F	L	I	E	S		E	E	L
E	L	A	I	N	E		E	O	S		L	A	Z	E
S	E	L	E	C	T	S		M	O	D	E	M		
			D	I	E	T	S		N	O	O	S	E	S
J	I	M		L	A	R	A	M		S	N	O	W	Y
A	R	I	D		R	O	B	I	N		A	D	E	N
V	A	L	E	T		H	I	M	O	M		A	R	E
A	N	K	L	E	T		N	I	L	E	S			
		M	E	D	O	C		C	O	N	T	O	U	R
Q	U	O	D		P	H	D		S	T	E	R	N	O
U	R	N		C	H	E	E	S	E	H	E	A	D	S
A	G	E		P	A	S	S	E		O	L	L	I	E
D	E	Y		A	T	T	I	C		L	E	E	D	S

44

B	R	E	W		M	O	B	Y			J	A	N	E
O	O	Z	E		O	B	I	E		S	I	L	A	S
U	A	R	E	O	N	E	Ⓑ	A	C	K	T	O	S	Q
T	R	A		N	E	S	S		U	I	N	T	A	S
			E	S	T	E		A	B	L	E			
B	L	I	M	P	S		R	A	I	L	Y	A	R	D
A	U	D	I	E		M	E	R	S			W	O	O
L	C	I	R	C	L	E	Ⓒ	O	M	E	S	F	U	L
E	R	O			A	S	O	N		L	O	U	S	E
D	E	M	I	J	O	H	N		M	E	W	L	E	D
			C	I	T	Y		R	E	V	S			
S	E	V	E	N	S		T	I	D	E		E	B	B
P	T	I	C	K	E	T	Ⓡ	O	U	N	D	T	R	I
A	T	L	A	S		O	U	T	S		E	N	I	D
S	E	E	P		M	E	S	A		Y	A	M	S	

45

C	O	I	F		A	S	K	E	D		C	E	D	E
R	U	S	E		S	C	I	F	I		O	X	E	N
I	C	E	R		T	A	L	O	S		D	E	S	I
T	H	E	M	I	R	R	O	R	C	R	A	C	K	D
			I	N	A				R	E	S			
O	D	E		S	L	A	N	T	E	D		S	A	C
F	O	R	G	E		F	I	A	T		O	H	I	O
F	I	N	E	T	O	O	T	H	E	D	C	O	M	B
O	L	I	N		A	R	E	O		O	T	T	E	R
N	Y	E		S	T	E	R	E	O	S		S	E	A
			D	O	C				V	E	T			
G	I	V	E	T	H	E	B	R	U	S	H	O	F	F
E	D	I	T		A	V	A	I	L		Y	E	A	R
N	O	S	E		F	I	L	L	E		M	I	N	E
T	S	A	R		F	L	E	E	S		E	L	S	E

46

A	B	B	E		C	A	R	A		M	I	L	L	E
W	E	A	K		U	P	O	N		A	D	A	I	R
A	L	B	E	R	T	S	O	N		N	E	W	E	R
R	O	B		H	I	E	D		D	E	A	R		
D	I	L	L	I	E	S		S	E	S	T	E	T	S
S	T	E	I	N			C	H	I		E	N	I	D
			K	E	R	O	U	A	C			C	P	A
B	A	N	E		A	D	O	R	E		D	E	S	K
E	L	I		D	E	M	P	S	E	Y				
T	A	C	T		I	T	O		R	A	M	B	O	
E	S	K	I	M	O	S		T	O	A	D	I	E	D
			L	E	A	S		F	A	S	T		A	T	E
E	M	A	I	L		N	I	C	H	O	L	S	O	N
G	A	U	N	T		O	D	I	E		A	M	O	S
G	A	S	S	Y		B	E	T	A		B	A	K	E

47

```
G O I N . R A S P . R A I S E
R U N E . A R L O . E X C E L
A C R E . F R O M . V I E W S
S H E D A F E W P O U N D S .
. . . F I T S . N E G . . . .
A M E L I A . I T S . P A D .
L O N E R . A F R O . B O N A
L O D G E A C O M P L A I N T
A R E S . S H E A . E R N I E
N E D . C H E . A G A T E S .
. . . A R E . D E S I . . . .
H O M E S R I G H T I N O N .
B I M B O . I A G O . F O R E
A R I E L . O N E R . F R A N
D E T R E . S A D E . Y A L E
```

48

```
F R I J O L E S . D A R T E R
E N S E N A D A . E N R O L L
M A R A T H O N . E D S E L S
. . . N O R M A N D Y . . . .
S C R I P . . B E S T B O Y .
T H E E . O U N C E . O A K S
L A B . S I T U . . A P R I L
. L I T T L E B I G H O R N .
B O R E D . I R A S . I A M .
A N T S . T S A R S . P E W S
. A S H T R A Y . S A R A S .
. . . Y O R K T O W N . . . .
Y E H U D I . A N T I E T A M
E R A S E S . N U R S L I N G
R E W A R M . S T A S S E N S
```

49

```
G A R B O . B A Y E D . N O W
A L I E N . O L I V E . A V A
T A B L E H O P P E R . M I X
. . G N A T S . N I C E N E .
S A T I E T Y . D I V I D E D
C R E A S E . L I N E A R . .
O M E N S . T A N G S . O R T
L O N S . S I Z E S . E P E E
D R Y . C O M E R . E X P O S
. . B L A M E D . F A C E I T
C R O O N E R . M I S E R L Y
. R I P S A W . T A S E R . .
A S P . S H O W S T O P P E R
V E E . T A P E S . U T T E R
E R R . A T S E A . T S A R S
```

50

```
A T O M . F O R M S . N A S A
D I V E . E L I S E . I N O N
D R A W B R I D G E A H E A D
S O L . L A V E . D M I T R I
. . . C O L E . U T I L . . .
A P A R T . S A T I N . G O B
S E T A T . S A M . I R A E .
K E E P O F F T H E G R A S S
. E L I S . I L E . R A D I O
D E N . E V E R S . A T E S T
. . . S T E W . H O T E . . .
S E D A N S . B I T E . G A L
P R I V A T E E N T R A N C E
E I N E . A G A T E . M A M A
D E A R . R O T O R . S T E P
```

51

```
S A H L . D I N G . S C A B S
O L E O . O R E O . C A R A T
B L A C K J A C K . A L I N E
. . . T O R O . K A R L . S T E
A S H . I S H . R E D H E A D
P A R I S . O A T S . I S M S
B O O M T O W N . P E T . . .
. . W H I T E K N I G H T . .
. . . O N E . H U N G E R E D
I C B M . L O S T . E R A T O
B L U E F L U . S O D . C A T
I A N . I O T A . N O A H . .
S I G M A . G R E E N B E A N
E R E C T . U L N A . B A L I
S E E M S . N O E L . A L I T
```

52

```
R B I S . C O L O N . R O M A
A L O E . O R A T E . U K E S
P U N C T U A T I O N M A R K
. E S T O P . S N A P P L E .
. . . M E T S . . S L I E R .
L I C I T . I N V I T E . . .
O R O N O . N E E R . P I P .
P A N A M A C A N A L C I T Y
E N E . S A K I . E A S E L .
. . . I R E N I C . A W A R E
. . A E T N A . N E I N . . .
T R O T T E D . S T E A K . .
I N T E S T I N A L O R G A N
L I E N . A N O D E . G O R E
T E S T . L O R D S . O G L E
```

53

C	H	E	R		D	E	B	T		D	R	U	G	S
L	A	L	O		I	T	E	R		E	E	R	I	E
O	L	I	N		V	A	L	E		P	A	I	N	T
G	O	O	D	W	I	L	L	S	H	O	P			
	S	T	O	O	D		I	S	I	S		A	R	I
			S	V	E	N		M	E	R	L	I	N	
O	P	S		E	N	A	C	T		A	I	D	A	
F	R	I	E	N	D	S	H	I	P	S	E	V	E	N
F	O	N	T		T	I	T	L	E		E	R	E	
E	X	C	E	S	S		O	A	R	S				
R	Y	E		H	E	I	R		T	I	L	E	D	
		P	E	A	C	E	O	F	F	I	C	E	R	
A	C	A	R	E		I	N	D	O		C	O	L	E
S	I	M	O	N		N	E	E	R		E	L	L	E
H	A	I	F	A		G	E	R	M		R	E	A	D

54

C	A	M	A	Y		A	L	E	U	T		M	A	R
O	H	A	R	E		B	I	L	K	O		I	C	E
P	A	N	T	S	P	O	C	K	E	T		S	H	A
			D	A	R	K			E	N	S	O	R	
D	I	L	B	E	R	T		J	I	B	B	O	O	M
U	V	U	L	A	S		B	A	T	A	A	N		
P	A	C	E	R		S	O	B	I	G		E	F	T
E	N	I	D		G	L	O	B	S		T	S	A	R
S	A	L		L	L	A	M	A		T	A	C	K	Y
		L	A	Y	U	P	S		V	E	N	U	E	S
P	R	E	L	I	M	S		D	E	S	S	E	R	T
	R	A	B	I	N			A	I	N	T			
O	V	A		G	I	M	M	E	A	B	R	E	A	K
B	E	L		T	R	A	I	T		A	D	D	L	E
E	L	L		O	K	I	E	S		N	A	T	T	Y

55

B	I	T	E		M	A	T	A		C	L	U	E	D
A	Q	U	A		A	M	O	R		L	A	N	A	I
A	S	T	R	O	K	E	O	F	G	E	N	I	U	S
		R	I	N	K		R	A	G					
O	L	D	H	A	N	D		P	O	V	E	R	T	Y
B	E	R	I	N	G		F	A	C	E		E	E	E
S	T	I	N	G		N	O	D	E		R	T	E	S
I	F	E	E	L	Y	O	U	R	P	A	I	N		
O	T	T	S		E	L	L	A		U	N	T	I	E
O	B	E		L	A	O	S		S	T	O	L	E	N
H	E	R	M	A	N	N		M	O	O	N	E	R	S
			E	S	T		S	E	L	F				
T	H	A	T	T	O	U	C	H	O	F	M	I	N	K
N	I	G	E	L		M	A	T	E		A	C	R	E
T	E	A	R	Y		A	T	A	D		S	H	A	Y

56

S	I	L	O		B	A	L	S	A		S	H	O	P
O	R	A	L		A	S	I	A	N		P	A	N	E
H	A	N	D	I	N	H	A	N	D		O	R	C	A
O	N	E		S	T	E	M		E	M	O	T	E	R
			A	L	E	S		C	R	A	F	T		
A	M	B	L	E	R		L	O	S	T	S	O	U	L
D	E	L	I	S		C	A	N	O	E		H	B	O
A	L	O	T		R	O	U	E	N		G	A	O	L
M	E	W		B	E	R	R	Y		C	O	R	A	L
N	E	B	R	A	S	K	A		C	H	A	T	T	Y
		Y	O	K	E	S		F	O	A	L			
E	M	B	L	E	M		A	L	L	I		S	O	B
V	I	L	A		B	L	U	E	O	N	B	L	U	E
I	R	O	N		L	A	D	E	N		I	O	T	A
L	E	W	D		E	D	I	T	S		T	E	S	T

57

M	E	S	S		S	C	A	L	P		S	H	A	M
O	T	T	O		T	A	B	O	O		T	A	X	I
C	H	I	C	K	E	N	O	U	T		U	Z	I	S
K	E	N		A	R	T	Y		A	R	N	E	S	S
S	L	E	A	Z	E			T	O	T				
			G	O	O	S	E	G	O	S	S	A	G	E
R	A	D	I	O		W	A	R	E	S		J	A	Y
E	B	A	N		D	I	V	A	S		D	A	Z	E
N	O	R		L	I	N	E	N		H	I	R	E	D
D	U	C	K	I	N	G	S	T	O	O	L			
			A	R	E			T	O	L	L	E	D	
C	A	C	H	E	T		E	S	T	E		A	V	A
A	L	O	U		T	U	R	K	E	Y	T	R	O	T
I	M	I	N		E	G	G	A	R		N	U	K	E
N	A	N	A		S	H	O	T	S		T	E	E	D

58

S	A	Y	S		A	W	A	C	S		A	R	I	D
U	T	A	H		Z	E	B	R	A		S	O	R	E
E	A	S	Y	S	T	R	E	E	T		S	C	A	N
T	R	I	N	I		E	T	T	A		U	K	E	S
		I	R	E	N	E		S	E	N	T	R	Y	
			S	E	A	M			H	E	R	B	S	
R	A	H	S		G	A	R	A	G	E		O	A	K
U	S	A		M	A	H	A	T	M	A		A	L	I
M	I	R		E	N	I	G	M	A		O	D	D	S
S	A	D	A	T			S	T	I	R				
	D	R	A	M	A	S			S	M	A	S	H	
H	A	R	I		A	L	A	W		O	C	C	U	R
A	S	I	S		N	A	T	H	A	N	H	A	L	E
H	A	V	E		I	N	E	E	D		E	L	A	N
A	P	E	S		C	A	S	T	S		S	E	N	D

59

```
B R A C E · I S I S · S C A M
A E R O S · N O T E · H A L E
O N T O P O F T H E W O R L D
B A I L · P A T E · A R I A ·
A T E · A T N O · E V E L Y N
B A S E H I T · I C Y · L I U
· · · L E M · A R C · W O N T
· S U M M I T M E E T I N G ·
O H N O · S I T · N I L · · ·
P O D · C T S · S T R E A M S
S W E L L S · G O R E · M A T
· T R E E · T A V I · U P T O
T I P O F T H E I C E B E R G
I M I N · H O L E · L E R O I
N E N E · O U S T · I R E N E
```

60

```
C U B E · S L A S H · P I P E
A P E X · M A I N E · O V I D
P O R T L A N D O R · C A N I
E N G · U R G E · O R A N G E
· · · A R T E · I C E T · · ·
S M I L E Y · P R O C E S S
W I L L S · G O O P · L E M A
A L O E · N O O N S · L O A N
T E N N · O N L Y · C O U L D
R A T I N G S · R E I L L Y
· · · O N U S · W A R D · · ·
A V O W E R · A A R E · W O E
N E O N · B E T H E S D A M D
C A P P · A L T O S · O R I G
E L S A · N O N O T · A N T E
```

61

```
R I O T · S M O G · C A F E S
O S H A · P I M A · A D O R E
S N I T · A R N O · M A R N E
H O O T E R V I L L E · T I M
· · · O A T · S C R I B E S
D E C O R A T E · D A D A ·
A P O · S N E L L · S A X O N
M I C H · S A G A S · S T L O
S C O O P · L A M P S · E D S
· A L E S · R E H E A R S E
A L B E R T A · A L L · · ·
D I E · S P R I N G F I E L D
A L A M O · I T O N · E T U I
M A C O N · E C R U · N C A A
S C H W A · S H A M · S H U N
```

62

```
B A C K · B A B U · T I M O R
A L E E · I R I S · I M A G E
H O L Y R O M A N E M P I R E
N E T · O L E S · D O O M E D
· · · B U O Y · B I T S · · ·
D O I N G · B A C H E L O R
M I N G D Y N A S T Y · U T A
O P E D · O N S · A C T I
O S T · O L D D O M I N I O N
G O O D B Y E S · A N T E S
· · · A V I S · A R C S · · ·
S I N G I N · A S T A · E R A
T H E M A G I C K I N G D O M
A I M A T · T H E N · B I L E
S T O R E · S E W S · S T Y X
```

63

```
S P C A · H E L I · A S S E T
K A H N · O X E N · N E A T O
E G A D · R I T A · D E L T A
T O N Y O R L A N D O · B A D
C D E · D I E T · I R M A ·
H A L F O F · S T R A N G E
· · A R I S T A · A R D E N
P A C T · C A N D O · G O O D
S T O I C · S T A B L E · ·
C O M M U T E · D E S P O T
· M A R E · A G U A · E L O
D N A · S A N F E R N A N D O
R O N D O · O O N A · S C A T
A N D O R · S U I T · T I G E
B O O T Y · E L I E · I L E D
```

64

```
S A H I B · F L A B · R O A M
E L I S E · R O B E · O N C E
P A P E R T I G E R · C E D E
A M P E R A G E · A C K A C K
L O O · I I I · E T C H · · ·
· · · E L D · R I C O T T A
C A N I S · P I N · U R A L
O W A R · S L A N G · N I K E
M O T O · C A D · E D G E S
B L E N D I N · S P A · · ·
· · · H O E D · T O R · O P S
D I S O W N · D A M N A B L E
O D O R · C L A Y P I G E O N
T E N S · E A V E · N E S T S
S A G E · S P E D · G E E S E
```

65

```
A S C A P   M I D A S   F T C
R O O N E   A D O L L   O R O
C H A T T A N O O G A   R I B
H O T O R C O L D   M E T E R
        N E E R   O D E S S A
V I G I L S   S U N U N U
A R E A   M O R O N   M S G
L I T   A S A L A R K   T O E
E S T   L O C A L   S E A M
      Y E L L E R   S C A R P S
P A S T E D   P E R M
A M B O Y   E M O T I O N A L
L O U   C H I C K A M A U G A
E U R   A E R I E   E N N U I
O R G   T H E I R   A S S A D
```

66

```
O F F E R   H O P I   D O Z E
C R E T E   A V O N   E M I L
H E R E S   G E N T   V A N S
O D D   T O U R D E F O R C E
      E C O L E   R U T
M I L O R D   G I N S E N G
I R A T E   W A L E S   O A S
D O N E   C A S E D   O M I T
I N C   G R A S S   P A D U A
S E C R E C Y   A R R E S T
      A I D   C R I S P
C O U P D E G R A C E   L O T
A N N O   N O I R   S A U T E
R E I N   Z E S T   T I M O N
A R T S   A S E A   S L E E T
```

67

```
C O M A S   A K A   A T T A R
A V A N T   R O B   S H O V E
T E D D Y   C R O S S E Y E D
S N A R L   H E A L T H
    B E E   W A R Y   A J A R
S C O W   L A N D   G O R E
T A U   J A Y S   A D U L T S
E N T R A P S   S T E E L I E
P A Y E R S   Z I N C   Y E T
I D O S   L E G O   E R R S
N A U T   S O P H   P R O
    A L I G H T   R O G E T
H A P P Y D A Y S   A D E L E
E X I L E   N R A   T E R S E
P E T E S   S S W   E S S E N
```

68

```
L A R V A   D A N G   M O P
E L I O T   U S E R S   O V A
M I N U T E S T E A K   P E W
        S A N T A   T I G E R S
S O L   C R Y   H E R O D
T R A S H Y   S O F T B A L L
R A M I E   M I N U S   R A E
A C E D   P I X E L   I O T A
I L E   B O N E S   B R U I N
T E X T I L E S   G L E N N E
    C A C A O   S O U   D A R
P A U P E R   B A S E S
A M S   P O L I S H J O K E S
P I E   S I E G E   A R E A S
A D S   D A D S   Y E A R N
```

69

```
A H E M   S W O R D   G E N A
N O V A   P A T T I   U P O N
T W I N C I T I E S   N E E D
E L L I O T T S   S A G E L Y
        F E E   G O S H
  H O O D   F U L L H O U S E
S A U L S   O L I V E   N A G
H I N D   D O N N E   D I V A
A K C   G E T A T   M E T E D
Q U E E N B E E S   I C E D
      L A U D   A N A
D I S O W N   S O R E N E S S
A S A P   K I N G C O T T O N
Z A N E   E M I L E   E R M A
E Y E D   D A T E D   D E E P
```

70

```
C L U B   C A G E R   H O B O
H O N E   A L O N E   O V E R
E D I T   R O B I N   N A T O
F I T A S A F I D D L E
        A F T   A S T E R
N A T U R E   P L A Y T I M E
A R E N A   A L A S   T I C
C L E A N A S A W H I S T L E
R E T   B I T S   N I L E S
E N E R V A T E   S T R E S S
S E R U M   M I R
        T I G H T A S A D R U M
L E F T   R E M I T   R A R E
O B O E   I R E N E   E V I L
A B E D   T O N E R   W E S T
```

71

```
P R I D E   T S A R   B L A B
L O C A L   H E R E   R U L E
A T O N E   O V E N   A S I A
T O N I C   R E N O   S T A N
      S T P   N A I L S
H I G H R O A D   R E H U N G
A N A   A N G E R   T A B O R
G O N G   G R A I L   T O N E
A N G L E   A D D U P   A C E
R E S U M E   L I N E A T E D
      T U M M Y   A R M
P S S T   M O S S   M O N K S
E C H O   E V I L   I R E N E
R A I N   T I N A   T A R O T
E N V Y   T E S T   S L O T H
```

72

```
D I C T   S A P S   B A N E S
E S A U   P L E A   A B O D E
P U T T   L I S T   R O U G E
O Z S   K I T T Y C O R N E R
T U C K I N   R U N T
    R U S T L E   L E S L I E
S P A R S   E X U L T   I N K
L A D D   S L A T S   D O T E
O I L   P H Y L A   S Y N O D
T R E M O R   T H A N E S
      I L E S   M O R S E L
P U S S Y W I L L O W   H U E
O P I U M   L I E U   B A B E
W O R S E   O M A N   A R I D
S N E E R   S E N T   T E E S
```

73

```
P A I R   C R A M   L A T H E
A L D A   H E R A   E R R O L
R E L I G I O U S R I T U A L
R E E L I N   M A O   S E R A
      A G E S   D O N
B R I T I S H S A T I R I S T
R A N   E A T   S P O R T Y
A C T E D   M R S   S T A R K
G E R M A N   A L P   N E E
G R O U P O F W A R S H I P S
      S P A   M O U E
A N K A   A W L   B R A V O S
F I N G E R N A I L F L E S H
A L I E N   E L S E   E R L E
R E T R O   D O O M   R O O S
```

74

```
M A R C   C A P E D   E G G O
A L A R   A G A P E   J O A N
J A V A   M I N I M   E A V E
W I N N E R S C I R C L E
      K O O L   J E T
P I S C E S   L A O S   C A P
E T H A N   M A T H   T A R A
T H I S D I A M O N D R I N G
R A V E   C A P P   E E R I E
I D A   D E M S   S C E N E S
      L O S   B L A H
K N O C K F O R A L O O P
A N O N   A L L E N   U T A H
T O N E   T O L E T   S T I R
E W E R   E G A D S   E O N S
```

75

```
S C A T   S H E E N   F A K E
T A B U   T A N G O   E V A N
A L O T   A R I E L   L A T E
B L U E E Y E D S O U L
L I N E N   T A F F E T A
E N D   D I O R   D O O D A D
    P O N D E R   R E I D
B R O W N E Y E D G I R L
S A U L   R E P E A T
A L L I E D   S O N Y   I T T
D I E T E R S   L A M E R
    B L A C K E Y E D P E A
P E R U   P A U L O   L A N D
A G A R   E L D E R   E L S E
S O H O   S P O C K   R A Y S
```

76

```
S E W U P   S T A T   P O E T
A R O S E   T O M E   O N C E
G R E E N B A Y P A C K E R S
E S S   N E T S   R H E S U S
      T A L I   D D A Y
L I P S M A C K E R S   L A W
A Q U A E   E L O   D E L E
P U R R   C H E A P   R A G E
P I E S   R A N   S A V E D
S T E   L I N E B A C K E R S
      P U C K   A L O E
I S A I A H   A S I N   P O I
C O M P U T E R H A C K E R S
E L I E   O M N I   E A S E L
D E E R   N O O N   S T O L E
```

77

```
S T A G   T A L K   B A S S O
P A L E   E T O N   A N N U L
A L I T T L E B I R D T O L D
R E T I R E   S C A M   B U S
      T E T E   K N O B
A C T   S H A M   D U R E S S
B R A S   O R E M   T O N I C
Y O U C A N T D O T H I S T O
S O P O R   H O P E   L U A U
S K E T C H   C E R T   E R R
      S H U T   S M U T
A L L   D R A T   I N U R E S
H E Y B U T W H A T A B O U T
U M I A K   N A M E   A I R E
M A N S E   Y I P S   S L O P
```

78

```
D O O M   S A L T   E M B E D
U R S A   E D I E   A L L I E
M A S S   L O V E   S K U N K
B L A C K F R I D A Y   E S E
      O I L E D   R O A M
B A T T L E   D E F R O S T
U N I   O S S I E   F E N C E
T E L L   S I N A I   A D E N
T A T E R   D E R M A   A N O
E R U D I T E   P L A Y E R
      E A S E   S W O O N
A B S   O N A N Y S U N D A Y
C A D E T   M A L T   E A V E
T R A I T   E R I E   A R I A
S A Y S O   N E E R   L T D S
```

79

```
A L D E R   A B B R   L E C H
Q U I R E   S O R E   E L L A
U N C A P   H O E S   A V O W
A G E   T I C K L E D P I N K
      A I D A   R E E S E S
B U B B L I N G O V E R
U T I L E   E W E R   J I B
R A K E   P I N E D   Z A N E
R H O   L I L I   F A V R E
      W A L K I N G O N A I R
V I S A G E   A I R Y
O N C L O U D N I N E   R P M
C O A L   P A I L   V O I L A
A N N E   O N C E   E L L E N
L E T T   N E E D   R E L A X
```

80

```
B A C H   S T R A W   A P S E
A C R E   C A I R O   S E A L
T H E M A R X B R O T H E R S
S E W   G E E S   A E R I E
      L E A D   M E T S
T A O I S M   D I R T   G A S
A I R S   F O L I O   R U T
S L A P S T I C K C O M E D Y
T E T   P A R K S   A B E L
E Y E   L I E S   S E R E N E
      B A L D   R U N S
I S L E S   W E L D   U B I
T H E T H R E E S T O O G E S
C O A T   E M B E R   F L E E
H O P E   D U S T Y   T Y P E
```

81

```
H A N E S   F R A T   R I M E
E Q U A L   R A G A   I R A S
C U R R Y F A V O R   V A C S
K A E L   A N I   G E N R E
      M I N T C O N D I T I O N
A L B E E   E L O I S E
L E E R A T   I O N   R T E S
A I R   L O T   N E T   A L E
S A G S   W A F   D A R N I T
      O P E R A S   C A G E S
B A S I L R A T H B O N E
E N T R Y   I R R   O R A L
A G E E   S A G E A D V I C E
K L E E   S C U D   D E N T E
S O D S   T E E S   T R E S S
```

82

```
A M A S   P S A T   G A U N T
L U F T   I N G E   A N N I E
A C R O   E O N S   U N I T E
S H O W E R W I T H L O V E
      D R Y   A L Y
G A R A G E   B R I E   K A T
A L I C E   T O O T   A E R O
P I P E D O W N W I L L Y O U
E V E S   G I G S   A L I S T
D E N   E R G O   S P I N E S
      U S E   G U S
S I N K S T O A N E W L O W
V I N C I   E N I D   A U R A
I L I U M   E T N A   R A C Y
M O T T O   N O S Y   D U H S
```

83

E	G	A	D		B	A	W	D		E	D	G	E	R
N	A	P	A		O	M	O	O		N	O	O	S	E
D	R	O	M	E	D	A	R	Y		C	R	A	P	S
S	A	T	E	D			S	O	L	O		D	O	T
U	G	H		S	T	A	T	U	A	R	Y			
P	E	E	P	E	R	S			H	E	E	H	A	W
	C	A	L	A	I	S		S	L	E	P	T		
T	E	A	R		M	A	O	R	I		P	R	E	S
S	P	R	I	G		I	A	G	R	E	E			
P	A	Y	S	U	P		T	O	O	R	D	E	R	
	H	A	I	L	M	A	R	Y		I	T	E		
S	P	A		N	C	A	A		C	I	T	E	D	
L	A	R	V	A		T	I	P	P	E	R	A	R	Y
A	N	T	I	C		I	N	T	O		A	R	N	E
Y	E	S	N	O		N	E	A	P		N	Y	E	S

84

S	I	F	T		L	A	T	I	N		B	A	B	E
H	O	L	E		A	B	A	C	I		A	W	O	L
A	T	O	M		M	Y	M	A	N		S	L	A	M
H	A	P	P	Y	A	S	A	L	A	R	K			
			I	R	S				R	E	A	M	S	
E	A	S	T	E	R		C	H	E	S	T	N	U	T
M	E	T	A	L		A	H	O	Y		N	S	A	
P	R	O	U	D	A	S	A	P	E	A	C	O	C	K
I	I	I		D	O	P	E		G	A	Y	L	E	
R	A	C	C	O	O	N	S		T	E	N	S	E	S
E	L	S	I	E			B	A	N					
	C	R	A	Z	Y	A	S	A	L	O	O	N		
N	O	N	E		R	O	O	S	T		A	B	L	E
O	D	O	R		A	L	L	I	E		S	O	D	A
R	E	D	O		B	A	K	E	R		T	E	S	T

85

P	A	R	R		A	D	A	M		A	P	R	E	S
O	B	I	E		L	O	B	O		I	R	A	T	E
L	I	G	H	T	E	N	U	P		R	E	G	A	N
A	D	I	E	U		T	E	L	E	C	A	S	T	
R	E	D	A	L	E	R	T		O	D	E			
	T	A	K	E	A	L	O	A	D	O	F	F		
A	R	M		E	L	L	A		L	E	V	E	E	
J	O	Y	R	I	D	E		P	R	E	S	E	T	S
O	W	N	E	D		A	S	T	O		N	E	T	
B	E	A	G	O	O	D	L	O	S	E	R			
	I	L	L		O	P	E	R	E	T	T	A		
C	A	S	C	A	D	E	S		I	F	E	E	L	
A	W	A	I	T		T	H	I	N	K	F	A	S	T
P	R	I	D	E		R	E	N	O		E	S	T	O
T	Y	L	E	R		E	D	A	M		D	E	Y	S

86

S	L	A	P		L	A	M	A		N	A	C	H	O
A	E	R	O		I	D	Y	L		A	G	A	I	N
R	A	M	P		S	A	C	K		Z	E	S	T	A
G	R	E	A	T	P	Y	R	A	M	I	D	S		
E	N	T	R	Y			O	L	D		A	D	A	
	T	R	A	F	F	I	C	C	O	N	E	S		
S	H	H		N	E	T		A	D	D	I	S		
H	A	Y	R	I	D	E		F	A	B	E	R	G	E
A	D	D	E	R		A	L	P		A	N	S		
P	E	R	F	E	C	T	C	U	B	E	S			
E	S	O		A	I	R		R	A	M	B	O		
	F	O	U	R	C	Y	L	I	N	D	E	R	S	
I	C	O	N	S		K	L	A	N		D	E	E	S
C	R	I	M	E		L	I	S	T		A	S	T	I
H	O	L	E	S		E	C	H	O		M	E	T	E

87

L	A	M	B		T	A	G	U	P			S	P	A
O	J	A	I		A	R	E	S	O		D	E	E	P
C	A	T	B	U	R	G	L	A	R		A	E	R	O
O	R	E		R	I	O	T		T	O	R	N	U	P
		H	A	F	T		S	H	U	T				
I	T	S	E	L	F		S	M	O	T	H	E	R	S
S	A	H	L		J	A	I	L		V	E	E	P	
A	X	E	L		M	O	N	T	E		A	L	B	A
A	C	E	S		A	N	K	H		D	E	A	R	
C	O	P	A	P	L	E	A		O	N	E	D	G	E
		N	O	D	S		S	P	U	R				
J	I	G	G	L	E		A	H	E	M		S	S	S
O	B	O	E		M	E	N	I	N	B	L	A	C	K
K	E	E	L		E	V	E	R	T		A	L	A	I
E	T	S		R	E	T	R	O		W	A	R	M	

88

G	I	B	B	S		E	B	B		B	O	F	F	O
A	D	E	L	A		R	I	A		E	N	L	A	I
B	O	G	A	R	T	A	N	D	B	A	C	A	L	L
L	L	A	M	A	S		G	A	T	E	W	A	Y	
E	S	T	E		O	M	B	E	R					
		N	O	I	R		M	A	A	M	S			
S	A	L	I	N	G	E	R		R	O	B	B	I	E
T	R	A	C	Y	A	N	D	H	E	P	B	U	R	N
A	C	C	E	S	S		D	E	F	E	A	T	E	D
T	H	E	S	E		B	O	I	L					
	E	A	G	L	E		L	O	O	M				
E	S	T	E	V	E	Z		C	L	A	I	R	E	
B	U	R	T	O	N	A	N	D	T	A	Y	L	O	R
A	M	A	T	I		A	I	D		T	E	E	N	Y
N	O	P	A	R		R	T	E		E	R	R	O	L

89

```
O Z O N E   C L A P   H A S P
T I D A L   H A R E   E L I A
H O I S T   A S A P   A L M S
O N E C O U N T R Y   D O I T
      A N N   A S A R U L E
C H A R   H A L T   D E T E R
P O X   K A R O   S D S
O N E C O N S T I T U T I O N
    O R D   T A R P   S R O
E C O L E   R E N O   A M O R
M O N D A L E   V A T
B O S S   O N E D E S T I N Y
A K I N   P E R U   P A S E O
R I T A   E G I S   C R A I G
K E E P   Z E S T   A S Y L A
```

90

```
I M A N   A B L E   A L L A H
R E N O   P A I X   L O I R E
A N T S   I L S A   L U M P Y
Q U I E T A S A M O U S E
        E R A   P R Y
P A S T R Y   R A T E   N O W
A F T E R   M A G I   T O P O
C O O L A S A C U C U M B E R
T O R E   C R E E   T E L L S
S T Y   C H E R   F I N E S T
      S A M   M A C
    S T R O N G A S A R O C K
A L L O T   A U N T   O P I E
S E I N E   S A S E   M A A M
P I P E R   A M E R   P L O P
```

91

```
J A M S   M E A R A   A G R I
O N E L   E T H E L   B L O B
B E G I N T H E B E G U I N E
S W A M I   M I X E D B A G
      E M I L   D I N H
S A G   I N I T   S T A T E N
E G O   T R O I S   B A D E
W A L T Z I N G M A T I L D A
E V E R   S E E N O   K I T
R E M I S S   R A K E   Y E S
      A N T E   R A C K
A F F L U E N T   A N G S T
B E E R B A R R E L P O L K A
B E A U   L O E W E   L E I F
A T T N   S L E E T   L E N T
```

92

```
C L A N   H A D J   S L A K E
O U S E   A R I A   H I T I T
C A S H M E R E S W E A T E R
O U T R E   S P H E R U L E
A S S U R E S   E O N
      S U P R A   T M A N
E M B A T T L E   Q U I T E
C H E C K O U T C O U N T E R
R O D E O   R E P E A T E D
U S E D   C H I D E
      W O O   E N I G M A S
A P P O I N T S   D R A M A
C H A R G E D A F F A I R E S
D I T C H   O A H U   D A B S
C L E A T   G R A M   S T A Y
```

93

```
I A G O   M E S A S   C L U E
S H U N   A M I S H   O A T S
M A R E   N O L I E   U S E S
  B U C K E T O F B O L T S
      A N T E   A R E
A D O R E   D O E   B E A D S
B E F A L L   F B I   W E E
B A T T L E O F B R I T A I N
E R E   T S E   E N R I C O
S Y N O D   U R N   T A T E R
      R E S   U T E P
  B E A S T O F B U R D E N
C O I N   A V O I D   O D I N
B O R G   G A L L O   O G L E
S K E E   E L D E R   R E E D
```

94

```
A L A S   A W O L   P E A C H
P E P E   M A K E   A C H O O
H A R P   E L A N   C L O M P
I V E T O L D Y O U M A Y B E
D E S   M I O   N A T
    B A A   A G I N   D U B
S A R A N   O S L O   L I S A
T W O M I L L I O N T I M E S
U R S A   A D A M   H E E D S
B Y E   E D E N   F E D
    S M L   O U R   P A P
N O T T O E X A G G E R A T E
E L I O T   M I L E   A C R E
C A D R E   A D E E   V E I L
K N E E D   S A S S   E R A S
```

95

J	A	N	E		B	O	T	C	H		G	L	A	D
A	B	O	Y		E	A	R	L	Y		R	E	B	A
B	L	U	E	P	E	R	I	O	D		I	V	A	N
S	E	N	S	O	R		C	U	E	S	T	I	C	K
				S	Y	N	O	D		O	S	S	I	E
B	E	S	E	T		O	L	S	E	N				
O	C	H	S		A	N	O		B	A	L	K	E	D
W	H	I	T	E	F	O	R	D	B	R	O	N	C	O
L	O	V	E	L	L		H	A	S		B	O	R	G
				L	Y	S	O	L		N	E	X	U	S
S	H	A	P	E		A	L	I	C	E				
P	A	G	A	N	I	N	I		R	U	G	G	E	D
A	L	A	I		R	E	D	H	O	T	M	A	M	A
N	E	I	N		I	S	A	A	C		A	R	M	Y
S	Y	N	E		S	T	Y	L	E		C	P	A	S

96

B	R	A		S	A	L	E	R	N	O		A	S	H
O	O	P		C	L	O	S	E	U	P		T	A	O
X	C	H	R	O	M	O	S	O	M	E		O	N	A
		O	N	T	A	P			B	R	A	N	D	X
C	A	R	A	T		E	M	O		A	C	A	R	E
A	L	I				D	I	P	S		C	L	A	D
M	E	S	S	E	S		S	A	T	I	E			
	X	M	A	R	K	S	T	H	E	S	P	O	T	
			W	R	I	T	E		M	O	T	L	E	Y
B	U	F	F		T	O	R	N				I	L	E
A	P	R	I	L		A	X	E		M	A	V	E	N
X	R	A	T	E	D			A	M	U	S	E		
T	O	Y		G	E	N	E	R	A	T	I	O	N	X
E	S	E		E	L	E	M	E	N	T		I	N	K
R	E	D		R	E	T	U	R	N	S		L	E	E

97

M	A	R	C		W	O	R	D		E	S	T	E	E
A	S	E	A		A	R	I	A		C	H	E	A	T
I	T	E	M		F	A	C	T		L	A	S	S	O
L	I	F	E	O	F	T	H	E	P	A	R	T	Y	
			O	S	L	O			R	I	P			
C	A	T		T	E	R	R	I	E	R		A	S	H
A	G	A	T	E			E	L	L		U	L	N	A
P	I	C	K	O	F	T	H	E	L	I	T	T	E	R
O	L	I	O		A	R	A			R	E	A	L	M
N	E	T		T	R	I	B	U	N	E		R	L	S
			S	A	G			S	E	N	D			
	S	A	L	T	O	F	T	H	E	E	A	R	T	H
C	A	R	A	T		R	E	E	D		R	A	R	E
O	L	I	V	E		E	A	R	L		T	I	E	R
S	E	D	E	R		E	L	S	E		S	L	E	D

98

M	A	R	Y		S	P	A	T	E		D	D	A	Y
E	Z	I	O		C	O	M	E	S		R	U	L	E
L	U	N	G		A	T	O	N	E		F	E	T	A
D	R	K	I	L	D	A	R	E		P	E	T	E	R
				E	S	T		M	E	T	E	O	R	S
P	A	N	D	A		O	N	E	I	L	L			
L	E	A	R	N	S		E	N	D		G	A	S	H
A	R	I	D		H	A	R	T	E		O	L	E	O
N	O	L	O		R	I	V		R	H	O	D	E	S
			L	A	U	R	E	L		A	D	A	P	T
S	Y	R	I	N	G	E		I	S	R				
M	E	A	T	Y		D	R	Z	H	I	V	A	G	O
I	S	I	T		M	A	I	Z	E		O	U	R	S
T	E	L	L		A	L	L	I	E		I	T	A	L
E	S	S	E		H	E	L	E	N		D	O	D	O

99

S	H	A	Q			P	G	A		A	P	S	I	S
N	A	S	A		U	F	O	S		S	E	E	M	E
L	I	S	T		S	C	O	T	C	H	T	A	P	E
		E	A	S	E		F	O	O		E	T	A	L
G	I	N	R	U	M	M	Y		N	O	S	A	L	E
H	A	T		P	E	A		M	A	V		C	A	Y
I	M	T	H	E		L	E	A	N	E	R			
	B	O	U	R	B	O	N	S	T	R	E	E	T	
			E	M	E	N	D	S		D	O	T	E	R
N	B	C		A	N	E		E	M	U		C	R	O
O	I	L	I	N	G		R	Y	E	B	R	E	A	D
T	E	E	S		A	S	A		L	S	A	T		
B	R	A	N	D	Y	W	I	N	E		Z	E	R	O
A	C	T	O	R		A	S	H	E		O	R	E	O
D	E	S	T	E		G	E	L			R	A	M	P

100

R	U	L	E	D		S	H	O	P		S	H	A	G
E	P	O	X	Y		C	O	L	A		T	A	R	A
E	L	O	P	E		A	B	E	L		A	R	I	Z
L	I	F	O		B	R	O	O	M	H	I	L	D	A
S	T	A	N	L	E	Y			E	I	R	E		
			E	E	G		B	E	T	S		Q	U	A
S	H	A	N	A		A	I	N	T		S	U	N	S
M	O	P	T	H	E	F	L	O	O	R	W	I	T	H
U	M	P	S		N	A	G	S		C	A	N	O	E
G	E	L		Y	O	R	E		A	P	T			
		I	G	O	R			S	U	T	T	E	R	S
V	A	C	U	U	M	P	A	C	K		E	R	I	E
E	R	A	S		I	O	T	A		R	A	N	D	D
R	E	N	T		T	R	O	D		O	M	E	G	A
B	A	T	S		Y	E	P	S		E	S	S	E	N

101

S	C	T	V		B	A	A	L		S	C	R	E	W
A	L	O	E		E	M	M	A		C	L	A	R	O
S	E	L	L		F	O	O	T		A	A	R	O	N
H	O	L	D	Y	O	U	R	H	O	R	S	E	S	
		T	U	R	N				P	E	P			
F	A	A		M	E	T	E	R	E	D		B	A	H
A	B	R	A	M		A	I	R			A	L	I	A
M	I	N	D	Y	O	U	R	M	A	N	N	E	R	S
E	D	I	E		V	A	N		I	N	S	E	T	
D	E	E		C	A	R	S	E	A	T		S	S	E
			O	R	R			A	C	R	E			
B	I	T	E	Y	O	U	R	T	O	N	G	U	E	
S	A	N	T	A		A	R	L	O		T	A	S	S
O	C	T	E	T		T	S	A	R		E	V	E	S
S	H	O	R	E		S	A	P	S		R	E	D	O

102

S	M	I	T		S	H	A	G		G	A	L	L	O
H	A	S	H		H	A	Z	E		A	V	A	I	L
A	G	A	R		I	R	O	N		L	O	R	N	E
H	I	Y	O	S	I	L	V	E	R	A	W	A	Y	
			T	O	T	E			A	H	A			
T	O	T	H	E	M	O	O	N	A	L	I	C	E	
C	A	R	L	O		S	H	A	D		D	D	S	
O	B	O	E		G	R	I	S	T		E	A	R	S
D	O	N		F	L	U	E			A	C	H	O	O
Y	O	O	H	O	O	M	R	S	B	L	O	O	M	
			O	R	O			T	E	E	N			
B	E	A	M	M	E	U	P	S	C	O	T	T	Y	
D	O	G	G	O		G	P	A	S		M	O	U	E
A	N	A	I	S		E	T	U	I		I	O	N	A
M	E	D	E	A		R	O	L	E		C	L	A	N

103

I	C	E	S		S	M	E	L	L		E	P	I	C
S	I	N	E		T	A	B	O	O		X	E	N	A
A	V	E	R		R	A	B	B	I	T	E	A	R	S
A	I	R	F	R	A	M	E		S	E	C	R	E	T
C	L	O	S	E	T		D	A	L	E	S			
			H	A	H		R	A	N		W	E	T	
P	L	A	Z	A		E	D	E	N		J	I	V	E
H	A	R	E	B	R	A	I	N	E	D	I	D	E	A
I	V	A	N		E	R	M	A		O	M	E	N	S
L	A	B		I	Q	S		S	C	I				
		K	N	U	T	E		A	N	N	U	A	L	
U	P	S	I	D	E		L	A	R	G	E	S	S	E
B	U	N	N	Y	S	L	O	P	E		R	A	T	E
E	R	I	K		T	Y	P	E	S		V	I	E	D
R	E	P	S		S	E	E	D	S		E	R	R	S

104

A	G	E	D		A	M	E	N	S		S	N	I	P
R	O	M	E		M	E	D	I	A		L	O	R	I
O	T	I	C		S	L	I	C	K		O	N	E	S
S	I	L	K	S	T	O	C	K	I	N	G	S		
E	T	E		P	E	N	T			T	A	M	P	S
			A	I	L	S		S	C	H	N	O	O	K
E	D	G	E			O	R	O				K	E	Y
G	O	O	D	Y	T	W	O	S	H	O	E	S		
E	R	G		U	S	S			A	I	R	Y		
R	E	F	R	A	M	E		H	U	R	L			
S	T	I	E	S		R	E	P	S		B	A	A	
		S	T	U	F	F	E	D	S	H	I	R	T	S
H	O	H	O		L	I	E	G	E		H	A	R	I
O	L	E	O		O	N	S	E	T		A	V	I	A
T	A	S	K		W	E	E	D	S		D	E	A	N

105

G	O	S	H		C	O	M	F	Y		D	A	T	E
O	B	E	Y		A	M	O	R	E		U	R	A	L
L	O	W	E		B	I	T	E	S		A	I	L	S
D	E	N	N	I	S	T	H	E	M	E	N	A	C	E
			A	N	T				A	X	E			
H	A	S		G	A	R	M	E	N	T		A	R	T
A	C	C	T		N	E	R	D		R	E	F	E	R
T	H	E	A	D	D	A	M	S	F	A	M	I	L	Y
C	O	N	D	O		D	O	E	R		T	R	A	M
H	O	T		G	R	E	M	L	I	N		E	Y	E
			T	I	E				S	E	C			
L	E	A	V	E	I	T	T	O	B	E	A	V	E	R
O	P	U	S		G	O	A	P	E		J	I	V	E
S	I	T	E		N	O	T	R	E		U	S	E	D
S	C	O	T		S	L	A	Y	S		N	E	R	O

106

G	O	B	S		W	A	D	I		L	A	V	E	R
A	N	U	T		E	B	O	N		I	G	A	V	E
M	Y	R	A		S	U	R	F		B	A	S	I	E
E	X	P	R	E	S	S	Y	O	U	R	S	E	L	F
			V	E	E				B	A	S			
V	E	R	T	E	X		F	L	O		I	M	A	M
O	N	A	I	R		G	R	E	A	T		E	R	E
L	O	C	A	L	A	N	E	S	T	H	E	S	I	A
T	R	E		Y	E	A	R	S		R	O	T	O	R
A	M	S	O		R	T	E		P	I	N	A	T	A
			P	O	I			A	R	F				
L	I	M	I	T	E	D	E	D	I	T	I	O	N	S
O	B	E	A	H		O	X	E	N		D	R	O	P
S	A	N	T	E		O	P	E	C		E	A	S	E
T	R	U	E	R		M	O	P	E		A	L	E	X

107

```
C A R G O   S P A S   R I T Z
A L I E N   M O R N   A R I A
S A O N E   U O M O   H E M P
S I T T I N G R O O M S
    S L A G   R T E   P O T
P O S   L O L A   S C R A P E
A C T A   M I L T   C A R P E
S T A N D I N G O V A T I O N
C A R N E   G A M A   S A S S
A N V I L S   E A R N   H E Y
L E E   L A S   R I O S
    W A L K I N G S T I C K
J U N E   T A R O   H E N R I
A S I A   E T A L   E A R E D
Y A N K   D E E D   S L E W S
```

108

```
M A L L   U T T E R   R O A D
A S I A   S U E D E   E R G O
T H E B R O N X I S U P B U T
H E N I E   T E A R O S E S
    A T I C   S L I T
G A S L I G H T   E S T A T E
E S T   N O I R E   E X O D
T H E B A T T E R Y S D O W N
N E E R   S N O U T   N I A
O N L A N D   T S A R I S T S
    G O E S   E N A S
T I E G A M E S   T H R E E
I T S A H E L L U V A T O W N
P E A R   A M A N A   A X E D
S M U T   N A T A L   R Y N E
```

109

```
O P A L   P A L E D   S A S E
S E M I   A M O U R   C Z A R
S N O B   T I A R A   R U N G
  D I R T I S N O T D I R T
    E R O S   E P E E
A M I T Y   L E G I T
L O O T   U N I T E S   E G G
B U T O N L Y M A T T E R I N
S E A   O N E A L S   A I D A
    C H A T S   A S K E W
  E C H O   O I L Y
  T H E W R O N G P L A C E
S H O W   O H A R A   C O Z Y
T O R E   T O M E S   E L I A
U S E D   C H E S S   S T O P
```

110

```
B O I S   C R A B   P I Q U E
R U N E   H E R A   S P U N K
A T T A   I S U P   A S I D E
W H O L E L O T T A L O V E
L I T   J E R   I B M   E R A
S T O N E   B O Z O   G R A S
    A C K   N E D   N E C K
H A L F T I M E R E P O R T S
U N I T   T U T   S E M
E T N A   K R O C   R E M I X
D I G   W A D   A D D   I S E
  Q U A R T E R P O U N D E R
G U I L E   R I N G   E A U X
T E N O N   E T U I   M I L E
E D I T S   D A T E   O R T S
```

111

```
G A I T   B R I E   R O M P
A D L I B   L O L L   O V A L
G O L D I L O C K S   S E R E
    B L I N K   I B E R I A
D E F I L E D   K N O B B E D
E M O T E D   B R O G U E
F I R S T   H E A R   D A T E
A L B   S C O F F E D   R I D
T E E S   O M I T   A G I N G
    A V O C E T   G R U N G E
S T R E A K S   T A N A G E R
C H A L K S   A R L E N
R A N T   U N B E A R A B L E
O N C E   R U E S   S C I O N
D E E R   E N D S   O N U S
```

112

```
T R A P   T E E M   S O M E
S A L I C   O R E O   U B E R
P I G E O N T O E D   M A S S
  M E R C I E S   E G A D S
W E B   K L M   A S O C I A L
E N R O B E   T I T O   A G E
S T A R R   S E L L S   H E X
      E A G L E E Y E D
P U P   I R O N Y   N I G H T
I K E   N E T S   T E P E E S
T U R E E N S   M A C   O R K
    L I N D A   M I L K E R S
R E D S   D U C K L E G G E D
A L O U   E S M E   D O I L Y
P E T E   S E X Y   S A F E
```

113

```
N A B S   L E H A R     T L C
A R L O   O X E Y E   S H E A
S T A N D U P A N D C H E E R
A S H   R I O T   O U T R E
    B A S S   P A R L A Y S
E N R A G E   S A U N A
L A I R   S T Y L E   A B E
S I T B A C K A N D R E L A X
A L E   P L A T E   G A L E
  R O U T E   S P O R E S
P A R O L E E   D U O S
I D E A L     G O B S   A H A
L I E D O W N O N T H E J O B
L E S S   A B D U L   N A P E
S U E   C A S T E   E X I T
```

114

```
C O P E   O M E N   S Y R U P
U P O N   N A M E   H O U S E
J U N G L E J I M   A S H E R
O S S   E D O   O B V E R S E
    B E A R D   L E M
S P A R K Y   O B E D I E N T
L O G O S   T O E S   T R I O
A N N A   C O D E S   E M E R
I C E D   O L A N   P S A L M
N E W W O R L D   C H A S S E
    A C E   S C R I M
P L A Y E R S   E E L   D E F
O U I J A   P E C O S B I L L
P I N O N   E V I L   L O S E
E S T E S   D A L E   T R E E
```

115

```
T E M P   F A D S   C L A D
A R C O   I R A E   B R I N Y
J A I L   L A Z E   L U N G E
  L A T T E R L A D D E R
A S S U M E     I D E A L S
W E T T E R W E D D E R
A L I E N   H E E D S   P A N
K E N S   D I R T Y   R A M A
E S T   B A S I E   C Y N I C
  B I T T E R B I D D E R
A L S A C E     A T E A S E
M U T T E R M U D D E R
A L O O P   I B I D   C U R D
N U N N S   S E M I   U S E R
A S E S   T R E E   P A V E
```

116

```
P A P A S   A C R E   G A M A
C L A S P   F L A X   R E A R
S I T K A   R A M P   E R I C
  T H E T R O U B L E W I T H
    D U O   S O O T   A R E
E A T   L O W     D U E L E D
T H E R A T R A C E I S
S A T E   E M U   A I D A
  E V E N I F Y O U W I N
W A L L O P   F O P   O P T
A R A   L I S T   W I T
Y O U R E S T I L L A R A T
L U R E   T E T E   T U L I P
A S E A   L A L O   E S T E R
Y E L P   E D E N   S T O R Y
```

117

```
U N C L E   D E E R   E V A N
S O L A R   R A K E   M I N E
A M O U R   O R E S   U S E R
F E U D   W O N D E R L A N D
  D E C A L   T O A S T S
C O N R A D   B E S O T
U N I   D I C E D   T E S L A
E O N S   S A L E M   S H O W
D R E A R   F I N A L   A B E
    L E V E E   Y A W N E D
R E G A L E   S O B I G
I V O R Y T O W E R   E R S E
P A R I   O S H A   A L I E N
E D G E   E L A L   I D L E D
N E E D   D O T S   T S A R S
```

118

```
H A G A R   D R A W   B L U R
A L I C E   E A S E   L A N E
I L L T H I N K A B O U T I T
    S E N S E   R E C T I
A L P   A G E   B A N S H E E
R E L A T E   C A R E T
O V A L   B A L E R   S A G
M A Y B E Y E S M A Y B E N O
A R S   L A I T Y   A R G O
    P A W N S   R U G G E D
S H A R I N G   A Y N   E L S
L E N I N   T R A C T
A S K M E A G A I N L A T E R
I S L E   C A R S   O C A L A
N E E R   H Y P E   G O T I T
```

119

M	A	T	S		O	L	G	A		R	E	A	T	A
E	L	A	L		D	U	O	S		E	L	L	I	S
A	G	H	A		D	A	L	I		D	M	A	R	K
N	A	O	M	I	J	U	D	D		H	E	R	E	S
S	E	E	S	T	O			E	D	E	R			
			T	B	A	R		U	N	F	A	I	R	
C	L	A	R	O		P	A	L	E		U	L	N	A
A	E	R	O		D	E	V	I	L		D	A	F	T
S	A	N	G		I	S	E	E		A	D	I	O	S
	T	H	E	E	N	D		L	U	B	E			
			R	O	O	T			A	R	A	B	I	A
S	W	A	M	I		B	I	L	L	Y	B	U	D	D
C	A	M	U	S		I	D	Y	L		A	S	E	A
A	N	O	D	E		L	E	N	A		T	E	S	T
N	E	R	D	S		L	E	N	D		E	S	T	E

120

B	A	K	U		E	T	T	A		F	A	C	E	S
A	S	I	N		L	A	W	S		I	N	A	N	E
S	T	E	T		E	R	I	C		N	A	V	E	L
H	A	V	I	N	G	A	G	O	O	D	T	I	M	E
			L	A	I			T	K	O		L	Y	S
U	M	P		P	A	S	T		R	U	T			
P	E	R	F	E	C	T	W	E	A	T	H	E	R	
I	G	O	R		E	E	L		I	V	A	N		
A	W	E	S	O	M	E	S	C	E	N	E	R	Y	
			E	T	H		D	E	A	L		N	E	E
T	W	A		A	I	R		B	I	G				
W	I	S	H	Y	O	U	W	E	R	E	H	E	R	E
A	S	T	O	P		D	A	L	I		O	D	O	R
N	E	H	R	U		E	G	A	D		S	N	A	G
G	R	E	A	T		R	E	N	E		T	A	R	O

121

A	Z	O	R	E	S		S	H	O	W		C	A	L
B	O	D	E	G	A		L	A	M	E		A	R	E
C	O	S	T	A	R		I	V	A	N		R	I	G
			A	N	A	R	M	A	N	D	A	L	E	G
S	A	K	I		E	E	N		E	A	S	Y		
C	L	A	N	T	O	N		A	L	B	S			
R	I	B		A	M	A	N		A	R	O	M	A	S
A	B	U	S	H	E	L	A	N	D	A	P	E	C	K
P	I	L	E	O	N		H	A	L	S		T	H	U
			R	E	S	T		F	E	S	T	O	O	N
M	O	L	T		E	A	T		R	O	O	K		
A	Y	E	A	R	A	N	D	A	D	A	Y			
B	V	D		A	L	P	O		A	V	O	I	D	S
E	E	G		S	L	I	P		N	O	U	G	A	T
L	Y	E		P	A	N	T		A	N	T	O	N	Y

122

G	I	L	T		T	O	R	A	H		I	H	O	P
I	G	O	R		A	R	O	M	A		N	O	N	O
B	A	T	E	S	M	O	T	E	L		S	L	I	T
E	S	T	A	T	E		S	T	R	A	I	T	S	
			S	U	R	G	E		S	A	N	D		
A	R	G	O	N		A	N	T		T	E	A	S	E
W	O	R	N		A	R	T	I	S	T		Y	O	M
A	D	A		B	L	A	R	N	E	Y		I	D	O
R	E	N		L	E	G	A	T	E		G	N	A	T
D	O	D	G	E		E	N	E		S	E	N	S	E
		H	E	E	L		T	R	A	P	S			
B	L	O	N	D	I	E		T	A	T	T	E	R	
M	I	T	T		P	L	A	Z	A	S	U	I	T	E
O	R	E	L		I	M	P	E	L		R	E	N	D
C	A	L	E		D	O	O	N	E		E	R	A	S

123

D	A	B	S		B	O	S	S	A		O	B	I	S
O	R	E	S		A	T	T	A	R		N	A	D	A
O	G	R	E		J	O	E	Y	B	I	S	H	O	P
D	Y	E		C	A	S	A	N	O	V	A			
A	L	A	M	O		M	O	R	A	L	I	S	T	
D	E	L	I	M	I	T			N	E	H	I	S	
			R	E	M	O	R	S	E		O	D	E	
	A	L	E	X	A	N	D	E	R	P	O	P	E	
S	R	A		S	E	A	L	S	I	N				
E	N	L	A	I		A	T	L	A	S	E	S		
C	O	O	L	C	A	T	S		E	N	T	R	E	
	D	E	R	A	I	L	E	D		A	H	A		
A	N	N	E	S	E	X	T	O	N		S	C	A	B
L	E	A	R		N	E	E	D	I		H	E	R	E
L	A	B	S		A	D	D	E	D		H	Y	D	E

124

G	E	N	O	A		I	S	N	T		S	W	I	M
O	V	E	N	S		S	T	A	R		O	H	N	O
R	E	A	C	H	E	S	A	V	E	R	D	I	C	T
A	N	T	E		P	U	N	Y		O	A	T	H	S
N	T	H		L	I	E	D		E	A	S	E		
			T	E	C		S	H	A	M		S	O	N
O	R	I	O	N		A	C	E	S		D	A	M	E
L	O	N	G	A	R	M	O	F	T	H	E	L	A	W
E	L	S	A		A	I	N	T		E	B	E	R	T
G	E	T		K	I	E	V		T	N	T			
		E	D	E	N		I	O	U	S		B	A	N
S	T	A	R	R		I	C	O	N		B	R	I	O
O	R	D	E	R	I	N	T	H	E	C	O	U	R	T
L	E	O	S		A	L	E	E		I	N	N	E	R
D	E	F	S		M	A	D	D		A	N	O	D	E

125

S	L	A	P		D	E	A	F		A	D	M	A	N
I	O	L	A		U	G	L	I		P	I	A	N	O
G	O	I	N	G	T	O	E	X	T	R	E	M	E	S
H	I	C	K	E	Y			E	W	E		A	W	E
S	E	E	Y	A		G	A	R	I	S	H			
			R	E	M	U	S		S	E	E	D	Y	
O	H	M	E		M	A	C		S	K	I	D	O	O
G	O	I	N	G	I	N	T	O	H	I	D	I	N	G
R	A	N	O	U	T		I	D	A		I	T	S	A
E	X	I	L	E		L	O	D	G	E				
		A	S	I	A	N	S		S	W	A	T	H	
E	G	G		S	I	P		S	T	E	R	E	O	
G	O	N	E	W	I	T	H	T	H	E	W	I	N	D
A	B	A	S	H		O	B	I	E		O	S	S	A
D	I	T	T	O		P	O	N	D		N	E	E	D

126

C	A	A	N		C	A	T	E	R		I	B	I	S
A	L	D	O		A	T	R	I	A		T	A	L	E
R	O	D	S	E	R	L	I	N	G		A	R	I	A
O	N	E		X	M	A	S		P	E	L	H	A	M
B	E	R	A	T	E	S		M	A	R	I	A		
			C	O	N		C	A	P	S	C	R	E	W
L	A	P	E	L		M	A	N	E	T		B	R	O
A	N	O	S		S	A	N	E	R		C	O	L	E
M	D	S		D	U	K	E	S		C	O	R	E	S
P	I	T	V	I	P	E	R		M	O	P			
		H	I	K	E	R		P	A	R	A	P	E	T
T	R	A	D	E	R		T	U	R	F		A	M	I
H	O	S	E		S	T	I	C	K	U	P	M	A	N
U	P	T	O		P	E	N	C	E		A	P	I	G
G	E	E	S		Y	A	S	I	R		D	A	L	E

127

F	U	S	E		D	A	L	I		S	I	L	O	
O	N	T	V		R	U	I	N		L	U	C	A	S
O	T	O	E		E	N	T	R		O	B	E	S	E
D	O	W	N	I	N	T	H	E	M	O	U	T	H	
			I	O	C			I	S	R				
U	P	I	N	T	H	E	A	I	R		B	A	A	S
T	O	N	G	A		L	U	T	E		D	L	I	
T	R	U	S	S		I	D	A		S	A	L	A	D
E	T	S		P	H	I	L		C	L	A	R	E	
R	E	E	L		O	U	T	O	N	A	L	I	M	B
			A	N	N			E	M	S				
B	E	S	I	D	E	T	H	E	P	O	I	N	T	
L	E	A	S	T		A	R	I	D		U	H	O	H
E	E	R	I	E		T	I	L	L		L	O	V	E
I	S	L	E			S	O	L	E		S	P	A	N

128

C	R	A	P	S		C	L	A	Y		B	A	R	B
P	I	P	I	T		R	O	S	A		O	H	I	O
A	G	E	N	A		E	R	I	N		N	O	D	S
S	A	D	A	T		S	N	A	K	E	E	Y	E	S
			T	U	L	S	A		E	L	Y			
P	L	E	A	S	E		R	E	G	A	L	E	D	
R	A	D		S	A	B	U		A	R	E	N	A	
E	I	G	H	T	T	H	E	H	A	R	D	W	A	Y
S	N	E	E	R		M	E	R	C		I	T	A	
S	E	R	R	A	T	E		L	E	S	S	E	N	
			I	I	I		P	L	U	S	H			
L	I	T	T	L	E	J	O	E		T	A	P	E	S
O	D	E	A		R	U	S	E		A	D	U	L	T
B	O	N	G		E	N	I	D		T	E	S	L	A
E	L	S	E		D	O	T	S		E	S	S	A	Y

129

L	O	G	E		A	T	L	A	S		F	O	R	E
A	V	I	D		P	O	I	S	E		A	W	O	L
M	A	G	I		P	A	S	T	E		L	E	E	K
B	L	I	T	H	E	S	P	I	R	I	T			
			O	A	T			R	E	H	A	B		
R	E	C	A	L	L		L	I	B	E	R	A	T	E
E	M	A	I	L		B	E	S	O			W	O	E
J	O	L	L	Y	G	R	E	E	N	G	I	A	N	T
E	T	O		A	I	D	E		A	R	I	E	L	
C	E	R	A	M	I	C	S		A	T	T	I	R	E
T	R	Y	S	T		S	R	O						
		H	A	P	P	Y	W	A	R	R	I	O	R	
S	P	E	C		A	R	M	O	R		I	D	L	E
M	E	G	A		C	O	C	O	A		F	E	E	D
U	P	O	N		A	D	A	P	T		T	A	O	S

130

S	T	O	M	P		L	I	M	P		S	A	N	S
P	A	L	E	O		U	V	E	A		U	H	O	H
O	C	E	A	N		L	A	M	S		R	O	P	E
I	K	I	D	Y	O	U	N	O	T		E	Y	E	D
L	Y	C	E	U	M			R	A	P	T			
			P	E	R	K	Y		A	H	O	L	D	
L	I	L	Y		R	A	N		F	R	I	D	A	Y
E	R	O	O		T	H	E	D	A		N	O	D	E
N	E	B	U	L	A		L	I	L		G	R	A	D
A	D	O	B	E		A	T	A	L	E				
			E	A	S	T		A	R	A	B	I	C	
F	A	S	T		A	B	S	O	L	U	T	E	L	Y
E	X	E	C		T	A	T	A		P	A	N	I	C
T	E	C	H		U	T	E	S		T	R	I	A	L
A	S	T	A		P	S	S	T		S	I	N	C	E

The New York Times Crossword Puzzles

THE #1 NAME IN CROSSWORDS

NEW
Ultimate Crossword Omnibus
Monday Through Friday
    Volume 2
Tough Crosswords Volume 11
Large-Print Daily Crosswords
Crosswords for Your Beach Bag

SPECIAL EDITIONS
Will Shortz's Favorite Crosswords
Crossword All-Stars
Bonus Crosswords

DAILY CROSSWORDS
Monday Through Friday Puzzles
Daily Omnibus Volume 12
Daily Omnibus Volume 11
Daily Crosswords Volume 63
Daily Crosswords Volume 62
Daily Crosswords Volume 61
Daily Crosswords Volume 60
Daily Crosswords Volume 59
Daily Crosswords Volume 58
Daily Crosswords Volume 57

EASY CROSSWORDS
Easy Crosswords Volume 4
Easy Crosswords Volume 3
Easy Crosswords Volume 2
Easy Omnibus Volume 1

TOUGH CROSSWORDS
Tough Crosswords Volume 10
Tough Crosswords Volume 9

SUNDAY CROSSWORDS
Sunday Omnibus Volume 7
Sunday Omnibus Volume 6
Sunday Crosswords Volume 28
Sunday Crosswords Volume 27

LARGE-PRINT CROSSWORDS
Large-Print Omnibus Volume 4
Large-Print Omnibus Volume 3

VARIETY PUZZLES
Acrostic Puzzles Volume 9
Sunday Variety Puzzles

PORTABLE SIZE FORMAT
Super Saturday Crosswords
Crosswords for the Holidays
Sun, Sand and Crosswords
Weekend Challenge Crosswords
Crosswords for Your Coffee
    Break
Crosswords for Your Work Week

FOR YOUNG SOLVERS
New York Times on the Web
    Crosswords for Teens
Outrageous Crossword Puzzles
    and Word Games for Kids
More Outrageous Crossword
    Puzzles and Word Games
    for Kids